D1271253

THE STRAIT GATE

The Strait Gate

Thresholds and Power

in Western History

Daniel Jütte

Yale UNIVERSITY PRESS

New Haven & London

Published with assistance from the foundation established
in memory of Calvin Chapin of the Class of 1788, Yale College.

Copyright © 2015 by Yale University.
All rights reserved.
This book may not be reproduced, in whole or in part, including illustrations,
in any form (beyond that copying permitted by Sections 107 and 108 of the
U.S. Copyright Law and except by reviewers for the public press), without
written permission from the publishers.

Yale University Press books may be purchased in quantity for educational,
business, or promotional use. For information, please e-mail sales.press@yale.edu
(U.S. office) or sales@yaleup.co.uk (U.K. office).

Set in Walbaum MT type by Newgen North America
Printed in the United States of America.

Library of Congress Control Number: 2015931017
ISBN 978-0-300-21108-5 (cloth : alk. paper)

A catalogue record for this book is available from the British Library.

This paper meets the requirements of
ANSI/NISO Z39.48-1992 (Permanence of Paper).

10 9 8 7 6 5 4 3 2 1

I am the door: by me if any man enter in, he shall be saved.

—John 10:9

The door speaks.

—Georg Simmel, "Bridge and Door" (1909)

CONTENTS

CONTENTS

INTRODUCTION

B Y THE SPRING OF 1918, with the Great War in its final phase, the Central Powers, headed by Germany and Austria-Hungary, were facing certain defeat. Yet actual capitulation was slow in coming, and meanwhile, the burdens imposed on the population intensified. Public anger reached fever pitch in Germany and Austria-Hungary in early 1918, when officials ordered that all door handles and knobs be removed from homes and shops.

General provisions were already very scarce among both the general population and soldiers at the front. In particular, the scarcity of metals—indispensable for producing armaments—placed a massive strain on the war effort. For several months, military leaders had been searching for new sources of industrial materials such as copper, brass, and iron. Church bells and kitchen pots were among the first to go, along with washbasins and oven doors. Now the people had to surrender their window handles and latches as well as their doorknobs, door handles, door latches, and bolts to the so-called *Metallzen-trale*.[1] This sacrifice was one step too far.

Resistance was swift: in Vienna, the mayor and citizens protested against the new measures.[2] In Berlin, the Zentralverband der Haus- und Grundbesitzervereine Deutschlands (Central Association of Home and Real Estate Owners) published a brochure containing a scathing denunciation of the planned confiscation, decrying the "severe intrusion upon the rights" of homeowners and foretelling material damage "of enormous proportions."[3] The press spoke of the "simply unbelievable demand that our homeowners *lay a hand* upon their own houses"—an expression that, in German, also implies taking one's own life, as if removing door fixtures were tantamount to suicide for the household.[4]

The critics' position was clear: before taking such drastic action, the government and military should make every effort to requisition all useful metals from their *own* buildings and offices. Some of the proposed alternatives came close to *lèse majesté:* "Even in the Reichstag we still have objects that we could sacrifice without much pain, such as the two statues of the Emperor standing in the dark in the vestibule," one opponent declared.[5] But the protests were in vain: in 1918, metal door parts disappeared from thousands of houses and shops across the country. Whenever homeowners did not obey, the authorities sent in so-called Removal Convoys (*Ausbaukolonnen*) to complete the job.[6] The proponents of these measures later calculated that Austria-Hungary alone took in 250 truckloads of copper in this manner.[7]

To date, this popular resistance to the confiscation of door handles and bolts has received almost no attention from historians. Granted, in the larger context of the war, it did not play a momentous role. The war dragged on until November 1918, likely aided by armaments made from recycled door fixtures. Afterward, metal door handles and bolts gradually returned.

Why did this measure trigger such an outcry? And why did it strike people as a kind of house-suicide? In our everyday lives, we tend to pay little attention to doors and their fixtures. We open and close them dozens of times every day; we regard them (if at all) as a means to an end, as mere devices for entering a building or room. But might not we, too, react with a great deal of discomfort and anxiety if we knew our doors and locks would soon stop working as they should?

This is a study of doors, gates, and keys and a history of the hopes and anxieties that Western culture has attached to them. Since my main focus is the premodern period, it may seem strange to have begun with a scene from World War I, but let us linger there for just a moment longer, specifically in 1915, three years before the confiscation of door fixtures became a political issue in German-speaking lands. At that time, a largely unknown writer in Prague by the name of Franz Kafka published a short story titled *Vor dem Gesetz* ("Before the Law").[8] "Before the Law stands a doorkeeper," opens Kafka. "To this doorkeeper there comes a man from the country and he begs for admittance to the Law." The story then proceeds along its Kafkaesque course: it is possible to go through the door, the doorkeeper responds, but not at the moment. After some deliberation, the man accepts this and installs himself in front of it, waiting "days and years" to be admitted. He makes many attempts to enter, but the doorkeeper keeps him waiting. When finally his life is coming to an end, a radiance begins to emanate "inextinguishably from the doorway." Desperate, the man asks why, in all these years, no one else has ever asked for admittance. In response, the doorkeeper roars in his ear: "No one else could ever be admitted here, since this entrance was intended only for you. I am now going to shut it."

This parable, which Kafka later incorporated into his novel *The Trial*, is just two pages long in most modern editions, but it has given rise to hundreds of pages of interpretation. One reason for this is the archetypal situation that it depicts, which each of us has encountered at one time or another: the sense of helplessness, of powerlessness that comes from being denied entry or even being locked out, and standing at the doorway in vain.

In these examples, we see two facets of our culture's complex relationship to its doors and doorways: more than just a functional place of passage, the door is an object onto which we project our anxieties and hopes, as well as a site of power, exclusion, and inclusion. This is one of the reasons it was (and remains) a locus of multiple, conflicting meanings. And for this reason, historians need to avoid the temptation of oversimplification. Doors, for instance, can exist in more states than merely open or closed, and even the meaning of an open or closed door is not constant. It has been observed that doors can function as a "communication system" and that "door position is a communicator of socializing intent."[9] In principle, this is correct; however, the content of the message and the way we perceive it are always contingent upon the specific situation and its sociocultural context. Thus, holding open a door is, in many situations, still considered a particular sign of respect. In the same vein, a door that is intentionally left open is often understood as a gesture of hospitality, an invitation to enter, or at least a sign of readiness to communicate. It is no coincidence that we speak figuratively of an "open house" for an occasion when a building or institution is open to a large number of people to whom entrance is otherwise prohibited. Significantly, the term "open house" and its corresponding German and French expressions, literally meaning "day of the open door" (*Tag der offenen Tür; journée portes ouvertes*), have entered the common lexicon precisely because they describe an *exception* to the rule, highlighting the infrequency of this situation: usually, the doors of a public building are open to the general public only one day in the year. (In the American context, "open house" can also refer to a different but similarly exceptional event: the showing of a house that is for sale.) However, an open door can also have negative connotations: a door we cannot close, or one that stands open for no obvious reason, will arouse—as during World War I—our mistrust, or worse, our fear.

Conversely, closed doors often signal protection to those who are inside and enable withdrawal from the outside world. Closing a door sends the message that one wishes to retreat to the interior of a dwelling and not be disturbed. As anthropological studies have demonstrated, doors in our society constitute "object[s] of fundamental importance for a sense of feeling at home."[10] Living in a building with a solid, lockable door has come to feel like a necessity in most Western countries. Thus, a history of our notion of security—postulated by the French historian Lucien Febvre half a century ago—would have to include a history of the door.[11]

Any kind of dwelling, be it a Stone Age cave, a medieval house, or a modern apartment, is marked by the same tension: it can be a place of protection, but it also has the potential to become a trap. The idea of not being able to open a door from the inside is the stuff of nightmares. And indeed, in emergency situations, the ability (or inability) to open a door from the inside can mean the difference between life and death. For this reason, public buildings are required to have emergency exits and, in many cases, panic exit devices; private buildings are sometimes subject to similar regulations.[12] But even when lives are not at stake, the loss of (individual) control over the opening of a door threatens our sense of personal freedom and essentially embodies the legal definition of imprisonment. Prison doors have no handles, and indeed millions of prison inmates around the world, irrespective of their crimes or backgrounds, are ultimately connected by a shared fate: the inability to open the doors behind which they live out their sentences. This feeling of powerlessness is a core and particularly humiliating aspect of the prisoner's punishment.

However, the inability to open a door from the inside is not the only nightmare associated with locked doors. Standing *outside* of a locked or impassable door can be equally frustrating and dispiriting, as Kafka's story illustrates. In the New Testament, too, the idea of standing before the gates of heaven, excluded from salvation in Christ, is one of the situations in which we find the proverbial "weeping and gnashing of teeth."[13] Conversely, in reality and in literature (the tale of Bluebeard, for example), locked and "secret" doors can also attract and fascinate us.

Between the seemingly binary states of open and closed, there is what the philosopher Gaston Bachelard called the "cosmos of the Half-open"—which is, in its own way, as complex as the completely open or closed door.[14] As Claus Seligmann has noted, "the half-open position is necessarily the most ambiguous of all," because it sends an inconclusive signal to its surroundings, so that "the potential for misunderstanding is very high [and] a well-structured social context is required to offset the inherent risk."[15] In Western culture, the half-open door has rarely been perceived in a positive light. This is particularly evident in Western iconography, where it often signifies unclear relationships or even the approach of death. Also, a partly open door at the center of a scene—in Dutch genre painting, for instance—often represents an irresistible invitation to eavesdrop (Figure 1).

Doors have always been more than simply a functional technology, and certainly more than just an aperture in a wall. As sociologist Georg Simmel remarked, the unstructured wall of a room is mute, but the door speaks.[16] Doors are truly storytellers: their design as well as the practices that any given

Figure 1. Nicolaes Maes, *The Eavesdropper*, c. 1655.
Wellington Museum, London.

society attaches to them can offer a wealth of information,
not least to the historian. Still today, doors are used to iden-
tify the style and period of historical buildings; Romanesque
and Gothic churches, for instance, are easily distinguishable
by their doors. Tellingly, the reverse sides of Euro banknotes
show stylized portals, explicitly selected—alternating with
windows—to symbolize specific periods of European history.

Clearly, then, the door, to borrow a term coined by Ernst
Cassirer, is an important "symbolic form," not just an object,

but rather a "part of the human world of meaning." Such forms, according to Cassirer, have the potential to embody mentalities and features of an epoch, since, more broadly speaking, "the mental content of meaning is connected to a concrete, sensory sign and made to adhere internally to it."[17] In addition, the door is one of the "most insistently rectangular elements" of our living space and has a *frame,* which in turn creates a resemblance to the form and visual effect of paintings.[18] And even the noises that a door makes may carry a message or a story: just think of the masterly way in which the femme fatale Clawdia Chauchat plays with the different registers of door-slamming in Thomas Mann's *The Magic Mountain.*

This book hones in on some of the stories told by doors. By peering into the past through doors, it explores a chapter in the cultural history of the West not yet probed and demonstrates how doors, gates, and related technologies such as the key have shaped the way we perceive and navigate the domestic and urban spaces that surround us in our everyday lives. This leads to the general question, then, of how, historically, we developed a fragile routine of orienting ourselves anew each day in the amorphous thing called "space."

The technical and material evolution of doors is an important part of this story, but there are other equally significant aspects that are visible only from the perspective of cultural history. For doors were and are more than the sum of their material parts, more than mere architectural elements of a building. This is why we also need to explore the rich variety of ways in which doors and doorways have served as symbols and metaphors in the course of European history. In this context, they emerge as remarkable examples of what Jacques Le Goff has called the "spatialization of thought."[19]

But if a purely technical perspective represents one extreme, then an exclusively metaphorological treatment would be the other. The historian does best to avoid both of these extremes and instead strike a balance by looking at the many practices that are associated with doors and embedding them within the broader context of cultural and everyday history. In other words, the historian must take into account that the door is above all a social and cultural convention.[20] Seligmann rightly observes that in Western culture, "only the door provides acceptable access to or egress from continuously bounded space. Climbing in or out windows, however conveniently located, or hacking one's way through walls, however flimsily constructed, are behaviors proscribed by the convention; we interpret them as odd or criminal."[21] But not every act of entering through a door is acceptable. Throughout history, doors have marked the place where the interior of a building begins and the exterior world ends, thus raising the question of who has the right to enter the *social* cosmos of the house, and who does not. As Pierre Bourdieu notes with respect to family life, doors play a crucial role in the "idealization of the interior as sacred, *sanctum*" by protecting the home's intimacy and separating it from the external world.[22] Depending on the type of building, doors can differentiate between further spheres as well. The French anthropologist Arnold van Gennep concluded in his classic study about rites of passage that "the door is the boundary between the foreign and domestic worlds in the case of an ordinary dwelling, between the profane and sacred in the case of a temple."[23]

In this context, the door's character as a threshold comes prominently to the fore. To be sure, not every threshold is a door, but every door is indeed a threshold. One could even go a step further and say that the omnipresence of doors in everyday life makes them the most important thresholds in the world we inhabit. The ceremonies and rituals of our religious and social lives reflect this. This quality, along with the "betwixt-and-between state of liminality" that doors embody, is primarily what has attracted the attention of researchers.[24] In their attempts to understand their own and foreign cultures, anthropologists have often focused on those particular symbolic rituals in which "to cross the threshold is to unite oneself with a new world."[25] The now largely forgotten folklore scholar Henri Gaidoz demonstrated as early as 1892 that throughout the course of history and in various cultures, numerous medicinal healing rituals have been connected with the idea of passing through a doorway. In archaic and animistic societies, this was largely connected to objects in nature: Gaidoz pointed to ancient tribal healing customs involving the act of passing between two special tree trunks or two halves of a sacrificed animal. Common to almost all of these rituals is the assumption that the illness will be transferred to the object of passage if the ritual is enacted properly.[26] Seen from this perspective, passing through a doorway for ritual and religious reasons represents a further development and a domestication of transitional rituals that were originally carried out in nature. A few years after Gaidoz's study, Arnold van Gennep took up this topic in his pioneering theory laid out in *Rites of Passage* (1909). Gennep concluded that in many cultures and many areas of life, "rites carried out on the threshold itself are transition rites."[27]

These and other anthropological studies inform this book in important ways.[28] At the same time, it must be stressed that much of the previous research on this subject has dealt with the role of the door or threshold on special occasions rather than in everyday life. The rites of passage that have been most thoroughly researched are those connected with exceptional situations (marriage, adoption, initiation into a particular community) or even unique situations (birth, death) in the life of an individual or of a community. Many of these occasions still exist in our modern world. However, as Walter Benjamin claims, the rites associated with them have become "ever more unrecognizable and impossible to experience."[29] Granted, there is a good deal of nostalgia in Benjamin's ambitious but unfinished *Passagen-Werk* (*The Arcades Project*), in which he set out to investigate a particular society at a particular time—Paris in the nineteenth century—along the lines of its once present and visible threshold locations and experiences.[30] By contrast, Benjamin saw his own time as a period in which "we have grown very poor in threshold experiences." He even claimed that the only threshold experiences we have left are those of falling asleep and waking.[31]

Of course, we need not follow Benjamin quite that far. In this study, we will see time and again how certain social practices are still bound to threshold locations, and conversely, how deeply rooted the "hesitancy to enter" remains to this day.[32] But it is also true that many of these practices are no longer as visible or as colorful as those mythically and religiously charged archaic threshold rituals that have captured the attention of anthropologists. If we take seriously what Benjamin called a "theory of thresholds" (*Schwellenkunde*), and if we wish to investigate the full spectrum of practices, ideas, and experiences associated with them, we must consider not only the special-occasion rites carried out at the threshold, but also those basic cultural skills that we have developed throughout history in order to handle doors in everyday life.[33]

A study of these everyday skills will enable us to approach the question of how, in Western culture, the door, like the house as a whole, has become an object "that gives mankind proofs or illusions of stability."[34] From a purely material perspective, doors have rarely been indestructible: they are generally made of little more than a slab of wood — or glass, in some modern cases — and thus are not an invincible guarantee of security, but rather a surface onto which we project our ideas of and need for security, privacy, and shelter. At the same time, doors reflect our related anxieties, as we saw in the example from World War I. The balancing act between these two poles requires a complex set of rules that govern our interactions with doors in our everyday lives. This book begins with that challenge: it is primarily devoted to cultural practices that have developed over the centuries for handling doors and, by extension, for making sense of the spaces that surround us.

Starting this thread, the first chapter explores the rich variety of ways in which doorways have served as sites of power, ritual, and religion. According to the Gospels, Christ referred to the entrance to heaven as a "strait gate" and famously compared himself to a door: "I am the door: by me if any man enter in, he shall be saved." Not only was this theological connection widely reflected in art and literature, it was also one of the primary reasons why premodern church portals were so frequently magnificent and profusely ornamented. I argue that this complex theological meaning of the door sheds light on why and how doors in general came to serve as sites for legal proceedings, as backdrops for political ceremony, and as indicators of social status and honor in everyday life.

Chapter 2 investigates the history of opening and locking doors. It refutes the view that it was common among premodern Europeans to keep their doors open because of an ostensibly lower sensibility for privacy and security. Instead, I demonstrate that premodern Europe was a society in which the question of who held the key had great importance. This is reflected, for instance, in the "power of the keys," an idea that had vast ramifications in a variety of contexts: it was inseparably connected to the hierarchy of the sexes in family life, the concept of property in law, the question of political influence in state affairs and at court, and the ideas of papal power and absolution in religion.

Chapter 3 opens with the observation that in Western culture, to this very day, crossing a home's threshold is often a ritualized procedure. The various practices and conventions related to passing through a door reflect a complex interplay of rational and superstitious assumptions. For centuries, doors were sites of magical customs, such as ritual burials under the threshold or the affixing of apotropaic objects. But it is not just exotic practices such as these that provide us with deeper insight into the way people in the past tried to control and tame the dangers associated with doors. Three everyday practices that exemplify this aim will be explored here: knocking on doors, passing through them, and protecting them from both physical and spiritual contamination.

Chapter 4 begins with the story of the most famous door in European history—namely, the main door of the Castle Church of Wittenberg, where Martin Luther, on 31 October 1517, is said to have posted his Ninety-Five Theses criticizing the Catholic Church, sparking the Reformation. Yet to this day it is not clear whether the posting of the theses actually happened, or whether that story is a product of legends from a later time. Using the events of 1517 as a starting point, this chapter reconstructs the general significance and meaning of doors in premodern Europe as places of publicity and the circulation of knowledge, but also as sites of controversy and conflict.

The final chapter focuses on a particular type of doorway that for centuries was among the most striking and visible features of the European city, often referred to as the "door of the city"—namely, the city gate. This chapter illuminates the effect of city gates on premodern daily life and what it actually meant to enter a city in the past. It also depicts the eminent political, legal, and symbolic functions of city gates in premodern Europe. Against this backdrop, it becomes clear that the razing of gates and walls, which began in full force during the nineteenth century, marks one of the most radical transformations in the long history of European cities.

Of course, this book cannot detail all the practices that have developed around doors throughout the centuries. The reader will likewise note that the focus is primarily on doors that separate an *interior* space from an *exterior* space. The term "interior space" may refer to a house or a sanctuary, and "exterior space," too, can take on various meanings depending on the context—a city street, for instance, or natural surroundings in the countryside. What all these constellations have in common, however, is that the door is where two spaces that are perceived as diametrically opposed—interior and exterior— meet one another.

One could object that walls likewise fulfill the function of separating interior space from exterior space. But on the conceptual level, this misses the mark. As Georg Simmel noted, "Precisely because it can also be opened, the door's closure provides the feeling of a stronger isolation against everything outside this space than the mere unstructured wall."[35] We could also say, taking after Henri Lefebvre, that the door "serves to bring a space, the space of a room, say, or that of a street, to an end."[36]

Along these lines, I cannot devote much space in this book to doors within building interiors. These doors, to be sure, have their own rich stories to tell about the expectations and associations that Western culture attached to them. In fact, the custom of installing solid doors in interior spaces developed earlier in Europe than in other societies. But rather than being a sign of cultural superiority, this was simply a matter of different preferences. Historically, in the Islamic world and in India and East Asia, the prevailing tendency was to separate rooms with curtains or sliding screens.[37] Both of these methods were also in use in classical Europe: archaeological research has shown that ancient Greek and Roman houses had interior curtains as well as doors.[38] But over the centuries, textiles, paper, and other flexible materials became less popular for enclosing interior rooms. Their disappearance corresponds to the rise of the opinion, now virtually unchallenged, that doors should fundamentally be "hard and resilient."[39]

What has not changed, however, is that interior doors, then as now, serve to differentiate a building's interior space, dividing it into areas with different functions. If these kinds of doors are not the focus of this study, it is precisely because it would lead us too far from the central topic of the book—namely, the question of how the door achieved the crucial role that it has played in Western culture toward the constitution of the categories of interior and exterior.

Clearly, these categories are not uniquely European. Each society, however, has its own distinct ways of defining and enacting them. If we look at Japanese culture, for example, traditional architecture is marked by a tendency to think of interior and exterior less as opposites than as unity. As a result, house and garden are not categorically separate, but ideally flow smoothly into one another. As we will see in Chapter 2, sliding doors played a much greater role in traditional Japanese architecture than hinged doors. Pushed to the side, they give the impression that the wall has been canceled and that the border between house and nature is fluid. In European architecture, by contrast, interior and exterior have often been perceived as opposites, and convention demands that they be kept distinct, not conflated. By and large, the transitional space between the two zones was not (and is not) meant to be blurred, but rather to be made as visible as possible, and the task of demarcation has been assigned to the door more than to any other architectural element in the house.

Here we reach one of the essential functions of the door, and at the same time one of the reasons for its symbolic power. For doors were and are far more than purely physical boundaries: they are also places of separation and hierarchization on a social level. This was especially evident in premodern times: at the entrances of private houses, doors generally distinguished between residents and strangers; in the case of government buildings, between rulers and subjects; in churches, between believers and nonbelievers; and in urban spaces, where we encounter doors massively expanded into city gates, between citizens and foreigners. The distinction between interior and exterior thus was not purely a spatial one, but frequently also carried explicit moral and ideological dimensions.[40]

Clearly, the idea of the house as sanctum, and the need for a quiet, private life within one's own four walls, can be traced much further back than the beginning of modernity, which is too often—and incorrectly—hailed as the birth of the notion of privacy. Premodern Europeans did assign great importance to issues of privacy and security, and they were vigilant about the state of their doors. In fact, they considered an intact door an indispensable component of a house—nay, a civilizing achievement. Tellingly, no less eminent a philosopher than Immanuel Kant used doors to illustrate the difference between humans and animals: in a 1762 essay, he rejected the idea that

"an ox's representation of its stall includes the clear representation of its characteristic mark of having a door." By extension, he denied that "the ox has a distinct concept of the stall."
For Kant, "only the being who forms the judgment: *this door
belongs to this stable* has a distinct concept of the building, and
that is certainly beyond the powers of animals."[41] Kant was not
alone in this opinion; some of his contemporaries, including
jurists and architects, expressed more generally the opinion
that doors and windows constituted those parts of the house
that distinguish it from "the dwellings of brute animals."[42]
From this followed the rule that doors and windows should
be particularly visible and that "their proportions and decorations" should be well planned and elegantly formed.[43]

Such statements remind us that doors and windows have
unmistakable commonalities, and the history of the window is
a fascinating topic in its own right. However, for the purpose
of this study, the differences are quite significant. Although,
like the door, the window is an opening in a wall, it is not a
threshold. And the respective importance of door and window
to the concept of the house also differs greatly: the window is
an option, but the door is a necessity, "the device that makes
architecture possible."[44]

This distinction is especially striking from the perspective
of historical *longue durée*. Archaeological studies, for example,
confirm that doors appeared earlier in history than windows.[45]
And especially in the distant past, the function of the window
was not as self-evident as it might seem to us today. This can
still be seen in the etymology of the word "window," which
derives from the Old Norse word *vindauga*, literally "an eye

for wind." Indeed, in parts of northern Europe until the early Middle Ages, windows were little more than vents for wind and smoke.[46] Windows that served primarily to let in light or provide a view of the outside—let alone glass windows—took centuries to develop. As late as the nineteenth century, in parts of the southern Italian countryside, so-called *trulli* were still being built—stone roundhouses that were always equipped with a door but rarely with windows in the conventional sense. Instead, they had tiny openings in the upper portion of the wall (or sometimes just a single opening in the ceiling) for venting smoke.

Today, very few of us would be willing to live in a *trullo*, but this is a matter of comfort and not a sign that we cannot tolerate buildings without windows. On the contrary, modernity has actually perfected the windowless building: with the triumph of electricity—together with artificial light and climate control—it is now possible to live and work in entirely windowless rooms. Each of us has been in one of those department stores, theaters, cinemas, libraries, or laboratories—buildings that often get by without any windows. Doors, by contrast, remain indispensable; and in some of those windowless buildings, it is actually the doors, especially glass doors, that constitute the only window to the external world. And while it is generally unacceptable in our culture to use windows for entering and exiting, we have no objection if a door, albeit one made of glass, assumes the function of a window.

Yet the increasing number of glass doors in Western architecture should not be misinterpreted: their transparency does not mean that they are more likely to be kept open or that we have become lax about closing them. On the contrary, one particularly well-known type of glass door, the revolving door, is ready for use in any position but at the same time is always closed. This type of door was introduced in 1888 by the American inventor Theophilus Van Kannel, along with the telling advertising slogan: *Always closed.*[47] A look at the statistics confirms that glass doors create only an illusion of openness: as early as the 1950s, when the popularity of these doors was on the rise, the United States saw "an average of 40,000 serious accidents per year due to people walking [into] or falling against glass."[48]

But even for buildings with façades featuring both doors and windows, a damaged window is considered far less problematic and dangerous than a damaged door. A broken window can have a variety of meanings, and it is no coincidence that a famous sociological theory is known by exactly this name. The "broken windows theory" maintains that broken window-panes left unrepaired and easily visible to passersby are one of the first indicators of the gradual decline of a neighborhood, with all the attendant social problems.[49] Yet precisely this observation also points to a further cultural difference between doors and windows. Indeed, the central argument of the broken windows theory is that individuals and communities *can* regard an unrepaired windowpane with indifference; but we cannot easily ignore a damaged door or write it off as merely a sign of "urban disorder." Rather, we see it as evidence of criminal activity, even as a source of danger. And this brings us back to the war-torn year of 1918. The order to dismantle window handles and latches upset German householders, yet the idea of intentionally damaging one's own door caused far greater anxiety and uproar.

Insights await us not only in looking at the history of the door, but also in looking at history *through* doors. Now, let's step inside.

CHAPTER ONE

"I Am the Door"
Portals of Salvation and Status

I F WE COULD TRAVEL BACK in time and walk through a premodern city, we would likely find the sensory experience unusual. The ambient smells were often rank compared with those of our modern cities, while the now normal clamor of machines and electronic devices was blissfully absent.[1] Today, we must rely on textual sources to help bring these experiential aspects to life. By contrast, it is far easier to conceive of what a premodern city *looked* like, because of the historic districts that survive in cities throughout Europe: many churches, palaces, and houses have been preserved over the centuries and look very much like they originally did. However, this does not mean that we *look at* these cities in the same way that people of premodernity did. Here again, both written and visual sources of the time can help us piece together what people paid attention to when they passed through urban spaces—and it becomes clear that their perceptions were often quite different from ours. Francesco Bocchi's *Le bellezze della città di Fiorenza,* for instance, which first appeared in 1591, provides an extensive and popular description of the city of Florence. Although it was presented as a travel guide for foreign visitors, it can also be seen as part of the genre of laudatory descriptions of cities that allowed urban citizens to share their pride in their city's noteworthy sights.[2]

Let us spend a moment in sixteenth-century Florence, with Bocchi as our guide. We cannot help but notice the careful attention Bocchi pays, on his various city tours, to the doors of buildings. He presents the "skillfully executed doors" of a certain palazzo as witness to the "exquisite inventiveness" of the architect. Looking at another palazzo, he observes that "the portal is of noble appearance." And of a third he notes that "the very beautiful portal on the façade is made with rich and magnificent ornamentation." Bocchi also devotes attention to the less ornate private homes of ordinary citizens. At times he points to their "beautiful doors"; elsewhere he remarks that a particular "door is designed with much grace." Church doors always merit special attention: the two bronze doors by Donatello in the sacristy of San Lorenzo "are very highly prized by all artists." And of the doors on the right side of the nave at San Lorenzo, attributed to Michelangelo, he writes, "In the simplicity of the parts one recognizes such an elegant and refined understanding that all other work, no matter how exquisite, is surpassed." Yet the most extravagant praise of all is reserved for the famous bronze doors of the Florence Baptistery, designed by Lorenzo Ghiberti (Figure 2). According to Bocchi, they are "executed with such unique and uncommon workmanship that they are regarded as miraculous rather than merely outstanding. Truly, if these two doors by Ghiberti were

Figure 2. Lorenzo Ghiberti, *Gates of Paradise,* 1425–1452.
Baptistery of San Giovanni, Florence.

visible only on occasion, and not at all times, as is the case, there is no doubt that they would rightly be counted among the most valuable wonders of the world."[3]

Bocchi's close attention to doors is a productive but by no means unusual example. Indeed, doors at that time were not simply functional objects, and they carried far more meanings than we associate with them today. Even the doors of average private houses were more than just mechanisms for entering a building. They frequently served as sites for legal proceedings, as backdrops for political ceremonies, and as indicators of social status and honor. Thus the cultural historian cannot focus solely on the door's material appearance: it is also crucial to uncover the roles that doors played within the symbolic world of premodernity and within what Jacques Le Goff has called the premodern "spatialization of thought."

In this context, the religious symbolism of doors, especially church doors, springs to mind. It is no exaggeration to say that the church door was considered the archetype of all doors in premodern culture, and it frequently became the showplace for a range of religious rituals and ceremonies.[4] In other words, each church door, far from being merely an imposing and interchangeable backdrop, was believed to embody a specific religious meaning.[5]

This metaphysical dimension was closely connected to the contemporary understanding of salvation, a context in which doors and gates played an essential role. Indeed, premodern people were convinced that the decision between every soul's salvation or damnation would someday be played out in front of very real, though not earthly, doorways: the entrances to heaven

and hell. Remember those magnificent doors to the Florence
Baptistery, which Bocchi called a "wonder of the world" and
which the great Michelangelo himself saw—literally—as an
anticipation of the "gates of paradise." This designation has
lived on in the vernacular, although most of the Baptistery's
present-day visitors are probably not familiar with the depth
of this religious background. For us, the religious experience
of these doors has become a purely aesthetic one.

In premodernity, by contrast, most people firmly believed
that heaven and paradise would be reached through gateways
or doorways; they also pondered endlessly over who would be
permitted to enter, and what they needed to do to ensure their
admittance. Over the centuries, responses to this question—a
key issue in Christian theology—divided the various currents
within Christianity, particularly after the Reformation, but
there was consensus on the idea of a gateway to heaven, which
was confirmed by the Old Testament.[6] And in the New Testament, it was Jesus himself who, in a famous verse, described
heaven's gate as "the strait gate," where "there are last which
shall be first, and there are first which shall be last." He advised his disciples, "Strive to enter in at the strait gate: for
many, I say unto you, will seek to enter in, and shall not be
able."[7] Thus, the celestial door was open only to the righteous,
as can also be seen in several other New Testament passages.
One of these (Matt 16:13–20) is the source of the belief that
the Apostle Peter kept watch over this door and that Christ
himself entrusted Peter with the key.

Yet the exact location of this entrance to heaven was a
source of much disagreement. The influential doctor of the

church Isidore of Seville (c. 560–636) claimed that there must be *two* doorways, one to the east and one to the west.[8] This issue was further complicated because the Bible does not state definitively whether the *porta caeli* should be envisioned as a gate or a door. The Latin term *porta* was ambiguous in any case; in premodern times, it could designate a city gate as well as a house door.[9] Indeed, in Christian iconography we find both options: the entrance to heaven sometimes appears as an imposing city gate, while elsewhere it is a simple wooden door positioned in the firmament between the sun and the moon, as though part of a modest dwelling of that era (Figure 3).[10]

Here, we should also distinguish between the heavenly gates and the gate that stood, according to contemporary thinking, at the entrance to *paradise*—which here means the garden of Eden. For Christian teaching made a distinction between the earthly paradise and the kingdom of heaven. Certain authors, such as St. Augustine (354–430), pondered whether the two realms might not in fact be one and the same. But by and large, from early Christianity onward, the prevailing belief was "that an intermediate place of happiness or at least of rest, namely 'paradise,' receives the soul of the just until these recover their bodies and make the final ascent to the kingdom of heaven."[11] Well into the early modern period, theologians and travelers sought to locate paradise in various earthly places, primarily the Orient. It was widely presumed that the entrance to the garden of Eden had a gate, which had been locked since the expulsion of Adam and Eve. According to this interpretation, only Jesus could open this gate for humanity: shortly before his death on the cross, he promised the

Figure 3. Heinrich Seuse, *Das Buch, das Seuse heißt* (Augsburg, 1482), with detail showing the entrance to heaven as a plain wooden door.

Good Thief, "Verily I say unto thee, To day shalt thou be with me in paradise."[12]

Over the centuries, the Christian imagination built still more doorways on the path to salvation, further strengthening the door's role as one the most important symbolic forms in Christian eschatology. New doors emerged in the Christian economy of salvation as the idea of purgatory gained currency and influence during the Middle Ages.[13] According to this idea, some souls, though not actually barred from the kingdom of heaven, would not be allowed entry until they had served penance for their worldly sins and undergone a process of purification. While some early Christian authorities considered purgatory to be a spiritual state, theologians and believers during the High Middle Ages increasingly thought of it as an actual location. It was a "spacious" place, but also an "enclosed space."[14] This implied that there would have to be an entrance to, as well as an exit from, the realm of purgatory.

In the *Divine Comedy,* Dante gives a detailed description of his entrance through the gateway of purgatory, where an angel inscribed the letter *P* (for *peccatum,* "sin") seven times on his forehead with a sword. The realm of purgatory that lay behind this gate, according to Dante, consisted of a mountain with seven tiers, each representing a specific sin. The poet had to stop at each one in order to cleanse the wound of the corresponding *P.* Entering purgatory was thus a thorny procedure, yet Dante describes the portal in positive terms, as a "holy gate" (*porta sacrata*).[15] And indeed, this portal was relatively harmless compared with the one that led to eternal damnation.

It was at those gates of hell that Dante began his journey through the afterlife. In one famous passage he reported that this entrance bore, in dark letters, the fearful inscription:

> Through me the way into the suffering city,
> Through me the way to the eternal pain,
> Through me the way that runs among the Lost. . . .
> Abandon every hope, who enter here.[16]

The idea of hell as a city with barred gates can be found in numerous ancient religions, but Christianity visualized it in particularly gruesome detail, and Dante's grim description fits the nightmarish depictions of hell that were emerging from the eschatological imaginations of his contemporaries.[17] Furthermore, the entrance to hell, unlike that of purgatory, is explicitly mentioned in the Bible: the Gospel of Matthew (16:18) affirms, "The gates of hell shall not prevail against [the church]."[18] While Matthew did not specify precisely what awaited the damned beyond these gates, other books in the Bible, particularly the Book of Revelation, offered premodern believers a vivid portrait of the horrors associated with entering the realm of hell. Later contributions from clerics and poets, Dante among them, expanded on these horrors. In the fifth century, Bishop Caesarius of Arles offered a particularly terrifying vision of hell, which he imagined as a vertical pit with doors at the top: "No breathing space will be left, no breath of air will be available when the doors press from above. Those who say farewell to the things of nature will be cast down there; since they have refused to know God, they will no longer be recognized by Him."[19] The entryway in particular was often described in lively detail, and some authors even claimed to know that the doors were burning hot to the touch or that they creaked.[20] Protestants, too, embraced this vivid imagery. Indeed, Luther sharply criticized contemporary skeptics who argued that hell could not possibly have a wooden door; they reasoned that such a door would have burned down long ago. And while Luther acknowledged that humans cannot know whether the gates of hell (and their chains) are made of wood or iron, he did not reject the imagery associated with the entrance to the underworld, for "we have to visualize the things that we do not know or understand, irrespective of whether, in reality, they look the way they are commonly depicted."[21]

Indeed, Christian art offers numerous visualizations of the gates of hell. Particularly impressive is the psalter of Henry of Blois from the twelfth century, which portrays an angel locking away Satan and his ilk with an imposing key, as described in Revelation 20 (Figure 4). Pictures of the gates of hell also figure frequently in the rather different context of Christ's "Harrowing of Hell." The New Testament only hints at this episode, but it was fleshed out and popularized through the apocryphal Gospel of Nicodemus and was in line with theological thinking of the time, according to which souls who had been condemned to hell could not possibly escape the underworld by their own powers.[22] Yet one group of souls could still hope for redemption: those found in limbo, a place located around the edges of hell (the Latin word *limbo* means "boundary").[23] These were the souls of pagans who led righteous lives before the coming of Christ, as well as the souls of infants who had died unbaptized. Christ himself was believed to have appeared at the gates of hell after his death and to

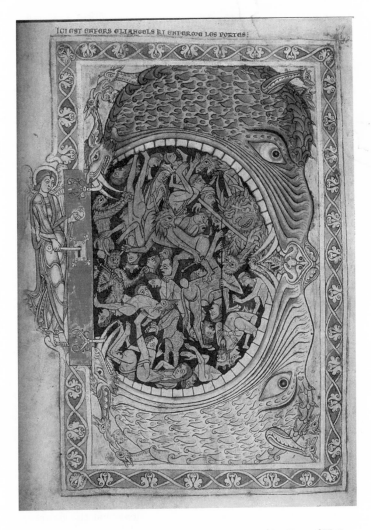

Figure 4. *The Last Judgment: An Angel Locking the Gate of Hell.*
Psalter of Henry of Blois (Winchester Psalter),
c. 1150–1250. British Library, London.

have opened them for the souls in limbo. Although the church never elevated the idea of limbo to the status of a doctrine, and theologians disagreed upon the extent to which Christ's appearance there could offer those souls true salvation, the episode remained a favorite subject in premodern Christian art.

The visual depiction of this scene was highly standardized. Typically, the entrance to hell is situated in a barren landscape, and the liberated souls gaze out in awe at their savior, who has just defeated the guardians of the underworld and unlocked the gates. Christ is often shown standing triumphant on the broken door, which has been torn from its hinges and thrown to the ground.[24] Incidentally, historians are indebted to these paintings: they are among the most detailed extant depictions of premodern doors, including the hinges on the ground and the nails from the doorframe (Figure 5). This precision of detail was no coincidence but a part of the message: the viewer should have no doubt about the all-conquering power manifest in Christ's breaking open the doors. It was also in line with the image from the Gospels in which Christ appeared to the apostles after his resurrection, and in so doing vanquished the locked doors (John 20:19), a miracle that premodern theologians regarded as further proof of his "not only natural, but also divine qualities."[25] By the same token, depictions of the Harrowing of Hell made it painfully clear that the damned would never be able to open the gate to the underworld from the inside. According to Nicodemus, after Christ appeared, he closed the gate of hell until the end of time, locking it from the outside with seven seals—or in words that in the Middle Ages were attributed to St. Peter Damian, a doctor of the

Figure 5. Fra Angelico, *Christ's Harrowing of Hell*, 1438, with detail showing the door to hell broken off its hinges and lying on the ground. Museo di San Marco, Florence.

church, "For those who are in hell prayer is useless, because the gates of mercy are closed to them and the hope of salvation forbidden."[26]

If faithful Christians wished to ensure their salvation and gain admittance directly to the kingdom of heaven, they were thus well advised to work toward it throughout their lifetimes. Indeed, according to the church, believers could have a glimmer of the divine feeling of passing through heaven's gate whenever they passed through a church door, the church being God's house on earth. In a statement attributed to St. Augustine, "There are two doors: the door of paradise and the door of the church: it is through the door of the church that we enter paradise."[27] This analogy between the two was a recurring theme in visual representations (Figure 6), and it influenced the architectural design of churches. In fact, this was one of the reasons why premodern church portals were so frequently magnificent and highly ornate.[28]

The theological underpinnings of the sacrality of the church door were largely based on two biblical passages. The more famous of the two — and the clearest expression of Christian door symbolism — comes from the Gospel of John, where Christ says, "I am the door: by me if any man enter in, he shall be saved" (10:9).[29] Thus Christ saw himself as the door to salvation. Some early modern theologians, such as the Protestant Martin Bucer (1491–1551), went as far as to argue that every door encountered in daily life should be seen as a reminder of Christ's reference to himself as the "door to eternal life."[30] While it is hard to know how many contemporaries shared Bucer's vision, familiarity with this biblical verse certainly

Figure 6. The elect entering the gate to heaven, which is fashioned in
the style of a Gothic cathedral. Detail from Stefan Lochner,
Last Judgment, c. 1435. Wallraf-Richartz-Museum, Cologne.

clarifies why so many premodern church portals feature an
image of Christ in a prominent place, usually the tympanum.[31]
The verse was also part of the Catholic rite for consecrating a
church and was inscribed above many church doors.[32] At the
Hagia Sophia in Constantinople, the largest cathedral in the

Christian world until its conversion into a mosque in the fifteenth century, it could even be seen above the majestic Imperial Door.[33]

The other biblical passage that influenced Christian door iconography and symbolism was the prophet Ezekiel's depiction of the eastern door of the temple: he described it as a *porta clausa,* an eternally closed door, through which only God himself could pass.[34] Premodern biblical commentators often allegorically connected this image with Mary's immaculate conception. Accordingly, premodern architects not only embellished the stone portals on their church façades, but also ensured that the doors displayed rich ornamentation in the *closed position.* For just as the open door, following John's description, was interpreted christologically, so the closed door symbolized the Virgin Mary. In fact, she was sometimes explicitly addressed as *porta caeli* and *ianua caeli* ("door to heaven").[35] In addition, the tendency to build three portals in a church façade was intended to be a reminder of the Trinity.[36]

Passing through a church door, then, was by definition more than a simple act of entering: it was charged with religious meaning. The solemn entrance into the church was a firmly established and carefully staged part of religious processions.[37] And in some churches, the congregant could even hope to receive an indulgence as a reward for passing through the door. The lavishly apportioned Holy Doors of the four papal basilicas in Rome were probably the most famous sites for this form of remission of sins. In a custom dating back to the late Middle Ages, a particular door in each of these four churches would be opened at the beginning of a Jubilee Year and would remain open to pilgrims for the rest of the year.[38] In other places, the remission of sins by passing through the door occurred on a regular basis. This was true of the Tomb of the Virgin Mary in Jerusalem, as we know from the report of the fifteenth-century German pilgrim Jörg Pfinzing: "Two small doors lead into the chapel. Whoever enters these two doors with sincere repentance and devotion will be freed of all his sins."[39]

In addition to religious rituals, certain architectural features also made passing through a church door a conscious and palpable experience. For instance, the doors of early Christian churches were often preceded by a narthex, an entrance hall that significantly expanded the transitory zone between profane outer world and the sacred inner space of the church. The narthex was often an imposing room in itself. This division of space into three parts also had a symbolic function because it mirrored the structure of the congregation: while the choir of the church was reserved for the clergy and the nave for the laity, the narthex created a space not actually inside the church but nevertheless sharing in its holiness. Its liminal quality also meant that it was open to those people who were not allowed to enter the sanctuary on special occasions, as well as to some groups who were barred altogether, such as penitents and heretics. Those awaiting baptism also had to remain outside the doors: tellingly, in Catholic teaching, baptism was considered the "gate to the sacraments" and to a Christian life.[40]

The narthex was a defining feature in the architecture of many early Christian churches. In cases of especially elaborate construction, a narthex might even boast five or seven "holy gates"—based on Christian numerology—leading into the actual church. Probably the best-known example of this is the Hagia Sophia in Istanbul, which actually has two narthices, both of which can still be seen today.[41] In the course of the Middle Ages, however, the concept of the narthex in Europe was gradually replaced by the ideal of a freestanding church façade. This choice made it easier to highlight the elaborate artistic design of portals, and this, in turn, facilitated an unobstructed display of their symbolism as gates of heaven (*porta caeli*).[42] Front portals with multiple nested arches that narrow toward the inside became a hallmark of Gothic churches (Figure 7). This characteristic visual effect not only refines the appearance of these imposing entrances, but also literally draws the believer into the church space.[43] In the same vein, the lavishly ornamented portals of large medieval cathedrals were not simply an aesthetic choice: their primary purpose was to convey a theological message. In his famous account of the Abbey Church of St.-Denis, for example, Abbot Suger records an inscription on the door:

> Whoever thou art, if thou seekest to extol the glory of these doors,
> Marvel not at the gold and the expense but at the craftsmanship of the work.
> Bright is the noble work; but, being nobly bright, the work
> Should brighten the minds, so that they may travel, through the true lights
> To the True Light where Christ is the true door.[44]

Of course, the grand portals of cathedrals were sometimes reserved for special and solemn occasions, and in daily life

Figure 7. Chartres Cathedral, western façade: the "Royal Portal" (c. 1145–1155), a masterpiece of early Gothic architecture. Nested arches create the effect of drawing the viewer into the church.

churchgoers would instead use the smaller side portals. It is also true that many churches were of humbler appearance than the great cathedrals. But even in these cases, believers had to be aware that in entering a church they crossed the threshold between a profane external space and a sacred interior—a threshold that the bishop himself had blessed in a ritual purification at the church's consecration.[45] In Le Puy-en-Velay, a medieval city in southern France, churchgoers and pilgrims were reminded of this special character of the church threshold as they climbed the imposing stairway leading up to the western portal of the cathedral: the final flight of stairs displayed a medieval Latin inscription admonishing impenitent criminals to refrain from touching the church's sacred threshold.[46] In every Catholic church there was also near the door a font of holy water, with which worshippers would cross themselves to complete their passage from the profane into the sacred sphere. This is still the case today, though the act of entering tends to receive much less attention; and it has been rightly observed that, since most visitors today focus on the interior of the church, the moment of entrance, and especially opening the heavy portal doors, is actually more likely to be felt as an obstacle.[47]

What has completely vanished from churches today is the custom of having a doorkeeper at the entrance. In Late Antiquity, the church doorkeeper even had a special name: *ostiarius* (from the Latin *ostium*, "door"). This term, which forms the etymological root for the English word "usher," harks back to the *ostiarii* of Roman antiquity, slaves who guarded the entrances to the villas of wealthy Romans. The early Christian communities appropriated the term but transplanted the position into a religious context. The ostiary became an ordained cleric entrusted with certain door-related duties. Since, in early Christendom, certain groups were not permitted to attend the celebration of the Eucharist, the ostiaries had to ensure that those people left the sanctuary after the liturgy of the Word, and they would then close the doors to the sanctuary. The ostiaries were also responsible for ringing the church bells and safeguarding the church doors from enemies, particularly during services. It was their task, as Bishop Isidore of Seville stated in the seventh century, to "watch over everything inside and out, and, making judgment between the good and the bad, they receive the faithful and reject the unfaithful."[48]

After Christianity became Europe's dominant religion, fear of physical attacks began to wane, and churches gradually opened up to the unbaptized as well. However, while the need to defend the church diminished, it was still necessary, then as now, to lock the church doors in certain situations and at certain times of day. Starting in the early Middle Ages, lay sacristans increasingly took over the door-keeping duties of the ostiaries. Yet the term "ostiary" survived in church language, even though little was left of its original meaning: for centuries, *ostiarius* remained the official term for the lowest rank of the minor orders of the church, and as late as the twentieth century, ordination to the rank of ostiary required the candidate to kneel before the bishop and touch a key with his right hand. The rank was not removed from the church hierarchy until 1972, when the term also disappeared.[49]

The premodern church also had other names for doorkeepers, and some of them, unlike *ostiarius,* are still quite familiar to us today, especially "porter" (from the Latin *portarius*) and "janitor" (from Latin *ianua,* "door"). Of course, we now generally use the latter to mean "custodian." But in premodernity both of these terms were used for the doorkeepers who guarded monastery gates. Only highly trustworthy people were eligible for this important responsibility. As early as the sixth century, the Rule of St. Benedict stipulated, "A wise old man, one who knows how to take a message and reply to it and whose age does not permit him to be idle, should be placed at the door of the monastery."[50] Like so many cultural phenomena related to doors, these terms, which live on today in the secular world, originated in religious contexts.[51]

This is true also of other practices. Indeed, church doors played a role in various administrative, political, and legal contexts.[52] Throughout premodernity, they functioned as bulletin boards and as sites for circulating information because of their high visibility in the urban landscape. Partly for this reason, too, they were also used for various legal transactions. For example, the area in front of the church portal was used for trials and for the execution of sentences in many parts of medieval northern and Central Europe. And to this day, the portals of some medieval churches show grooves caused by the whetting of swords, probably in connection with legal rituals.[53] Portals used as sites of court deliberations and punishment were often called "red doors," and this was no coincidence: red, the color of blood, was a symbol of jurisdiction, and the architects and builders were well aware of this. In the *Schedula diversarum artium* (*On Divers Arts*), a twelfth-century compendium describing various techniques for artists and artisans, there is a chapter titled "How to Redden Doors." While the red color has long since vanished from these portals, the custom has left traces on a linguistic level. In Dutch, if a man says he has to "go before the red door" (*vor de roode deur moeten gaan*), he means he must appear in court—even though the court, of course, has long since moved away from the church portal, and the doors of Dutch courtrooms are no longer red.[54]

Although its use as a court was already on the wane from the late Middle Ages onward, the church portal retained its importance for other legal transactions, such as the signing of contracts and swearing of oaths.[55] We know that in the early modern Venetian territories, for which recent studies have provided reliable figures, 5 percent of all notarial legal transactions were still carried out on church thresholds.[56] This may seem a modest amount, but we should remember that, especially in the Republic of Venice, many alternative locations for legal affairs existed, among them the offices of public notaries and the chancelleries of the governing authority. In short, the importance of the church door as a legal location was not entirely supplanted by the increasing institutionalization of the law. To the contrary, the significance of doors and gates in law remained sufficiently important for entire legal treatises to be written about the subject.[57]

Doors and thresholds also retained a role in a legal ceremony connected to an important rite of passage: marriage. Well into the early modern period it was common in many parts of Europe for the first part of the marriage ceremony to take place not inside the church, but at the church door. Specifically, the marriage vows and the exchange of rings took place outside the door, since these were legal transactions, while the celebration of the mass, which in Catholicism highlighted marriage as a sacrament, was reserved for the church interior. The Christian iconographic tradition emphasized and legitimized this custom, often depicting wedding scenes—particularly Mary's—as taking place in front of or at church portals. This also clarifies what the Wife of Bath in Chaucer's fourteenth-century *Canterbury Tales* means when she says that "Housbondes at chirche dore she hadde fyve."[58]

What is more, this custom left traces in the very architecture of churches: numerous medieval and early modern churches had a special lateral "bridal portal," in front of which the legal, secular part of the marriage ceremony would take place (Figures 8 and 9).[59]

By the same token, church doors played a significant role when marriages were dissolved. From early modern Scotland and Ireland, for example, we know that a divorce was considered complete when the former spouses left the church via

Figure 8. Bridal portal of the late Gothic St. George's Minster in Dinkelsbühl, an imperial city in southern Germany. A statue of the Virgin Mary stands in the central section of the tympanum.

Figure 9. The wooden doors of the bridal portal, as seen from inside St. George's Minster. The doors, along with their exquisite ironwork decorations, were made in 1725/26.

two separate doors.[60] And church doors also became a stage for dissolving a different kind of union: between believer and church. Thus the formal act of excommunication customarily took place at the church entrance. Excommunicants literally would be "shown the door" and thereby excluded from the house of God. To return to the fold, they would have to do penance and swear to improve, prostrating themselves on the ground before the church portal. Only then would the bishop take them by the right hand and lead them back into the church.[61] This same location played a role in other rituals of repentance as well. The chronicler and abbot Regino of Prüm, writing around 900, described the rites of Ash Wednesday as follows: "all penitents taking on a public penance shall present themselves before the doors of the church to the Bishop of the diocese—clad in a sack, with bare feet, face pointed to the ground, thus bearing witness to their guilt in their clothing and demeanor." After the penitents were led into the church and strewn with ashes, the bishop was to "command the servants to cast them out the church doors. . . . On Maundy Thursday they should return to the entrance of the church."[62] But this ritual seems relatively painless compared with what Raymond VI, Count of Toulouse, had to undergo in 1209. The previous year he had ordered the murder of a papal legate and was consequently excommunicated. When he showed remorse for his deed, the church authorities gave him a special penance: he was led naked through the streets of the town of Saint-Gilles du Gard to the portal of the abbey church (*adductus est comes nudus ante fores ecclesiae*). There, in the tympanum, he could see a depiction of the Second Coming of Christ—an explicit reminder that he, too, would someday have to justify his deed to the savior.[63]

Conversely, people who sought the protection of the church at a time of persecution (just or unjust) knew that grasping the church door, particularly the door ring, was often their last hope. For this act entitled them to asylum in the church and gave them at least temporary respite from their persecutors or from the authorities. The idea that a church should offer sanctuary was appropriated from pagan temples in Late Antiquity, probably an attempt by the early church to keep up with rival cults in terms of general appeal.[64] Indeed, during the Middle Ages and early modern period, when feuding and vigilantism often challenged the state's developing monopoly on power, the church's offer of asylum was not a purely theoretical scenario, nor was it unusual. Machiavelli, who watched the political struggles and vendettas in Renaissance Florence, noted that "all those who for public or private cause are persecuted are accustomed to take refuge in churches."[65] In medieval England, we have estimates of roughly 800 cases of church sanctuary each year, and even during the early modern period, we find 332 recorded cases of *petitio immunitatis* in the cathedral of Durham alone during the years 1464–1524. The actual number may be far higher, since the Durham registers listed only asylum seekers who had committed serious crimes, primarily murder.[66] Only in rare instances did a church refuse sanctuary; in all other cases the fugitive could at least achieve a standoff by grasping the door ring. And although a lengthy stay in the church grounds was generally not possible, extradition was out of the question. On the whole, these situations could be resolved only through a compromise, in which the revenge seekers renounced their violent intentions on condition that their opponent leave the city and go into exile.[67]

A breach of church asylum, by contrast, could be harshly punished. This was the experience of a group of government officials in the French city of Sens in 1304, as reported in a contemporary source. Suspecting a clergyman of a crime, they "ripped him forcefully away from the doors of the church and its ring, which he had been grasping, whereby they multiply breached and shamelessly infringed upon the immunity of the church." The officials were subsequently dismissed and required to do penance and pay a monetary fine to the church.[68] Harsher still was the punishment imposed on a bailiff of the Earl of Leicester who, in the year 1200, removed a fugitive thief from a church in Brackley (Northamptonshire) and had him hanged at the gallows. The bishop of the diocese subsequently ordered that the bailiff and his accomplices be excommunicated. The punishment was not lifted until the men underwent a gruesome penance: they had to appear before the gallows in the middle of winter, barefoot and dressed only in their undergarments, to dig up the thief's decaying corpse and carry it on their bare shoulders back to the church of Brackley, about a mile away. There they had to carry the corpse once around the sanctuary building while being scourged by the clergy; then they had to prepare an honorable burial for the corpse. And finally they had to walk barefoot to distant Lincoln, the seat of the diocese, where once again they had to repent before the portals of the local churches and endure further scourging.[69]

The houses of worship of Europe's most visible religious minority at the time—namely, Jews—played a similar role. Indeed, the synagogue door also functioned as a distinct legal space and a place of publicity in everyday life. It was commonly used for the cancellation of deeds and seal, as, for example, in the public announcement of the death of a debtor.[70] Minor lawsuits and lesser legal transactions were likewise decided there, particularly in Ashkenazic communities; and it was common in some places to swear oaths while holding the door ring of the synagogue. An analogous custom can be found among Christians: in the absence of a legal codex or holy book, they were allowed to swear oaths with a hand placed on the church doorpost.[71]

For Jews, the synagogue door also played a vital role in the rituals that focused on belonging to the community. For example, the religious excommunication (*cherem*) of an individual was often made known by posting a verdict on the door.[72] Conversely, when Jews who were banned (or who had rejected their religion through conversion) displayed credible remorse and an honest will to return to the faith, the door of the synagogue was frequently the showplace for their readmission to the community. Depending on the severity of the case, sometimes renegades would be permitted reentry into the sacred space of the synagogue (and thus into the community) only after they had literally become an object of a transgression. The freethinker Uriel Acosta recorded this in a vivid account of his second return to Judaism in 1640. First he was bound to a pillar of the synagogue and scourged; "after this I put on my clothes, and went to the threshold of the synagogue [*ad limen Synagogae*], where I prostrated myself, the door-keeper holding up my head, whilst all both old and young passed over me, stepping with one foot on the lower part of my legs, and behaving with ridiculous and foolish gestures. . . . When they had all done, I got up, and being washed and made clean by the man who stood by me for that purpose, I went home."[73] But even a symbolic (and humiliating) ritual of this sort was not always enough to ensure a clean break between past and present for the affected individual or for the community. Acosta, in any case, was unable to return to a normal state of affairs, as the debasement—understood here quite literally—had so damaged the religious critic's sense of honor that he committed suicide a few weeks later.

The imposing architecture and religious significance of church doors also left traces in linguistic history. With the rise of Christianity in northern Europe, the common words for "door"—the Germanic precursors of the current English word (including the Old English *duru* and Old High German *turi*)—which usually referred to regular house doors, were felt to be inadequate for the lavishly appointed doors of the church. Already in the early Middle Ages church doors were often ironclad or ornamented with wooden carvings; some were even covered with leather or precious fabrics. As the difference between sacred and secular architecture became more and more apparent, the Germanic-Latin neologism *turiporta* was coined to describe church doors. This is actually a tautology, since the Latin *porta* also refers to an entrance. But precisely this tautological emphasis expressed the imposing nature of the church door.[74]

In comparison with church doors, the doors of private houses during the early Middle Ages were relatively modest. In the later Middle Ages, however, this began to change. Along these lines, the Renaissance architect Leon Battista Alberti argued in his influential treatise *On the Art of Building* (c. 1450) that doors should be given "a graceful appearance." Tellingly, he also felt obliged to caution that it was inappropriate to imitate sacred architecture too closely when building a residential house, or to build a home's doors of bronze or ivory. Instead, Alberti recommended the use of "modest materials."[75] Yet it was precisely in his time that we see heightened attention to doors in secular architecture, with architects of the Italian Renaissance focusing extensively on how they should be built and embellished.[76] The renowned architect Sebastiano Serlio (1475–1554) devoted an entire treatise to this theme, including fifty drafts for doors, portals, and gates, some of them in antique styles, others very extravagant.[77] For Serlio, doors and gates "could stimulate the qualities he most admired in the good architect, namely judgment and inventiveness."[78]

Another Italian architect engaged in this discourse was Vincenzo Scamozzi (1548–1616), who wrote extensively about doors in his theory of architecture. He drew a basic distinction between three sorts of entrances to buildings: the main entrance (*porte principali*), the less significant doors (*porte meno principali*), and the side doors (*porte accessorie*). The terms themselves make clear that the front door was the most important, not only because of its function but also because of its significance for the dignified appearance of the house as a whole. The main entrance was one of the "essential parts" (*parti essentiali*) of the house, prominently exposed to the gaze of guests and visible to all passersby. According to Scamozzi, it should be as attractive as possible; he considered marble an especially appropriate material for the doorframe. He also voiced clear opinions about the proper positioning of the door in the façade, claiming that the door is to the house as the mouth is to a living creature.[79] For Scamozzi, the analogy between door and mouth was primarily a lesson in the proper positioning of the entrance, in line with its importance to the overall appearance of the house. But some of his contemporaries took the analogy more literally, designing their front doors to *look* like oversized mouths: the most famous—and perhaps also most eccentric—example is the portal to the Palazzo Zuccari in Rome, built by the painter and art theorist Federico Zuccari in the 1590s (Figure 10).

The idea of the door as the house's mouth was, in itself, not new: it connects to an etymological explanation that went back to the Middle Ages, according to which the Latin word *ostium* ("door") was derived from the word *os* ("mouth").[80] In medieval architecture, however, this notion had found expression only in limited ways: in Romanesque and Gothic secular architecture, the position of the door depended largely on the practical needs of the dwellers.[81] During the early modern period, by contrast, architects like Scamozzi promoted the idea that the main door of a building should be placed as close to the center of the façade as possible. This preference emerged in Renaissance Italy, but it soon spread across northern Europe, where private houses with symmetrical façades became increasingly popular, featuring the door—like a mouth—at the center.[82] And it fits into this picture that the word "façade," tellingly derived from the Italian word for "face" (*faccia*), first came into widespread use across Europe in the early modern period.[83]

Princely palaces and other official buildings were ideal places for architects like Serlio and Scamozzi to realize their ambitious plans, and during the early modern period, these buildings frequently became loci for lavish expressions of

Figure 10. Mouth-shaped entrance to the Palazzo Zuccari, Rome.
Built by the painter and art theorist Federico Zuccari in the 1590s.

wealth and power. Magnificent doors, in particular, were seen
as reflections of the prince's status, so their effect had to be
maximized. Filippo Maria Visconti, the ambitious and eccentric ruler of Renaissance Milan, even ordered his architects
to move the location of the interior doors of his palace during

his absences so that he could derive new delight from these changes upon returning.[84] To be sure, many early modern castles were built not only for the pleasure of their noble inhabitants, but also to be admired by their non-noble guests and by foreign travelers; in fact, travel guides of the day recommended that visitors pay attention to the construction and ornamentation of the doors.[85] A poem about the Palazzo Medici in Florence, written in 1459, praised the building's intarsiated doors, claiming that some of them were so artfully executed that "no one could ever tire of looking."[86] Unsurprisingly, a door that failed to meet expectations would not escape criticism. According to the seventeenth-century German artist and art theorist Joachim von Sandrart, a stately building with "a narrow and dark entrance" was bound to appear like a "beautiful and well-proportioned body that has been given a crude and ugly head."[87] Along the same lines, Michel de Montaigne, on his visit to the small country villa of the Medici in Pratolino in 1580, praised the impressive gardens but commented to the gatekeeper that he "strongly condemned the ugliness of the doors and windows." The doors in particular displeased him: he thought they looked like "big pine planks, without shape or workmanship," far inferior to courtly architecture in his own country and to what he had seen elsewhere on his journey through Italy.[88]

From the Renaissance onward, architects and artists also devoted increasing attention to building lavish stairways leading up to the main entrance. These heightened the effect of the door from grand to monumental, but they served to extend the threshold and the moment of entrance in an almost theatrical fashion—in accordance with what some historians have called a deliberate "dramaturgy of the stairway" at the time.[89] A stage of this sort, of course, required actors who knew how to perform on it, and contemporary books on courtly ceremony contained detailed sections on the rules to be followed when receiving different kinds of guests: whether they should be greeted at the foot of the stairs, in the middle, or at the top; whether one or both wings of the doors should be opened; whether the door guards and footmen should make a gesture of respect—all this protocol was of greatest concern.[90] Common people were generally made to wait in front of closed doors in order to instill in them a proper sense of respect. This was also true for petitioners who wished to speak with the authorities, as well as for parishioners who sought audience with a clergyman. At times this must have caused frustration or anger in the people waiting. As the popular fifteenth-century preacher Bernardino da Siena observed, having to wait outside a dignitary's closed doors could have an important psychological effect: "Thou hast far greater reverence for him than thou wouldst have had hadst thou gone thither without having felt any longing whatsoever, and had found all the doors open."[91]

Courtly and official architecture were ideal settings for the flourishing theatrics of door and stairway, but the phenomenon also resonated in other strata of early modern society. In seventeenth-century England, even a clergyman admonished his readers that "a goodly building must show some magnificence in the gate."[92] And treatises such as Domenico de' Rossi's popular *Studio d'architettura civile* (1702–1721), the first volume of which dealt in detail with exemplary door designs, helped to supply architects throughout Europe with concrete examples and measured drawings.[93] Here, too, size was an important factor. In a 1788 treatise *On the Character of Buildings,* the anonymous author—now thought to be a high-ranking Prussian government official—proclaimed, "The first thing that we should look at when we see a door is its size . . . because it is the size of the door that will most easily let us determine the purpose, and thus the character, of the building."[94]

Granted, city homeowners—even when they belonged to the upper classes—were rarely in a position to surpass the houses of the nobility for displays of grandeur, but they nonetheless took pride in ornamenting their doors and gates as means permitted. In some places, this trend also left linguistic traces: in medieval France, for example, the term *huis* (from the Latin *ostium,* "door") was the most common word for the door of an ordinary house. Beginning in the sixteenth century, however, this word was gradually replaced by the term *porte,* which had previously been used in French for the larger and more elaborate doors and gates of castles.[95]

Early modern German lands also showed heightened attention to the design and ornamentation of doors: tellingly, in thriving cities like Nuremberg, the task of crafting doors increasingly shifted from carpenters to cabinetmakers, skilled artisans whose focus until then had been on creating furniture.[96] Unfortunately, we do not know what the front door of one of Nuremberg's most famous burghers, Albrecht Dürer, looked like, but we can assume that Dürer paid particular attention to its design. It is fair to say that no other artist of the time played as skillfully with the door motif and its symbolism as Dürer did in his oeuvre. Of course, this also owed to the fact that his German surname—a translation of the Hungarian word *ajtó* (door), reflecting the name of his ancestral hometown, Ajtós—was derived from the German word for door (*Tür*). Dürer was a virtuoso in using door imagery as part of his artistic self-fashioning: he incorporated a representation of a door in his coat of arms, and he even fashioned the capital *A* of his famous monogram A.D. in the shape of an open door (by stretching out the triangular form of the letter *A* and raising the horizontal bar to create the impression of a lintel). Dürer's placement of the monogram in his paintings sometimes seems to imply a message, especially in his religious works. In his Paumgartner altarpiece, for instance, the monogram conspicuously appears on the post of another liminal space: a wooden awning, underneath which lies the infant Christ (Christ himself, of course, also being a "door," according to the New Testament). Mary's gaze, in turn, passes right through the open door represented by the letter *A*. Given that Dürer, in his famous Munich self-portrait from that same period, did not shy away from presenting his likeness in a Christlike manner, it is possible that similar intentions are at work in the altarpiece. In this reading, the letter *A*, the doorframe of the monogram, doubles as a doorframe through which Mary's sacred gaze passes, thereby endowing the artist with divine inspiration.[97]

Obviously, the increasing attention to door design and ornamentation did not mean that the doors of *all* private houses became larger and more elaborate, but in many parts of Europe there was a distinct tendency in this direction. Referencing Palladio, seventeenth-century English author and diplomat Henry Wotton noted that the "principal Entrance" should never be "regulated by any certaine Dimensions; but by the dignity of the Master; yet to exceed rather, in the more, than in the lesse, is a marke of Generosity, and may alwayes be excused with some noble Embleme, or Inscription."[98] Indeed, in regions north of the Alps, not only were the doors more intricately carved, following Italy's example, but the area above the door also received great attention. Here we increasingly see artistic wrought-iron grilles, which also allowed light into the house; alternatively, the surface was decorated with carvings, inlays, reliefs, or paintings.[99] Frequently the family's coat of arms, or that of famous ancestors, was placed on or above the door, the so-called keystone being a popular place for it.[100] In addition, this space often contained an inscription noting the year of construction of the house or the date of the topping out ceremony, sometimes along with the name or initials of the builder or head architect (Figure 11).[101]

Although this trend could be seen in rural regions as well, it was more pronounced in cities, especially those in which a princely residence or seat of government was located.[102] Diplomats, who began to set up permanent embassies in these cities during the early modern period, virtually were obliged to display the coat of arms of their country and sovereign on the house portal. As a German author noted in the 1730s, this ensured "that they be all the more easily found, and that their houses be shown appropriate respect."[103] This quotation also reminds us that this was a time before house numbering: in many European cities, house numbers did not appear before the eighteenth century, and even then only gradually.[104] For

Figure 11. The lavishly ornamented wooden door of the
so-called Wintersches Haus, a well-preserved seventeenth-
century burgher house in the south German city of
Nördlingen. The inscription on the lintel indicates the date
of the door's creation (1697) while also displaying a Latin line
praising God (*Soli Deo Gloria:* "Glory to God alone").

centuries, decorated portals thus served as aids to orientation
in the city. At the same time, the ornamentation of the door
gave the house an individual character and projected information about the social status of the owner. According to a
seventeenth-century architectural theorist, homeowners were
free to decorate their doors as they wished, but he advised that

their front doors should indicate "something about the station of the inhabitant or the master."[105] It fits into this picture that young people were taught to pause before entering a house in order to take a careful look at the façade and door.[106]

In addition to providing something to look at, doors often offered something to read. This was especially true in university towns, where academics adorned their portals with inscriptions—to demonstrate their erudition—as well as with coats of arms.[107] These inscriptions and other decorations also became more common at the time because of the religious conflicts between Protestants and Catholics that had been raging since the Reformation. While Protestants often preferred their churches bare and unadorned, the same could not be said for their houses. On the contrary, many townhouses in Protestant regions were richly ornamented, which can be attributed partly to the fact that artists and stonemasons who had previously worked for the Catholic Church now had to find new sources of income. At the same time, many Protestants wished to use the façades of their houses to express their new faith. Thus passersby would often find the inscription *Verbum domini manet in (a)eternum* ("the word of the Lord endures forever") over the doors of Protestant houses.

This phrase expressed the Protestant belief that the essence of Christian life was the Word of God as recorded in the Bible, rather than acts of mercy as the Catholic Church maintained. It was an unmistakable statement of Protestant belief at this time, and some Protestants even had it stitched on their clothing.[108] We also see the general familiarity with such phrases from the fact that sometimes only an acronym was inscribed on the door—in this case, VDMIE. Thus, in cities where Catholics and Protestants lived side by side, doors became yet another battleground in the struggle between the faiths. Catholics might counter, for example, by displaying images of the Virgin Mary above their doors.[109]

The fondness for inscriptions can also be traced to a secular impulse shared by Catholics and Protestants alike, namely, the exhibition of wealth. "The blessing of the Lord, it maketh rich, and he addeth no sorrow with it" (Prov 10:22) appeared above many a burgher's door in central Germany at this time. Other wealthy burghers used the opportunity to lament the envy of their neighbors. One elegant seventeenth-century stone dwelling in Bielefeld bears the blunt inscription: "Oh God, it is my fate, that they should always hate me, though I do nothing to them; and when they do not begrudge me, they still give me nothing." Variations on this theme also appear elsewhere.[110]

Alberti had explicitly cautioned that doors to secular buildings should be more modest than their counterparts in church architecture. One might thus claim that the increasingly elaborate design of secular doors indicates a gradual "secularization of the door." But one could also argue the opposite: that doors in the secular sphere were gaining an increasingly sacred character. Of course, with regard to private houses, we are not dealing with a truly religious "sacredness," since these doors do not demarcate sacred and profane realms in the religious sense. Nonetheless, the door was "holy" (*res sancta*) in another sense, for it marked the transition from the outside world to the sheltered space of the individual—a distinction as significant in premodernity as it is today.[111]

I do not want to revisit here the question of whether the categories "private" and "public" existed at this time, or whether they are later inventions, for such polarization would not do justice to the complex realities of premodern everyday life.[112] A great deal of evidence supports the view that there was a sense of what we today call private and public. But perhaps more important than the notion of a *private* sphere was the idea that the threshold of the house was the junction of two different *legal* spheres: the legal space of the house and that of the exterior world.

The idea that the house constitutes a distinct legal space exists today as well, but it is not a modern invention; its roots extend deep into antiquity.[113] In Germanic lands, a related legal term took shape in the Middle Ages: *Hausfrieden* ("domestic peace").[114] This did not imply that there was a different form of law in the house than on the street; rather, the disturbance of domestic peace simply had distinct and more serious punishments. In some premodern codes of law, for example, the fine for a violent act or an insult committed inside a house was six times higher than for the same crime committed out in the street.[115] Clearly, the concept of *Hausfrieden* presupposes that there is a physical point where the house as a legal space begins. The front door was the most common line of demarcation. In some places, the domestic peace traditionally extended as far as the roof gutters.[116] Since the gutters often jutted out beyond the exterior walls, this definition technically extended *Hausfrieden* beyond the actual, inhabited space of the house. Yet the gutters, then as now, were located several meters above street level, so in practice this was a virtual boundary. And even where this approach was used, breach of domestic peace typically became an issue only at or inside the front door.[117]

In reality, therefore, domestic peace was chiefly linked to the integrity of the door. "What happens in the front doorway is treated as if it had happened within the house," declared Johann Heinrich Zedler's *Universal-Lexicon* in the eighteenth century, summarizing the traditional juristic opinion.[118] Violent acts against the threshold of a house were thus always more than simple vandalism, as they constituted a breach of *Hausfrieden.* This was the reason why, for example, a blow to the door (or a window) was punished more severely than a blow to a person in the street or the tavern.[119] It is telling that, in the legal literature of the Holy Roman Empire, the "malicious damaging of doors," even without intrusion into the house, was mentioned alongside real capital crimes and fell in the domain of High Justice.[120]

These strictures also applied to the authorities, who in many places were not allowed to intrude into their subjects' houses or forcefully open their doors. "No doors can in general be broken open to execute any civil process," summarized the noted English jurist Sir William Blackstone in the eighteenth century, and most legal commentators on the Continent concurred with this view.[121] Even in the case of a court summons, the court messenger was not allowed to force entry (*neque dure, neque violenter*) if the door was locked, nor so much as open it if it was closed. In such cases he was to read the writ of summons aloud in front of the door; to enter the house, according to prevailing legal opinion, would humiliate the residents and harm their honor (*injuria*). If the accused did not appear in court after several attempts at summons (or if there was a grave "criminal cause"), then the law allowed the authorities to cross the threshold and apprehend him or her in the house.[122] Regulations concerning interactions between the authorities and citizens' front doors were strict, and when these rules were broken, the public was quick to take it as a sign of unlawful, even despotic rule. This is vividly depicted in *The Massacre of the Innocents of Bethlehem*, a painting by Pieter Brueghel the Elder from the 1560s (Figure 12). Here, Brueghel moved the gruesome New Testament episode from Palestine to a snowy Dutch village during the time of Spanish oppression. Herod's officers, clad in Spanish uniforms, are shown going door to door, forcing entry as they carry out their murderous assignment.

Naturally, neighbors and strangers likewise were prohibited from entering a house against the will of the homeowner. Apart from emergency situations, any such intrusion counted as a breach of *Hausfrieden*.[123] Hermann Weinsberg (1518– 1597), a councilman and meticulous diarist from Cologne, knew this well when he recorded an unpleasant episode in his journal in 1568: as he and his brother were taking a stroll through the city, they passed the house of a goldsmith, where they saw Hermann's brother-in-law standing in the doorway.

Figure 12. Pieter Bruegel the Elder, *The Massacre of the Innocents of Bethlehem*, c. 1565–67, with detail showing officers forcing open the door to a villager's home. Kunsthistorisches Museum, Vienna.

This relative had long held a grudge against the Weinsberg family and so, in full view of passersby, he shouted, "There go the two villains" (*da gaint die zwein boiswichter her*). Though angered by the insult, the two men resisted the urge to go up to the door. The learned jurist Weinsberg knew that to do so would be to commit a crime; instead, he opted to pursue the matter in court. The incident ended with his brother-in-law apologizing.[124]

Whether an intrusion involved forcing the door or simply opening an already unlocked door was irrelevant in legal terms. Either way it was a breach of *Hausfrieden,* though the use of force might increase the punishment.[125] Clearly, such measures were meant to deter burglars, but theft was not the only threat against a house and its threshold. Feuds, neighborhood conflicts, and violence against social outsiders also led to intrusion, and not all protagonists showed as much restraint as Hermann Weinsberg. In fact, forcible entry, the so-called *invasio domus,* was quite frequent in day-to-day conflicts and was considered a form of extrajudicial punishment. In the English-speaking world, the now largely forgotten word "hamesucken" (in German, *heimsuchen*) describes this ritual, which was primarily designed to humiliate inhabitants rather than to burgle them.[126] Hamesucken, which could target an individual or a group, was related to other forms of contemporary vigilantism, such as *charivari,* or "rough music," but was far more violent. It usually involved breaking down doors and smashing windows and sometimes also caused significant damage to property inside the house.[127] However, its defining characteristic was forcible entry. Tellingly, the punishment for

hamesucken in several Germanic legal traditions was that offending parties had to pay a fine multiplied by the number
of times they had crossed the house's threshold during the
event.[128] In especially severe cases, hamesucken was even punishable by death.[129]

Obviously, part of the reason why doors (and windows)
were attacked during instances of hamesucken was because
they were the weakest parts of the house and particularly exposed. But it must be remembered that doors played a crucial
role in the effect of a building and thus also represented the
honor—and especially for the middle and upper classes, the
projected image—of the house and its inhabitants.[130] Indeed,
in most European languages at the time, the term "house" was
used synonymously with "family."[131] People who were seen as
dishonorable by their enemies or by society risked having that
disgrace made public in the very place where no one could
mistake it: their own homes.

These violent acts could take drastic, sometimes ritualized
forms when the population rose up against a hated ruler or his
dynasty—in other words, against his House. After the death
of Pope Sixtus IV (1484), raging Roman citizens stormed the
palace of a count who had been associated with him. According
to a contemporary chronicler, "they took the house by storm
and plundered and tore down what was left in the palace, rav-
aged and destroyed all doors and marble window frames with
iron clubs; . . . as one can still see, not a door or window was
left unharmed."[132] In other Italian cities, too, palace doors and
windows—as well as the residences of wealthy individuals—
were vandalized and sometimes even stolen during revolts.[133]

In the major trade city of Antwerp in the sixteenth century, the authorities warned the citizens not to attack the doors of Italian bankers or crowd around them.[134] Jews were another group repeatedly assaulted in this way, as happened, for example, in Vienna in 1700, when a workman got into an argument with a member of the household of Samuel Oppenheimer, a wealthy court Jew. Out of the brawl grew an anti-Jewish mob, which gathered in front of Oppenheimer's house, destroyed the doors and windows, and then looted the building while the inhabitants hid in an underground vault. The violence continued until the city guards intervened: "as a warning," one contemporary observed, they hanged the Christian ringleaders from an iron grille above the entrance to the house, for obvious symbolic reasons.[135] Yet the authorities did not always act so decisively to stop attacks against Jewish homes, and when the mob maintained the upper hand, the door might be the stage for the execution of the inhabitant. In reports of the Rhineland massacre during the First Crusade (1096), Jewish chroniclers record that Christian attackers hung the body of a murdered Jew at "the entrance to his house" (*petach beito*), in order to "mock" him.[136] Throughout premodernity this could also be the grisly fate of Christians in episodes of mob violence and intrareligious conflict, and here, too, it was seen as a humiliation for victims and their houses.[137]

The front door of a premodern house, then, was the stage on which the status of the dweller played out in both positive and negative ways.[138] And as with church doors, the special status of the front doors of private houses is evident in a range of legal contexts beyond the punitive. For example, in real estate transactions, as well as in other less voluntary changes of ownership, the claim to the whole house was symbolically expressed at the door as its *pars pro toto*.[139] For example, when a house was seized, it was common as early as the Middle Ages to affix a seal to the front door to indicate that the owner no longer controlled the entrance, and by extension the house. Naturally, this seal was a source of anger and humiliation for the affected party, who would frequently attempt to break it off and get rid of it.[140] Creditors could then legally resort to more drastic (and no less symbolic) action: removing the door altogether.[141] Authorities could exercise the same right if a household refused to pay taxes for an extended period of time. In the Netherlands, it was still common in the eighteenth century to unhinge the front door of a house if the inhabitants did not pay their taxes after two or three reminders.[142]

Another legal ritual that marked the transfer of property to new owners—in this case, by voluntary sale—was called "transfer by door" (*traditio per ostium*). The new owner would announce his or her acquisition of the house by grasping the doorpost, knocker, or hinge with the right hand, or by placing the right foot on the threshold.[143] In early modern German, the word *Antast*, now understood simply as touching (*Antasten*), could be used to designate this form of legal transfer.[144] Similarly, the formal opening and closing of doors could publicize acquisition, and in certain circumstances, an entire society could pass into the hands of new leadership in this way. Consider the colorful but unexceptional case of the small village of Castel Menardo in the Abruzzi and its transfer to its new feudal lord in 1561. A contemporary notarial report attests

that the new lord sent an official proxy to the village for this
purpose:

> [This agent and] several bystanders of the same village went
> to the house of usual residence of the court. He went inside
> and took into his possession, via an inventory, all the papers,
> both civil and criminal, of that same village, walking up and
> down that same house, opening and closing its doors. And, as a
> continuation, he went to the holy Church of the Sacred Cross,
> in which the community of the said village is accustomed to
> gather, going inside, praying, walking up and down, ring-
> ing the bells, opening and closing the doors, and doing other
> things etc. And, as a continuation, he went to the gates of the
> same village and fortress, and, opening and closing them, he
> walked up and down through the village and fortress, doing
> and carrying out other things as a sign of a true taking and
> proper act of possession of the said village or fortress and of
> all its territory.[145]

Such rituals could become far more complicated, even to
the point of scandal, when rival claimants to power and ownership clashed. One notable example comes from northern
Germany in 1665, when Duke Christian Louis of Brunswick-
Lüneberg died after a long illness in the city of Celle. The
duke was childless, and his death brought to a head the long-
smoldering conflict over his succession. His two brothers disagreed on the correct interpretation of their father's will on
this point, but the prevailing legal opinion at the time was
that power should pass to the eldest brother, George William.
At the time of the duke's death, however, George William was
abroad, which the younger brother John Frederick seized to
his advantage. On the evening of the duke's death, John Frederick ordered soldiers to march into Celle and close the gates

of the ducal palace as well as those of the city. He then seized official control of the duchy, in the palace and in the presence of notaries and witnesses. Essential to this act was holding and opening the doors of the palace. George William's supporters tried to do the same, but they were a few hours too late. Indeed, George William had left authorized representatives in the city before leaving on his journey. But when they went to the ducal chancery to seize the door—and with it, control of the duchy—there in the doorway stood one of John Frederick's officers, who told them they had come too late and that the new duke had already "seized" (*ergriffen*) control. He then shut the door and thus (*re ipsa*) made it clear that sovereignty had already irrevocably transferred to John Frederick. The delegates then attempted to claim power for George William by ritually seizing other doors throughout the city: they held ceremonies at the doors of the main churches and city hall, putting up placards and their lord's coat of arms as proof. However, the new duke's men tore them all down the same day. Not until several months later did the brothers finally negotiate a resolution to their conflict.[146]

Chipping at the door, literally cutting off small slivers of it, was another legal ritual in which the door represented the house *pars pro toto*. This custom was practiced throughout Germanic lands and possibly beyond in premodern times, and it survived well into the nineteenth century, even in larger cities like Frankfurt am Main; yet there is almost no historical research on it. Like certain other legal customs noted above, chipping at the door could be used to announce or formalize a transfer or claim of ownership: in these cases it was often the buyers or heirs who documented their legal claims in this way. By contrast, when a transfer of ownership was ordered by a court, as in cases of seizure, a specially appointed court clerk would carve out a sliver from the door and present it to the new owner. This custom was also practiced in criminal investigations. In cases of homicide, intentional or otherwise, the local authorities had to document that they had visited the scene in order to reserve the right to investigate. For this purpose, authorities frequently took chippings from a door at or near the scene of the alleged crime. Occasionally, parts of the corpse were taken instead, but naturally this sort of evidence was not very durable. Wood chippings, accompanied by an explanatory note, were much easier to stow away with the investigation files. In some rare cases, these objects still survive in archives.

In southern Germany a special term was coined for such objects: *Fraischpfand* (using the Franconian word *Fraisch*, meaning "casualty" or "crime"). It is no coincidence that the practice of taking *Fraischpfänder* was particularly prevalent in southern Germany, a region with many coexisting and competing subterritories that were prone to border disputes and rival claims concerning jurisdiction. The first authority to succeed in taking a *Fraischpfand* could then claim jurisdiction over the location. In this context, the extensive use of this custom, especially in the seventeenth and eighteenth centuries, both owed to and played into the territorial fragmentation of the Holy Roman Empire.[147]

Legal rituals such as *traditio per ostium* or the taking of *Fraischpfänder* are further evidence that doors were of particular interest to authorities in much of early modern Europe. It is worth noting, however, that premodern European law did not treat doors solely in symbolic ways. Throughout Europe, homeowners were required to lock their doors at night. In France, well into the early twentieth century, the external doors (and windows) of residences were taxed—a fiscal measure that exploited the fact that no house can get by without a door.[148] For the same reason, doors were used for the statistical assessment of an urban space. In Milan, as early as the thirteenth century, the authorities recorded the number of residential front doors, independent of any census of inhabitants.[149]

To us, governmental and legal interest in doors may seem just as alien as the importance of doors in the sphere of religion. But ultimately these aspects all merge into a coherent image of a society in which doors received far more attention than they do today. As we saw in Bocchi's tour of sixteenth-century Florence, premodern people had a refined sensibility for doors and their ornamental details, irrespective of whether they were sacred or secular. And while church doors gave a foretaste of the experience of salvation, doors of private houses gave extensive information about the social status, wealth, and education of their inhabitants.

Doors were both emblematic and widespread in another and perhaps surprising context: the knowledge economy of early modern Europe. Indeed, the trope of entering through a door or other passageway often figured in artists' depictions of the exploration of new worlds both real and imagined. In fact, door and gate—more broadly, the idea of passage and transition—functioned as a key paradigm for the discovery and acquisition of new knowledge. Consider Columbus's discovery of the Americas: the Spanish kings, noted patrons and profiteers of this discovery, celebrated it explicitly as crossing a threshold that no other nation had yet crossed. They also situated the threshold at a specific (though imagined) location: the fabled Pillars of Hercules in Gibraltar. Since antiquity, the idea persisted that the imaginary gate between Gibraltar and North Africa created by these pillars marked the end of the Mediterranean Sea and thus the limit of the known world. The mythological hero Hercules had inscribed the pillars with the warning *non plus ultra* ("nothing further beyond"). The discovery of the New World in 1492 defied this mythical warning, and soon after the discovery of the Americas was made known, the Spanish kings modified their coat of arms to include the motto *plus ultra* ("further beyond").

This could of course be seen as mere wordplay, but it was nonetheless characteristic of an approach that became dominant during the early modern period: the systematic urge to *transgress* the boundaries of existing knowledge. Tellingly, a famous depiction of the Pillars of Hercules embellishes the frontispiece of Francis Bacon's *Instauratio Magna* (1620), the influential treatise in which Bacon called for the start of "a total reconstruction of sciences, arts, and all human knowledge."[150] The Latin motto between the pillars, *Multi pertransibunt & augebitur scientia* ("many will pass through and knowledge will be augmented"), based on Daniel 12:4, is an explicit appeal to pass through this virtual gateway. According to Bacon, scientific understanding can progress only when many people transgress the boundaries of present knowledge. The context here is no longer just the discovery of the Americas, but of a different New World: that of the New Science. In contrast to medieval theologians, who tended to regard human curiosity (*curiositas*) as a vice, Bacon legitimized the human desire for knowledge as a positive force. And in Bacon, as in other early modern authors, the act of passage symbolized by the gate functions as the epitome of *curiositas*.

In the Middle Ages, by contrast, there were no passage metaphors of comparable importance. Indeed, the acquisition of knowledge was not perceived as a transgression of existing boundaries but rather as an accumulation of a specifically *vertical* nature: the great scholars of the Middle Ages imagined their task to be like adding building blocks to a body of knowledge towering heavenward. The ideal of striving toward the heights, particularly in the Gothic period, could also be felt in other cultural manifestations, from script to architecture.[151] The quintessential expression of this was the idea of *Summa*, which appeared in the titles of numerous treatises and encyclopedias during the Middle Ages. In the early modern period, however, people began to envision the acquisition of knowledge—whether new or inherited from the luminaries of the past—as a horizontally configured *passage* rather than an upward stacking. The number of books with titles including the words "door" or "gate" increased rapidly.[152] Among them we find a work titled *Porta linguarum* (Gate of Languages), a systematic introduction to the study of languages, by the polymath and education reformer Jan Amos Comenius (1592–1670). Later editions of this very successful book appeared under the slightly altered title *Ja-nua linguarum* (Door of Languages). True to its title, this was a work in which, according to the author, "the gate of tongues [is] unlocked and opened."[153] A few years earlier, using the same metaphor, the Irish Jesuit William Bathe (1564–1614) published a guide to learning Latin, English, French, and Spanish under the title *Ianua linguarum*.[154] Scholars in other fields made similar efforts: in the sciences, there was Charles Blount's 1684 treatise titled *Janua scientiarum* (Doors of the Sciences), which declared itself "a compendious introduction to geography, chronology, government, history, philosophy, and all genteel sorts of literature."[155] And in theological literature, there was Bishop Joseph Hall (1574–1656), who structured the introduction to his popular *Art of Divine Meditation* as a "portal" and invited his readers to step through the "common entrance into this work."[156] Further examples from this time are easy to find.

These titles clearly tie in with a general early modern tendency to convey the acquisition of knowledge through metaphors of space. For instance, many books appeared with the word *theatrum* in their titles, depicting the world of knowledge as a stage.[157] If we look to a prolific writer such as Comenius, we find a range of other titles that use spatial metaphors, such as *Via Lucis* (The Way of Light) and *Orbis Sensualium Pictus* (The Visible World Pictured). But doors and gates occupied a special place in the imagery of knowledge: many books portrayed themselves as "portals" not only through their titles, but also in their visual presentation, with title pages fashioned after doors or gates urging the reader to enter (Figure 13).[158]

Figure 13. One of many early modern title pages showing
a gate or door. Samuel Daniel, *Delia: Containing certaine
sonnets, with the complaynt of Rosamond* (London, 1592).

Similarly, at the beginning of Comenius's *Porta linguarum*,
we find a poem by a contemporary admirer who exhorts un-
decided book buyers not to miss the opportunity to enter
through this open gateway:

> Not that thou't let this work at any rate
> Presume I fixe a bill upon thy gate:
> The Portall speakes it is already prest,
> And stands wide open for a Princely Guest.[159]

In an age that was already grappling with the problem of "information overload," books also featured new tools for orientation, particularly what we now call indexes.[160] With the rise of the printing press, which enabled the production of identical copies of a book, the frequency and importance of indexes increased significantly.[161] And tellingly, authors and readers again harked back to door imagery, often referring to the index as a *key*.[162]

Today, door-related metaphors are no longer used as extensively in the knowledge economy as they were in the past, and the terms "gate" and "door" rarely appear in the titles or frontispieces of books, let alone scholarly ones. But in certain contexts, they persevere. For example, we speak of "gatekeepers" when referring to the people who ensure the quality standards of their field, such as journalism or academic publishing. And in the digital world we have witnessed a resurgence of these metaphors: we speak of "portals" and "gateways" that structure our path toward digital knowledge. But, ironically, we can gain access to these digital doorways only through the "windows" on our screens. Indeed, the window has become the most prominent spatial metaphor of the digital world. That, however, is another story, for another book.

CHAPTER TWO

The Power of the Keys

W HAT WOULD HAPPEN "IF SOME barbarous American should among other pieces of Shipwreck, thrown by the Sea upon the Shore, light upon a Key of a Cabinet"? This question occupied Robert Boyle (1627–1691), one of the leading English natural philosophers of his time. In Boyle's view, the answer was clear: with a mixture of disdain and pity, he reasoned that since Native Americans had a naïve and spiritual relationship with objects, did not inquire into causes or usefulness, and had "never seen a Lock," they would understand a key as little more than "a piece of Iron."[1]

A century and a half later, another European remarked on the character of Native Americans, though this time supported by close-up observation: German naturalist Alexander von Humboldt (1769–1859) visited Venezuela in 1799 in the course of an expedition, where he noted that "in most houses the doors remain open, even at night: so good-natured are the people here."[2]

Leaving open the question of how valid Boyle and Humboldt's observations actually were, their perception of natives' indifference to keys and locks reveals more about the observers than it necessarily does about the observed: Boyle saw it as a sign of a "barbarous" mentality, while Humboldt admired the unspoiled and good-natured character of such "primitive" peoples. What both assessments have in common, however, is that they show the Europeans' astonishment when faced with societies in which the use of lock and key was unusual. For both men, as for the vast majority of their European contemporaries, these devices pervaded everyday life. But why could they not imagine daily life in Europe without locks?

Any historian who addresses this question should avoid the trap of oversimplification and idealization that we see in Boyle and Humboldt. Yet the way in which some historians speak of premodern Europeans' use of locks shows just as much misplaced self-assurance. Even in more recent historical studies, we read that "doors [were] only seldom locked" in premodern Europe and that open doors were a common sight, even at night.[3] On closer inspection, such claims are hardly tenable: the European cultural practice of locking doors has a centuries-old history, and the same holds true for the key as a technology. This chapter delineates this history. More particularly, it probes the fears and claims to power that were bound up with keys and reflected in their symbolic meaning. In fact, the history of locking doors offers historians a key, as it were, to the history of security and power in premodern Europe.

■

In a number of ancient cultures, some doors closed simply with bolts and latches, while others could be locked with keys. Both the Bible and the literature of Greco-Roman antiquity speak frequently of locks and keys, and from archaeological discoveries we know that these keys were sometimes lavishly crafted.[4] This is particularly true for ancient Egypt and for postclassical Greece, and it is not surprising that the locks and keys originally fashioned from wood were slowly replaced by more sophisticated variants in bronze and iron.[5] Accordingly, the material value and production costs of keys were often considerable. Yet this was not the primary reason why losing a key might be the stuff of nightmares. In his *Oneirocritica,* a manual on the interpretation of dreams, the second-century Greek author and diviner Artemidorus described the case of a man who dreamt that he lost the key to his house while traveling. On his return, he discovered his daughter dead inside the house. Artemidorus interpreted this upsetting dream as a hint "that things at home were not safe"—the loss of the key signifying not only the insecurity of the house, but also a loss of control over the fate of one's family.[6] In fact, there is ample evidence that in antiquity house doors were not randomly left open. In ancient Rome, for example, doors were left wide open only when the paterfamilias was home and receiving guests or clients.[7]

In contrast to other technical achievements of the time, which only came to light again during the Renaissance, knowledge of how to produce keys was not lost during the Middle Ages. For one thing, this technology had been known in Europe—among the Celts, for instance—independently of the influence of Greco-Roman civilization.[8] As for need, the recurring periods of violence and lawlessness during the Middle Ages were precisely what made it essential to lock one's home. Admittedly, keys from the Gothic and Merovingian periods were still relatively simple.[9] But the later Middle Ages were "reputed as a period of great progress in producing locks and keys of highly artistic design," and France, Germany, Italy, and Spain in particular emerged as centers for the production of ever more intricate keys (Figure 14).[10] By that time, European locksmiths had already switched from wood to metal: since the tenth century, locks and keys had been made primarily from iron or bronze.[11] Thus on journeys to the Levant, early modern European travelers were surprised to find that the doors there were more often ironclad than in Europe, yet the locks were frequently made of wood.[12]

In early medieval Europe, the most elaborate locks—now often showpieces in museum collections—were primarily intended for trunks and chests rather than for doors.[13] They were particularly necessary in churches in order to secure relics, the most precious items, in custom-made receptacles.[14] In domestic settings, too, lockable chests, trunks, and cupboards remained an important mode of storage throughout premodernity. But this does not mean that people were indifferent to the security of doors, or that anyone could enter a house at will. Rather, secure containers were needed because, in general, more people lived in each house than today, and the house itself had fewer separate rooms with lockable doors than modern houses.[15] It was therefore more common for several people to share a

Figure 14. Lock and key, late fifteenth century, south Germany.
Bayerisches Nationalmuseum Munich, Inv.-No. E 10.

single space, and anyone wanting to keep his or her belongings private did well to lock them away in a container.

Various activities, of course, required that doors be left open, such as certain crafts or, in the country, work in the stables. In southern Europe—at least in agrarian areas, during the summer—the climate may also have led to a certain ease about leaving doors open during the day. Yet one should not infer that open doors were the rule or the ideal state in everyday life, as some historians have.[16] Early modern people were well aware that their houses had to be secured. Whoever could afford the protection of a door lock did not hesitate to buy one, and as excavations and estate inventories have shown, this was true in the city and the countryside alike.[17] Differences in the technical quality of locks were mainly related to cost, and this explains why rural householders' locks were often less elaborate and ornamented than those of city burghers or the aristocracy. It also explains why Michel de Montaigne was so disappointed in the 1580s, during his journey through Italy, when he saw "locks like those in our villages" in the Medici villa in Pratolino.[18] But one should not conclude from this that country people cared less about security. In fact, it was sometimes particularly important to them, especially if they lived isolated from their neighbors. In eighteenth-century England, for instance, travelers observed that houses in rural areas were often "barricaded, bolted, barred and double lock'd fast, both public and private, backside and foreside, top and bottom."[19]

For more evidence disproving the idea of constantly open doors in premodern times, we might look to the profusion of warnings from upper-class authors and found throughout folk culture. In nearly all major European languages, there were proverbs to this effect as early as the Middle Ages: "It is good to close one's door when night falls," goes a saying in French.[20] And in Spain: "My door is closed, my head is guarded."[21] Other proverbs pointed out that a closed door offered personal safety as well as a barrier to annoyances such as beggars and other people who "ask for much and bring little."[22] The French poet François Villon (1431–c. 1463), who was familiar with the lives of vagrants and criminals, knew what he was talking about when he cautioned, "The house is safe, but be sure it is shut tight."[23]

Warnings to secure the house were also common in the extensive early modern literature for heads of household, and the point was well taken.[24] In a world without industrial mass production, replacing stolen belongings could be difficult and costly. Since savings banks were uncommon, the possessions inside the house comprised the primary net worth of many families—and insurance in the modern sense was nonexistent.[25] As a result, failing to lock one's doors meant putting a great deal at stake. No one knew this better than merchants and moneylenders, whose prosperity was tied to material goods and money reserves, which had to be secured.[26] The late medieval *Book of the Rules of the Moneylender and the Borrower*, written in Hebrew by an anonymous author, exhorts bankers to avoid having too many doors and windows in their buildings, "so as not to be exposed to the danger of burglary." Such anxieties were by no means unique to Jewish moneylenders.[27] In a manual written around 1350, Florentine merchant Paolo da Certaldo, a Christian, likewise cautioned his readers to close their doors and windows firmly at night.[28] In addition, he advised that the paterfamilias should always keep the key to the house in his chamber (*camera*) when sleeping or napping, day or night.[29] In a similar vein, the renowned pedagogue Jan Amos Comenius gave his seventeenth-century readers the following advice: "After thou hast past over the dore, shut it up, setting the barre against it, at the least bolting it."[30]

Was such advice repeated so regularly because no one paid any attention to it? This is certainly a legitimate question, but in this case the situation is more complex. Although some residents neglected or simply forgot to lock their doors, they were the exception. We know that "shutting-in" was a common idiom in English for nightfall.[31] The morning unbolting and opening of house doors was a firm daily ritual and marked the transition from night to workday.[32] And precisely because so much importance was ascribed to the nightly locking, it was sensible to reiterate the point in householder manuals and moralizing treatises, even if most people already locked their doors of their own accord. In other words, this particular reiteration of norms concerning individual and collective security had, as it often does, an affirmative rather than a prescriptive purpose.[33]

Samuel Pepys (1633–1703) in seventeenth-century London did not need any warning: for him, locking up went without saying. When he lost the keys to his office one day, it made him "very angry and out of order, it being a thing that I hate in others and more in myself, to be carelesse of keys, I thinking another not fit to be trusted that leaves a key behind their heels."[34] As we know from numerous passages in his diaries,

Pepys was particularly concerned about his savings, which he hid, like many of his contemporaries, at home. And his worries were not unreasonable, for most of his hopes for social ascent and a better life were bound up with his steadily growing fortune. In his journal, he meticulously documented the increase of his assets, and he locked the door to his house with equal care whenever he and his wife left it. He was therefore horrified when he returned from a visit one day to find the doors unlocked. It turned out that his servants, not burglars, were to blame. And although Pepys knew that it was not intentional, he did not hesitate to punish the responsible kitchen maiden for her inexcusable lapse of vigilance: he "gave her a kick in our entry, and offered a blow at her." From his diary, we know that Pepys's house doors were secured not only by lock, but also with a bolt that could be operated only from inside. Thus another problem arose: one night, Pepys and his wife returned home to find themselves locked out as the servant had fallen asleep after bolting the door.[35]

Pepys was not alone in his worries, which also extended to locking the doors to rooms within the house. The sixteenth-century diarist and councilman Hermann Weinsberg always locked his bedroom and the room in which he kept his documents (*schriffkamer*) whenever he left the house. With advancing age, he sometimes forgot his key ring. He never actually lost his keys: his sister, who lived with him, always found them in the end. All the same, these incidents caused him considerable worry (*wes ich mich besorgt*), because his bedroom contained his "secret documents, copybooks of correspondence, and money." He was particularly concerned that the eccentric stipulations of his will might come to light, and with good reason: after his death, the will did in fact cause endless squabbling among his relatives.[36]

From the historical picture that emerges, we can see that security considerations were no less important to premodern people than they are to us today. But there were certainly other reasons why people at the time were careful to lock their doors. Before the advent of central heating, people were loath to leave doors open during cold weather. In the early eighteenth century, the English poet Alexander Pope ridiculed those of his compatriots who, in their enthusiasm for Italy and antiquity, outfitted their homes with long exterior walkways and grand doors, to the detriment of their health: "[They] call the winds through long arcades to roar, / Proud to catch cold at a Venetian door."[37]

Likewise, we should remember the many superstitions associated with open doors. According to one widespread belief, if an unlocked door opened by itself, the spirit of a deceased person might enter the room; it could also be a sign of impending death. Conversely, it was customary at the moment of a death to open windows and doors in order to allow the soul of the departed to leave the house—further evidence that the exterior doors of residences were usually closed.[38] Superstition almost always dictated that house doors be kept closed at night. Otherwise, according to a folk belief common throughout Europe, the house would be invaded by evil spirits, or worse still, by the Wild Hunt, a horde of supernatural beings who gathered at certain times and whom one had to avoid provoking at all cost. People often attributed the nocturnal rattling of doors to such eerie creatures as well.[39]

In many places, the authorities, too, had an interest in residents locking their doors. In fact, they even had the power to make residents do so.[40] There were several reasons for this. For example, it was universally known that closed doors (and windows) could slow the spread of fire. This was an important consideration in premodern European cities, where dense construction and the use of highly flammable building materials meant that a single house fire could easily devastate an entire city—the Great Fire of London in 1666 being perhaps the best-known example of such a catastrophe. Thus, every preventive measure, no matter how small, had to be taken seriously. Although closing doors and windows at night would not preclude such a disaster, it could at least limit the flow of air to the fire and help prevent the flames from spreading to neighboring buildings.[41]

Even so, we should not lose sight of the fact that the authorities also had simpler security considerations in mind, like violence and night criminality. Starting in the late Middle Ages, many cities had a curfew that regulated when inns and hostels had to close their doors; only people with a good reason could be out at night.[42] This both protected possible victims and made criminals more conspicuous. For the same reasons, as well as to prevent burglaries, the authorities in many places required that the front doors of private residences be locked at night. Apparently, people did not see this as excessive government interference. In fact, the locking of house doors was an intentional analogy to the closing of city gates, which took place throughout Europe every evening in order to prevent unwelcome people from entering the city.[43]

Many European cities had night watches, either appointed by the authorities or set up by citizens to ensure safety during the night hours. Rembrandt's famous painting *The Night Watch*—the name was added later—does not actually represent a municipal watch carrying out its nightly duty; rather, it is a carefully composed group portrait of a civic guard. But the nightly supervision of the streets was indeed among the duties of such civic guards, who also ensured that house doors were properly locked. In London, for example, the night watchmen hit the house doors with their sticks for this purpose.[44] They even checked back doors: thus, the knocking of a watchman alerted Samuel Pepys one night that the rear door to his house was not closed.[45] Similar controls existed elsewhere in Europe, as well as in the Ottoman Empire.[46]

Premodern residents who did not fulfill their responsibility to close their doors at night had to contend with fines or even physical punishment.[47] As late as the eighteenth century, innkeepers and citizens who opened their doors to suspicious people at night without notifying the authorities, or who allowed guests to leave after curfew, faced particularly harsh punishment: in France, the authorities could even brick up the hostel door.[48] Of course, most citizens obeyed the curfew: after all, it was in their own security interest, and in the age before electric lighting, the path through unlit streets or even the dark of nature usually hid more dangers than enticement.[49] Young people, however, persistently challenged these night rules, for two reasons: for one, particularly during times of economic and social crisis, they tended to vent their frustration by acts of vandalism, such as battering or throwing stones at doors.[50] But these nightly excursions were also one of the few opportunities for unmarried youths to socialize with members of the opposite sex and engage in sexual adventures. In his autobiographical writings, the eighteenth-century German novelist and scholar Friedrich Christian Laukhard gives a frank account of his first sexual encounter as a teenager: in line with common practice at the time, his parents had locked the house from the inside when night fell, so young Friedrich had to climb out of the window in order to meet a washerwoman "who let me lie next to her."[51] Such episodes were one of the reasons why the authorities often warned parents not to allow their children out at night and not to trust them with the house keys. Those who did not follow these rules were threatened not only with worldly punishment, but also with the wrath of God.[52]

The punishments, however, were far more severe for individuals who intentionally crossed the threshold of a locked house with criminal intent. Germanic law books explicitly required a higher sentence for intruders who had broken through a locked door, and French law also distinguished between "breaking" (*éffraction*) and "simple theft" (*vol simple*).[53] At English common law, to this day, the acts of "breaking" and "entering"—as through a door or window—constitute the crime of burglary. The traditional interpretation of these elements dictated that entering through an already open door was not burglary: following legal precedent that went back to the famous jurist Sir Edward Coke (1552–1634), the judges of London's Old Bailey declared in the eighteenth century, "if the door of the mansion stand open, and a thief enter this is not breaking." And much the same, if a criminal were to find an open door or window and "with a hook or an engine draweth out some of the goods of the owner, this is no burglary, for there is no actual breaking of the house."[54] (Luckily, the common law has evolved on this issue.)

Housebreakers caught in the act were often branded with a glowing iron in the shape of a key.[55] The rationale behind this "mirror punishment" was clear: since the key was the symbol of legitimate access, its importance was impressed—literally, and very painfully, no less—on those who had violated the integrity and sanctity of another's home. At that time, moreover, justice was often meted out in several stages, and burglary was punishable by death in much of Europe. For a burglar sentenced to death, this branding was therefore a comparatively mild prelude to much worse punishment.[56] But even if the burglar got away without capital punishment, the plainly visible imprint of the key would serve as a sharp warning to potential emulators.

Those who made illegal copies of keys or tampered with locks also faced harsh punishment. The sixth-century *Lex Salica*, valid throughout Francia, expressly forbade the unlawful reproduction of keys or the manipulation of locks.[57] Sentences for these crimes varied throughout premodern Europe but were generally harsh. In late medieval Bohemia, culprits were punished by amputation of their hands.[58] As late as 1722, in France, a delinquent who had illegally reproduced and sold keys was broken on the wheel. Another common punishment for the crime was death by hanging.[59] In general, the commerce in keys was strictly regulated in early modern Europe. In many places, the law dictated that old keys could be disposed of only by selling them to locksmiths who belonged to a guild.[60] These guilds were essential to the quality of the locksmith's trade and the legal reproduction of keys. In 1411, Emperor Charles IV established the title of Master Craftsman for locksmiths in the Holy Roman Empire. In imperial cities such as Nuremberg, only one of these master locksmiths was authorized to produce or repair locks and keys for municipal buildings and city gates. Here and in other areas of Europe, locksmith guilds, which monopolized the production of keys, emerged from the late Middle Ages onward.[61]

Naturally, with regard to home security, homeowners, then as now, would have been naïve to rely on the mere presence of a lock on the door and on the moral integrity of locksmiths to protect them from determined criminals. As Milton noted in *Paradise Lost*, there was always the possibility that

> A thief bent to unhoard the cash
> Of some rich burgher, whose substantial doors,
> Cross-barred and bolted fast, fear no assault,
> In at the window climbs, or o're the tiles. (IV. 188–91)

In densely inhabited premodern cities, watchful neighbors could therefore serve as an additional form of crime control and prevention.[62] But precisely because relations with neighbors were closer (or more inevitable) than today, they were also a double-edged sword. Some medieval proverbs recommend locking doors and securing belongings as a good practice for preserving neighborly relations.[63] During the Renaissance, Leon Battista Alberti put it more negatively: he named thieves and neighbors in the same breath as reasons why "we should avoid having windows or doors open out."[64] It would be too rash to dismiss Alberti's remarks as cynical. In fact, to the extent that criminal statistics from this period are available, they seem to support his suspicions: in sixteenth-century Rome, for instance, more than 75 percent of documented burglaries that happened while the residents were away were committed by neighbors or relatives.[65] This was yet another reason why the authorities encouraged closing doors. By the same token, the law in some places guaranteed that a person "can neither be punished for nor required to explain what is said behind closed doors and with members of their household within their four walls."[66] This makes clear that the sense of a private sphere did exist in premodern times. In fact, we know that in houses divided into several units, occupants generally set up rules regarding access to different areas and usually kept both the internal and the external doors closed.[67]

In light of all this, what are we to make of the fact that many early modern paintings, particularly seventeenth-century Dutch art, show open doors and windows? And why are these paintings virtually the hallmark of certain contemporary painters, such as Pieter de Hooch (1629–1684) and Jacob Ochtervelt (1634–1682)? These are legitimate questions, yet it is precisely this conspicuous use of open doors that urges us to take a closer look.[68] Indeed, written sources from the Netherlands tell a rather different story: the Dutch, like other Europeans, generally kept their doors and windows shut, especially at night, which suggests that this aspect of the paintings does not reflect an actual practice, but rather was "staged." For the painter, open doors enabled experiments with perspective; for the viewer, they also—quite literally—opened a door onto the prosperity of the bourgeoisie, from whose ranks most of these paintings' buyers came.[69]

In view of this, the claim that "the open door was universally understood as an invitation" in premodern times is clearly an exaggeration.[70] At times, the exact opposite was the case, and a striking example of this can be found in fourteenth-century Venice. In 1310, the Venetian authorities discovered that several patrician families were planning to topple the doge. The heads of two families were executed as ringleaders. A third family, which was involved in the plot to a lesser degree, endured a rather different punishment: the authorities decreed that the main door of their house must remain open in perpetuity. This open door was meant to inflict great humiliation on the house (*casa*) and thus also on the family (*famiglia*), these terms being interchangeable in Italian, as in many other European languages. More than half a century later, the Venetian authorities reaffirmed the punishment, emphasizing that the door had to be secured with "good and thick chains of iron immured in the living stone" to ensure that it remain open forever. If the family were to remove the chains or close the door, they would be fined each and every time.[71]

There were other contexts in which an open door during the day was regarded as ambiguous or even negative. In moralistic literature, for instance, many negative connotations were attached to open doors. The influential Dutch moralist Jacob

Cats (1577–1660) argued that the family home was ideally a bulwark closed off to the outside world, in which the women could go about their household duties during the day without outside intrusion, while the men attended to business outside the home. Along these lines, Cats cautioned the matron to ensure that the keys be given to servants only when absolutely necessary and that the front door never remain open unattended. For when the door was open, danger threatened, not only from intruders, but also from gallants and seducers— particularly for the daughters of the house: "Open door, open bodice," Cats warned, his meaning unmistakable.[72] This analogy also functioned the other way: Cats disparagingly referred to a drunken woman as an open door and to an adulteress as a door without a lock.[73] Against this background, it is clear that in early modern art—in and beyond Cats's Netherlands—the motif of the unattended open door did not necessarily symbolize a bourgeois ideal but could actually suggest and problematize the "sexual availability of women."[74]

Obviously, this was a heavily male discourse, and male authors' warnings frequently related to male fantasy and to maintaining patriarchal structures. It fits a pattern also found in other places and earlier periods: in ancient Greece, for instance, a man's dream about a burning door was interpreted as an omen of immediate danger to, or even the death of, his wife.[75] In the same vein, the biblical Song of Solomon compares a young girl to a door that must be secured.[76] In other words, for centuries, people projected their anxiety about the integrity of the house, the moral integrity of the family, and the seduction of its women onto one specific part of the house: the door.

The physical shape of the door and its character as the most significant opening in the building may have been one reason why it became the focus of these kinds of fears. Both Christians and Jews found support in the Bible for the analogy between doors and the external female sex organs, most famously in Job's curse against the day on which he was born "because it shut not up the doors of my mother's womb" (3:10). In the Jewish tradition, these and other similar passages from the Bible led rabbinical authors to conclude that "just as there are keys to a house, so too there are keys to a woman."[77] Similar notions existed among Christians, and indeed it was the same door-related technology, the key, that was supposed to help protect—at least in male wishful thinking—the integrity of both one's house and one's wife's sexuality. Although it is a modern myth that women in premodern Europe wore chastity belts, with the keys kept by their husbands, visual depictions and polemical references to these belts existed throughout the early modern period.[78] The imagined analogy between the door and the external female sex organs also found expression on a vernacular level. In early modern Italy, the verb *chiavare*, which literally means "to put a key in a lock," was (and remains) a common vernacular term for intercourse; and in a similar vein, an illegal duplicate key was called an "adulterous key" (*chiave adulterina*).[79] In both a real and figurative sense, then, a husband had to ensure that access to his wife remained "open" only to him. In German lands, if one threatened to push a married man's "back door open"—a seemingly harm-less phrase—it was understood as a reference to adultery, real or intended, which is why jurists regarded the phrase as a seri-ous insult (*gravis injuria*).[80]

It follows that an open door could send an ambiguous message, particularly in relations between the sexes. Various medieval proverbs, directed at both women and men, indicate that one should stand at an open house door as briefly as pos-sible. This warning applied even to those with unblemished moral integrity, for "[t]he open door leads the holy person into temptation."[81] Such warnings were well in line with biblical accounts of the door as a place where sin loomed. The Holy Scripture's warning about a "strange woman" is stated in no uncertain terms: "Remove thy way far from her, and come not nigh the door of her house."[82] Similarly, on the first pages of the Old Testament, one reads, "But if you do not do right, sin couches at the door; its urge is toward you, yet you can be its master."[83] Perhaps alluding to such warnings, Boccac-cio, in the fourteenth century, included a bawdy story in his *Decameron* about a hermit in the desert who cannot contain his sexual desire when a young woman shows up at the door of his little house (*casetta*).[84] Of course, the *Decameron* is fic-tion, but its erotic constellations were perfectly plausible to Boccaccio's contemporaries. Erotic encounters at and in the doorway happened day in and day out in the densely populated cities of premodernity. Even the clergy were not immune to these temptations: in 1562, in the north German trading city of Stralsund, a tearful young woman named Ursula reported to the mayor how a deacon had involved her in an offensive conversation from the doorway of his house as she passed by. Hinting at what ensued, she asked the mayor to ensure that the deacon "not lay hands on her" in the future.[85] Whether the mayor took action is not clear from the sources. However, we do know that precautions were taken in premodern Europe for the reverse situation—where women were harassed at their doorways by men or where women "encouraged" intrusion through ambiguous or even lewd behavior.

In some parts of Europe at the time, views like those of Jacob Cats were actually established in law. For instance, in seventeenth-century Silesia, it was decreed that the heads of households "should keep all of their doors well closed and retain the key with themselves" in order to prevent outsiders from fornicating with children, wives, and maids, but also to avert comparatively harmless activities such as strolling and dancing at night.[86] Anxious husbands and religious authorities put forward such arguments as early as the Middle Ages in both the Christian and the Jewish communities of Europe. Writing in the Rhineland in the mid-fourteenth century, the Jewish moralist Eleazar of Mainz admonished young women to "always be inside their homes and not roaming about; nor may they stand at the doorway watching everything that goes by."[87] In very similar terms, the Catholic preacher Bernardino da Siena (1380–1444) warned young girls:

> O maidens! Learn how you must conduct yourselves at home, and how you must be upon your guard in respect of him who doth enter therein; for thou seest that the Virgin Mary stayed shut within her house, and would always see first who wished to enter there, and would know that which he wished.

> Maidens, you know not how strong and overwhelming are the
> desires of youth! There is naught better than to keep within
> doors, and not to do with men, or even with women.[88]

While Bernardino's compatriot Boccaccio evidently had very
few illusions about the efficacy of such warnings (as we know
from his stories), he nonetheless urged wives to keep the house
door bolted during the day. At the same time, he urged husbands to always be on their guard, lest they find themselves in
the same situation as the protagonist of another of his stories
in the *Decameron*, a poor and gullible mason who cries out: "I
thank you, God, that although you have made me poor, you
have at least given me the consolation of a good chaste woman
for my wife! You see how she locked the door behind me, so
that no one else could come in and pester her."[89] The irony of
this story lies in the fact that his wife actually makes every effort to open the door to her lover in secret. Among the works
of other authors of the time, there are plenty of morality tales
and erotic stories in which open or unlocked doors signify illegitimate sexual encounters.[90]

The clear sexual connotation of the door and the concerns
associated with it were one reason why it was far more common for women, particularly young girls, to use the window
rather than the door to watch activities in the street or converse with passersby. The balcony—an architectural element
that became increasingly popular in early modernity—was
another place that women often used for the same reasons.[91]
By contrast, sitting in the doorway was highly problematic
throughout the entire period. Early modern readers, for example, immediately understood that Cervantes was referring

to prostitutes when he described Don Quixote's arrival at an inn where "there chanced to be standing at the door two young women who belonged to the category of women of the town, as they say."[92] Similarly, when Cervantes's contemporary Michel de Montaigne traveled through Italy, he knew what to make of those women who come "to the doors of their houses, where they stand in the public view at the convenient hours."[93] In the eighteenth century, Zedler's massive *Universal-Lexicon* bluntly stated that sitting in the doorway had been the "sign of a whore" since time immemorial.[94] An honorable woman had to avoid giving this impression at any cost. Or, as lawmakers at the time put it, "A women who does not want to be a whore should not give the appearance of a whore."[95]

Consequently, young women were permitted to appear in the doorway only under supervision. Many authors maintained that only matrons and older women should be allowed to stand or sit at the door, and even then, only as long as the woman behaved honorably and did not do it too often.[96] Within these narrow limits, Leon Battista Alberti conceded in his treatise on family life: "On a few occasions, in order to teach her [the matron] a certain air of authority and to have her appear as she should in public, I made her open our own door and go outside practicing self-restraint and a grave demeanor. This led our neighbors to observe her air of discretion and to praise her, which increased the respect of our own servants."[97]

There were attempts to resolve the question of proper female behavior through architectural changes. For instance, one could add an alcovelike antechamber to the ground floor, with windows that opened onto the street: in this way, the women of the house could fulfill their household duties and simultaneously observe activities in the street and speak with passersby, all without having to cross the threshold. At the same time, from this protected interior room, they could guard the house and the front door. This architectural solution was particularly popular in the Netherlands, where it was referred to as a *voorhuis*. By contrast, the family's living spaces were generally located in the rear, and the storerooms in the upper part of the house. Thus, the *voorhuis* was the only part of the house that was "simultaneously public and private," and many early modern Dutch paintings show women and children in the *voorhuis*, which, though protected, was not entirely cut off from the outside world.[98]

In eighteenth- and nineteenth-century North America, the porch (from the Latin *porticus*) would come to play a similar role as the *voorhuis*: it, too, constituted a liminal space of the house that provided women a distinct place for socializing "at home yet not inside." For a woman, sitting on a porch was far less problematic than standing in the doorway. The porch allowed women, at least during the warm months of the year, to tend to housework and look after children without suffering domestic isolation.[99] Indeed, the porch made it possible for women to talk informally with passersby, including those who were considered socially or racially inferior (and who therefore would have been beyond the bounds of seemly contact even in the street). At the same time, such contact was permitted only on condition that the inferior party keep a certain distance from the porch and not cross the threshold of the house.[100] It should also be noted that the *voorhuis* or porch was less a female privilege than a patriarchal concession. Ultimately, the decisive question in the hierarchy and power structure of the house was who had access to the keys.

Unlike today, it was unusual in premodern times for each member and servant of the family to have his or her own key to the house.[101] According to convention, only one person in the house was entitled to the "power of the keys," and this was the male head of household. It was only on marriage that the power passed also to the matron of the house. This was not just a question of everyday importance, but also a critical legal issue. Since antiquity, the "power of the keys" had been understood as the right of a married woman to act in legal matters and to enter into financial obligations if necessary for managing the household.[102] In practice, this legal concept often came down to the question of how much money a wife could spend without consulting her husband and was sometimes the source of fierce arguments. In this patriarchal society, the power of the keys provided wives with room to maneuver. It also explains why married women commonly wore ostentatious key rings on their clothing, especially when undertaking legal transactions: strictly speaking, a wife who could not show her keys was unable to transact in a legally binding way. Thus, for Cicero, "to take away a wife's keys" (*claves uxori adimere*) was equivalent to abandoning her.[103] This was not simply a well-worn metaphor: throughout early modernity we find cases of husbands who punished their wives after fights by taking the keys from them, thus either locking them inside or out of the house.[104]

Against this background, it becomes clear why women were often depicted with a key ring on their belts in medieval and early modern art.[105] Far from being an ornament or a fashion accessory, the key ring was an explicit reference to a woman's legal and social status. We know from archaeological research that honorable women during the early Middle Ages were sometimes even buried with their keys.[106] Of course, a woman's right to carry a key was not only a legal privilege, but also came with significant responsibility. Jean Bodin, the influential sixteenth-century French legal scholar and political theorist noted approvingly that in ancient Rome, the law of Romulus permitted the husband to take his wife's life without due process of law if she committed one of four transgressions: adultery, passing off another man's child as her husband's, habitual drunkenness, and last but not least, "having duplicate keys."[107] Not every early modern male author went quite as far as Bodin, but there was certainly agreement that the female power of the keys entailed a moral duty to care for the welfare and honor of the house. In the words of the author of a moral treatise from eighteenth-century England, "By taking the trouble of the Keys, a young Lady may learn how to go through her domestic Offices."[108]

Tellingly, in visual representations of women from the late Middle Ages and the early modern period, one can often infer certain character traits of a woman from her keys. For example, in his *Schussenried Altar of the Virgin Mary* (c. 1515), now in Berlin's Gemäldegalerie, the German painter Bernhard Strigel prominently placed St. Anne's richly decorated key ring in the center of the panel, on a chest at the foot of the bed (Figure 15). St. Anne herself appears in bed, just after the birth of Mary, but her eyes are locked on her key ring: Strigel

Figure 15. Bernhard Strigel, *Schussenried Altar of the Virgin Mary*, c. 1515, with detail showing St. Anne's key ring displayed on a chest. Gemäldegalerie, Staatliche Museen, Berlin.

presents Mary's mother as an ideal matron of the house, who not only deserves the many keys on the ring, but also guards them and is aware of the responsibilities associated with them. In other works of art, Mary, in turn, appears with a key ring firmly fastened to her belt, highlighting not only her status as a married woman, but also her trustworthiness (especially as her husband Joseph is absent from so many paintings).[109]

The situation is very different in Israhel van Meckenem's *Couple Seated on a Bed* (c. 1495), an engraving with a worldly subject (Figure 16). In this seemingly modest depiction of two lovers, the young woman is revealed, on closer inspection, to be an adulteress (or a courtesan). The scene is unmistakably erotic: the man has his arm around the woman's back, his hand peeking out on the other side and touching her breast. Two details betray the illegitimate character of the encounter: the key and the door. From the young woman's loosened girdle, the key ring hangs suggestively and carelessly in her lap. What is more, the door in the background (on the left) is suspiciously bolted from the inside, even though a man is inside the room and it is apparently daytime (the candles in the candelabra are not lit). The carved monkey sitting atop the bedpost further underscores the inappropriate nature of this encounter.[110]

As such examples make clear, in premodern Europe the question of who held the key was extremely important. Albrecht Dürer astutely captured this point in a sketch in which he noted that "keys mean power" (*schlüssell betewt gewalt*).[111] And this observation was true in a variety of other circumstances, well beyond the context of marriage and family life. It held true, for instance, in politics. For centuries, both secular

Figure 16. Israhel van Meckenem, *Couple Seated on a Bed.*
Engraving, c. 1495. Kupferstichkabinett, Staatliche Museen, Berlin.

and religious authorities had a chamberlain, whose role was to manage and protect the fortunes and possessions of the government.[112] For this reason, he was granted the power of the keys: he held the keys to the ruler's buildings, chambers, treasuries, chests, and cabinets. At large courts, a single chamberlain could not possibly carry out these responsibilities, so a Lord Chamberlain (in French, *Grand Chamberlain;* in German, *Oberkämmerer*) was tasked with carefully selecting and supervising multiple chamberlains and doorkeepers. The position of chamberlain involved both responsibility and proximity to the ruler, which explains why it ranked high in the court hierarchy and was greatly sought after. Many chamberlains wore

Figure 17. Key of the Royal Bavarian Chamberlain from
the period of Prince Luitpold's regency (1886–1912).
Deutsches Schloss- und Beschlägemuseum, Velbert.

keys on their court attire (Figure 17), but these extravagant and decorative keys, much like medals, often had no practical function and served mainly as symbols of the office and its powers. The ostentatious display of keys continued even as the responsibilities and powers of the chamberlain slowly changed during the early period. In some royal courts, the position became a purely honorary title, while in others, it developed into an early form of the modern finance minister. In the latter sense, the term is still used today. Take, for instance, the City of London, where the office of the Chamberlain of London was first recorded in 1237. For centuries, the prime responsibility of the chamberlain was the custody of money, valuables, and documents, although he had many other duties as well; and at his death or retirement, the key to the strong room was handed over to his successor.[113] To this day, the finance director of the City of London is titled "Chamberlain." Real keys, however, no longer play any role in the position, particularly as the assets—as well as the debts—of cities like London far exceed the capacity of a traditional strong room.

In the political life of early modernity, the keys to the city gates played no less significant a role than those to government chambers. Indeed, a city gate that could not be locked was not considered a proper gate, but simply an arch.[114] In practice, of course, securing early modern fortifications required more than just a key, and a range of other technical devices were in place to ensure that gates were safely shut and bolted. However, this did not diminish the significance of the key in the iconography and ceremony of contemporary politics: it remained the prime symbol of sovereignty over a city. In German lands, keys can be found in the coats of arms of more than a hundred cities, among them important imperial cities such as Worms and Regensburg.[115] For centuries, if the city was subject to an external sovereign, municipal leaders had to hand the keys over to the ruler when he visited. This gesture of deference, the *traditio clavium*, entailed considerable risk, as the municipal authorities then technically lost the right to control who could enter and leave the city. The festive and highly ritualized ceremonies that marked the event were partly designed to cover up these risks.[116]

Against this background, the capture or confiscation of a city's keys held great symbolic meaning and therefore was often staged triumphantly, as illustrated by an episode from the fourteenth century. After Cardinal Egidio Albornoz had reconquered numerous rebellious cities in the Papal States on his military campaign in the 1360s, Pope Urban V demanded an accounting of the curial funds used in the effort. Albornoz is said to have presented a cart with the keys to the subjugated cities and exclaimed, "Here are the accounts" (*Ecco i rendiconti*).[117] But sometimes citizens, and not only conquerors and other outsiders, tried to seize the city keys in order to demonstrate their claims to power. This happened in 1514 in Worms when a group of citizens rose up against the city magistrate. After the magistrate's councilmen fled to the churches and monasteries for asylum, the victorious rebels demanded the keys to the city, and in order to keep the situation under control, they ordered that the city gates be closed. Council officials who hesitated to hand over the keys were brutally subdued.[118] In many other places in Europe, too, the capture of the city keys was a decisive moment in conspiracies and protests against the authorities.[119]

The bitterest battle waged over keys in early modernity, however, had to do with keys that had never actually been seen: the keys of the Apostle Peter. In order to understand this controversy, we must first call to mind a central passage from the Gospel of St. Matthew, where Jesus announces to one of his disciples, "Thou art Peter, and upon this rock I will build my church . . . I will give unto thee the keys of the kingdom of heaven: and whatsoever thou shalt bind on earth shall be bound in heaven: and whatsoever thou shalt loose on earth shall be loosed in heaven."[120] In a later passage (Matt 18:18), this privilege of binding and loosing is expanded to the rest of the apostolic community.

The importance of these words for the history of Western society and culture can hardly be overstated, for the Catholic Church derived two prerogatives from them that were vital to its authority and mission.[121] First, it derived the pope's claim to be Peter's successor and thus to act as the Vicar of Christ on Earth. Second, theologians extrapolated that Peter, in being entrusted with the keys to the kingdom of heaven, was also granted the specific Power of the Keys (*potestas clavium*), especially the authority to pardon sins ("to loose") or to deny their forgiveness ("to bind"). Building on this interpretation, medieval theologians, in particular the Scholastics, established a systematic doctrine of the Power of the Keys. In a general sense, the *potestas clavium* granted to Peter came to be understood as encompassing all clerical offices, services, and powers that Jesus had established for the salvation of the members of his church.[122] Thus, from the Power of the Keys, the Catholic clergy derived the prerogative to take believers into the church or to excommunicate them, as well as to decide on the dispensation of the sacraments. In practice, even the Crusades were justified through this doctrine.[123]

The Power of the Keys was therefore critical for legitimizing and bolstering the spiritual authority that church officials claimed for themselves. The original passage from the Gospel of St. Matthew does not indicate how the binding or loosing should occur or how the believer is supposed to imagine it visually (which is one of the reasons why many modern theologians prefer to use the expression "keys" in an abstract-metaphorical sense).[124] These uncertainties notwithstanding, many theologians and believers through the centuries associated the Power of the Keys with actual, physical keys. The early Christians already believed that St. Peter's opening and closing of the gates of heaven was the quintessential expression of the Power of the Keys (Figure 18). The definition widely accepted by the Scholastics, drawing upon the Venerable Bede, also makes use of this physical image in order to clarify the idea of the Power of the Keys: "The keys are a special power of binding and loosing by which the ecclesiastical judge should receive the worthy into the Kingdom [of heaven] and exclude the unworthy therefrom."[125]

As an institution, the church strongly encouraged this visual understanding. After all, the idea of the Power of the Keys was one of the pillars of its claim to power and could

Figure 18. St. Peter with the keys at the gate of heaven. Woodcut
from Werner Rolevinck, *Fasciculus temporum* (Utrecht, 1480).

be impressed more easily upon the faithful by visual means
than with abstract discussions. As a result, Christian iconography promoted the idea by depicting the two keys as the
most prominent attribute of St. Peter. In countless paintings
and sculptures, he was shown holding a pair of keys—often
clearly visible, sometimes even oversized.[126] Suffice it to mention Pietro Perugino's famous fresco *The Delivery of the Keys*
(1480–1482) in the Sistine Chapel in the Vatican, which depicts Jesus giving Peter the keys (Figure 19). The keys are
disproportionately large and occupy a prominent place in the
center of the foreground. The subject of the fresco later turned

Figure 19. Pietro Perugino, *The Delivery of the Keys*, 1480–1482,
with detail showing Jesus giving Peter the keys.
Sistine Chapel, Vatican.

out to be particularly fitting for this location, as the Sistine Chapel became the preferred site for the election of popes, and Perugino's depiction—which faces the cardinals as they cast their votes—underscores the papacy's claim to stand as the successor to St. Peter. Of course, the keys were an essential part of papal self-representation and iconography long before Perugino's time. In fact, ever since the Middle Ages, popes have included these two keys in their coats of arms. They also cultivated the custom of presenting as gifts keys made from precious metals.[127]

A similarly physical interpretation of keys also prevailed among those contemporaries who criticized the Catholic Church's monopoly on salvation and, mainly, the enormous power of the popes. Among critics of the papacy's moral decay was the anonymous writer of the Latin dialogue *Iulius exclusus e coelis* (*Julius Excluded from Heaven*), first printed in 1518.[128] No less than the famous humanist Erasmus of Rotterdam was suspected of being the author (and rightly so, modern scholars believe). This witty dialogue, published many times during the sixteenth century and translated into all major European languages, describes the futile attempts of the recently deceased Pope Julius II (r. 1503–1513) to gain entry to heaven. Hardly any pope before him had been as worldly, and tellingly, his contemporaries referred to him as "The Warrior Pope" (*Il Papa guerriero*). The dialogue begins with a scene in which Julius, much feared for his anger during his life, realizes that the gates of heaven are closed to him:

> "What the devil is this? The doors won't open? Someone must have changed the lock, or at least tampered with it."

To which his *Genius* replies:

> "Are you quite sure you haven't brought the wrong key? The
> key to your treasure-chest won't open this door—and anyway,
> why didn't you bring both of them with you?"

The pope, "seething with anger," begins to bang furiously on
the doors; in response, St. Peter, who guards the gate, ap-
proaches and remarks ironically:

> "It's a good thing our gate is as solid as rock or he'd have bro-
> ken the doors down, whoever he is. This must be some giant
> or paladin, some wrecker of cities. Immortal God! it smells
> like a sewer round here! I won't open the door directly, but I'll
> peep through the bars of this window and find out what kind
> of monster it is."

The dialogue then develops as an indictment of the morally
corrupt pope. Many contemporaries approved of its claims, not
least a reader by the name of Martin Luther.[129] But Luther,
who had set the Reformation in motion the year before the
dialogue appeared, went even further. For him, it was not only
individual popes who deserved damnation; he outright rejected the papacy and the idea of the papal Power of the Keys.
In his 1530 treatise *The Keys* (*Von den Schlüsseln*), he explicitly accused the popes of having "left the key that looses lying
idle, ruined and rusted" and of abusing the concept for their
own worldly and political interests.[130] According to Luther, the
keys that the pope claimed for himself were "not the keys to
Heaven of which Christ spoke, but rather the pope's keys to
the abyss of Hell."[131] This was not the only writing in which
Luther flatly rejected the papal claim to the Power of the Keys.
Yet he did not call the idea of two real keys into question. For

one thing, this physical image was in line with his custom of illustrating difficult theological questions in an accessible way. For another, it provided him (as it did Erasmus) with abundant opportunity for sarcastic puns. For example, a few years later, Luther again rejected the pope's right to the Power of the Keys, mockingly declaring that the Supreme Pontiff had converted them "into two skeleton keys to the treasure chests and crowns of all kings."[132] Luther's followers used the same type of polemical rhetoric: a Protestant broadsheet from 1617 shows St. Peter engaged in a bitter fight with the pope to prevent him from stealing the keys (Figure 20). In it, Peter warns the pope in no uncertain terms: "Give me the keys right now / Or else I will punch you in the mouth." The pope's response reveals the depth of his moral corruption: "Give me the key, / or I will take it by force, / Believe me, I don't care about you / or about Christ either."[133]

In the age of the Reformation, the issue of the Power of the Keys became one of the central bones of contention between Catholics and Protestants. After all, every Christian's ability to find salvation hinged on it. Despite their many internal quarrels, all Protestants agreed that neither the pope nor the priesthood had any authority to invoke the Power of the Keys to decide a person's right to salvation. In the Protestant view, the path to salvation led neither through clerical intermediaries who claimed to hold the loosing key nor through good works, but rather through the individual's faith, the grace of God, and belief in the Holy Scriptures. From this perspective, the binding key, too, no longer belonged to the priesthood, but rather—in line with Protestantism's alliance with

Figure 20. *The Pope's Sacrilege and St. Peter's Rage over the Binding and Loosing Key of Our Lord Christ.* Anonymous German broadsheet, 1617. Germanisches Nationalmuseum, Nuremberg.

secular authorities—to worldly rulers as the "new secular bishops."[134] At the same time, however, the power associated with the binding key was curtailed, for Luther saw the church as obligated to practice mercy. Thus, in contrast to Catholic practice, excommunication from the Protestant community was to be imposed only in cases of severe transgression, such as open heresy.[135]

It is beyond the scope of this chapter to go into all the details of the fierce Catholic-Protestant controversy concerning the Power of the Keys, especially as it raged equally between various currents of Protestantism, each accusing the other of possessing the "wrong keys."[136] In any case, it is clear that the *idea* of the Power of the Keys was not called into question by the Reformers, but rather was reinterpreted. Thus it is fair to say that, for centuries, discussion of sin and the power of forgiveness in Western culture was channeled largely through one metaphor: the key.

But how does all this relate to us moderns, who live in an age of secularism? While theologians still engage with the concept of the Power of the Keys, far fewer ordinary people are familiar with this term. In all likelihood, a considerable number of Christians today have never even heard of the doctrine of the Power of the Keys. This certainly has to do with secularization, but—strange as it might seem—it also has to do with our changed living conditions. In comparison to our premodern ancestors, Western people today live years, even decades longer. And according to historian Arthur Imhof, people have grown accustomed to these "gained years" as well as to the fact that the majority of the population now "experiences a biologically complete life with childhood, adolescence, maturity and old age."[137] And partly as a result of this longer lifespan, the belief in life after death has eroded. In a 2008 survey conducted in Western Europe, only 35 percent of respondents reported believing "quite" or "very much" in an afterlife.[138] As a result, the concept of the gates of heaven and the question of who will be able to pass through these gates no longer seems to have the same urgency as it did for premodern people.

But it would be rash to assume that this idea no longer exerts any influence on our thinking. In fact, the Russian philosopher Lev Shestov (1866–1938) argued that, in the transition to modernity, the idea of the Power of the Keys was not eradicated, but rather transformed. According to him, "we judge what is good and what is bad, what should be and what should not be, with the same assurance as did our predecessors, the Catholic theologians."[139] For the Nietzschean Shestov, this way of thinking was rooted in the pre-Christian period, yet it was Christianity that took the most blatant step: it took the keys entirely out of God's hand. "If God Himself announced from heaven that the *potestas clavium* belongs not to men but to Himself alone, even the gentlest would rebel," he wrote.[140] Thus, while in modern times the self-assurance and hubris of the West has ceased to wear theological robes, the idea of the Power of the Keys continues to exist under the surface of secular thought. In Shestov's view, no major European philosopher has been humble enough to renounce the idea at the heart of the *potestas clavium:* "Men are so accustomed to the idea that they possess and must possess this limitless power over earthly reality as well as over all possible realities that they could not bear the idea that they do not have, and could never have this power."[141]

Irrespective of whether one agrees with Shestov or not, it is clear that in Western culture, keys have been (and remain) more than just an aid in closing doors, chests, or cabinets. To recall Dürer's word, keys signify "power," and for centuries the question of who held power over certain keys was central in various contexts: in family life, the power of the keys was bound up with the hierarchy of the sexes; in law, with the concept of property; in politics and at court, with the question of political influence; and in religion, with the idea of salvation.

From this perspective, a society without keys was bound to appear technologically backward, or at least structurally different in terms of power. In their journeys of discovery, early modern Europeans found many such societies—and in their encounters with them, the Europeans considered the keys that they carried with them to be symbols of their civilizing superiority. Tellingly, when England sent a ship to China and Japan in 1580 to sound out possibilities for mutual trade, careful consideration was given to the question of which European products should be taken along "for a shew of our commodities" and to impress people in the Far East. In the end, along with luxury items such as fine glassware and ivory products, the English merchants decided to include "locks and keyes, hinges, bolts, and haspes &c., great and small of excellent workemanship."[142]

Europeans clearly considered their knowledge of locks and keys to be an economic asset, but they also used it to demonstrate their sophistication and power. This particular "power of the keys" could become very physical, in a way that is captured by the corresponding German term, *Schlüsselgewalt:* in German, *Gewalt* means both "power" and "violence." It was, in any case, a German passenger who recorded a revealing episode during Captain Cook's second voyage to the Pacific. The episode took place in September 1773, when Cook's men stayed a while longer in the Society Islands, giving presents to native women and girls. As the German eyewitness reports, one girl "incessantly importuned every one of us as long as she suspected we had a single bead left." Finally, one of the Europeans gave her a padlock that had drawn the girl's particular attention, as this technology was unknown on the island, and he then demonstrated its use in a malicious way:

> [H]e consented to give it her, and locked it in her ear, assuring her that was its proper place. She was well pleased for some time; but finding it too heavy, desired him to unlock it. He flung away the key, giving her to understand at the same time, that he had made her the present at her own desire, and that if she found it incumbered her, she should bear it as a punishment for importuning us with her petitions. She was disconsolate upon this refusal, and weeping bitterly, applied to us all to open the padlock; but if we had been willing, we were not able to comply with her request for want of the key.

Members of the tribe, including the chief and his wife, soon joined in the girl's urgent request and even offered costly gifts in return. Eventually, the Europeans showed mercy and "a small key was found to open the padlock, which put an end to the poor girl's lamentation."[143]

This brings us back to Boyle and Humboldt, with whom we started the chapter. Admittedly, these two thinkers did not

go as far as the men on Cook's expedition and were satisfied
to contemplate the relation between keys and the customs of
native people. Yet the very idea that keys played little or no
role in certain cultures remained perplexing to Europeans: it
was either a reason to mock them (as Boyle did) or to express
wonder at their "good-naturedness" (as Humboldt did). Both
conclusions are equally problematic. For while there were and
still are societies in which keys and locks play a smaller role
than in Western culture, this fact alone says relatively little
about the complexity of social life or the morality of people.
To illustrate this more fully, we need only look to traditional
Japanese culture and architecture.[144]

Keys and door locks have been known in Japan for centuries. Their use was first documented in the seventh century
CE, after the technological know-how for their production
arrived, presumably from China. Contrary to what European
voyagers like the English merchants of the 1580s thought,
Japan was certainly not a keyless society. Until the twentieth
century, however, keys did not play the same role in daily
life there as they did in Europe. This had a lot to do with the
structure of the traditional Japanese house. In Europe, even
in the premodern era, the walls of a house (preferably made
of stone) were designed to mark a clear boundary between
the building and its environment, not only in an architectural sense, but also in a legal sense. In Japan, by contrast,
the dominant ideal was that the home and its natural environment should be viewed as a unity rather than as opposing spaces. The transition from the living space to the artfully designed garden should be fluid, and accordingly, the

boundaries of the house should be flexible rather than static and permanent.

Consider the case of house doors: in premodern Europe, the few external doors of each house were made from massive materials. Irrespective of their sturdy appearance and importance for the display of status, doors were always seen as a weak point in the wall. By contrast, a typical Japanese house featured many external doors, each consisting of a wide wooden frame with wooden ribs in both directions, the interspaces lined with translucent and easily tearable paper. As a rule, these doors did not open outward, but by sliding. When closed, they let the daylight in, and when fully open—that is, slid to one side—the permanence of the wall seemed to be suspended and the boundary between house and nature blurred. Tellingly, there is no traditional Japanese word for the typical European door with hinges. Instead, and ever since the late nineteenth century, it has been referred to as *doa* (from the English "door").[145]

However, one should not conclude that security was not a consideration in Japan—quite the contrary. But the mechanism used was social rather than technological; people more firmly and systematically relied on family members and servants to guard the doors and allow visitors to enter. Door locks and bolts did exist, but they could often be operated only from inside. Thus, many houses could not be secured from the outside, and in practice the house was often left unlocked anyway. As Atsushi Ueda notes, locks served more as "symbolic seals," while the actual task of securing the house lay with its occupants. This was possible—and efficient—because in traditional Japanese society, several generations of a family usually lived under one roof. While the younger members worked, the elderly in particular guarded the house and its entryways. For a long time, locks were used only in places where no one lived, such as production facilities and warehouses.

This system, which historians have described as a specifically Japanese "national residential crime prevention system," functioned quite reliably until after World War II and declined only because of the accelerated structural change in Japanese society during the second half of the twentieth century: as the extended family gave way to the nuclear family unit, the social method of home security began to erode. In its place emerged a system of elaborate door locks of the Western variety, which is now the standard in modern Japan. Of course, these changes did not occur without resistance. During the early phase, men in particular criticized the appearance of lockable doors and feared that more widespread use would accelerate the decline of the traditional family order. As historian Jordan Sand has shown, their "main fear was that these things would lead to the liberation of women from the home. With fewer doors to the outside, small Western houses were easier to lock up and leave empty."[146] Ironically, the very technology that allowed for confining women to the home in Europe could be perceived as a means of female liberation in Japan.

Because of the qualms about Western-style doors, the transition in Japan from social to technological home security occurred only gradually, and it is significant that this transition period was also a time of heightened insecurity. During the 1960s, a statistical study from the Kyoto Prefecture police

concluded that "the most common form of entry by a burglar was through 'unlocked doors'" (31.2 percent) and that in
nearly 30 percent of burglaries, the door locks were defective.
In only about 10 percent of cases did the intruders have to
make an effort to break the locks. As one Japanese historian
of architecture noted, "it seems that the Japanese could have
prevented a great many robberies by paying a little more attention to their locks."[147]

Of course, some premodern European householders also
relied on extended family members or on neighborly social
control to secure their homes. In country areas, this can still
be seen today.[148] And although, as we have seen, this method of
protection had its critics, by and large it has existed in Europe
since the Middle Ages—not *instead* of locks, but *in addition*
to them. Indeed, one can say that in the West, door and lock
became an inseparable unit: every door had to have a built-in
lock by definition. But this unity, and the need for it, should
not be seen as self-evident, and Japan is not the only case in
point.

Another culture in which the practice of locking was quite
different from the Western model is premodern Iran. Although
a thriving locksmith trade existed in Iran for centuries, its focus was not the same as in Europe.[149] In fact, "the fixed lock
tended to be much less employed and, when used, to be far less
refined in workmanship than its European counterpart."[150] Instead, locksmiths primarily produced padlocks. These could be
fixed to a door, but also to an object; in other words, they were
mobile rather than permanent and could be used according
to need in a wide range of situations. For this reason, great

attention was paid to their technological sophistication and decorative design. Significantly, however, this attention did not extend to the keys that accompanied them: as one scholar of Iranian history put it, "the key almost invariably played a minor role from an aesthetic point of view."[151]

As these examples show, the unity of door and lock that emerged in European culture was not the result of an inevitable historical process. It tells us little about technological superiority, but a lot about individual and collective fears. Against this backdrop, it also becomes clear why the idea of societies in which doors were always open was as fantastical to Europeans as it was fascinating. Indeed, the idea of a house door that did not need to be locked figured prominently in utopian literature as far back as Plato, who stated in his blueprint for an ideal society that, among the Guardians, "no one is to have the kind of house or storeroom which cannot be entered by anyone who feels like it."[152] Taking up this thread in his *Utopia*, the sixteenth-century humanist Thomas More described a world in which house doors "open easily with a push of the hand and close again automatically [and] let anyone come in." In More's ideal society, locking was no longer necessary, because—as in Plato—"there is nothing private anywhere [in the house]."[153] Just a few years after the publication of More's treatise, this utopian vision seemed briefly to come true in continental Europe: in the wake of the Reformation, the Anabaptists—a movement of radical Protestants who aspired to live according to the New Testament in every respect—rejected the idea of individual property and followed the example of the early Christians in sharing all their worldly possessions. For this reason, as a contemporary observed, they "broke the locks off their doors, chests, and cellars." However, "as in the times of the apostles, it did not last long."[154] Indeed, the Anabaptists, whose radical communalism was perceived as a grave threat to the conventions of society, were relentlessly persecuted all over Europe. These examples are another reminder that in the Western tradition, speaking positively about open doors has rarely been free of moralistic or even utopian connotations, and this holds true also in our own time. To this day, older people like to point out in an idealizing way that during their childhoods doors were not locked, implying their awareness that it was, and is, an unusual custom.

Ultimately, Western culture has been marked by profound ambiguity with respect to doors: in *theory*, the idea of keeping the door open without risk is a utopian ideal; in *practice*, the open door was and often still is deeply suspect. Tellingly, the doors that Westerners perceived as being open by default were not their own, but those of other, non-European societies. We have seen this with respect to Native Americans, but the same expectations also underlay the colonial aspirations of the great Western powers in Asia. Take, for example, Commodore Matthew C. Perry in the 1850s: through the threat of military force, he succeeded in making Japan give up its centuries-long isolationist policy. Perry's contemporaries hailed this as an overdue "opening" of Japan. In addition to opening the doors to trade, Perry was also credited with unsealing the entire "hermetic empire" and ensuring that "the unnatural barriers by which it has so long insulated itself from the world have been broken."[155] The notion of an "open door" in Asia became an even more important goal of foreign policy during the 1890s when the Western powers fought to preserve their business interests in China: in this context, there was now explicit talk of an "open door policy," which the U.S. government in particular promoted. The open door policy meant that all imperial powers—the major European nations, Russia, and the United States—were supposed to enjoy free and unhindered access to the Chinese markets and ports. On paper, the national integrity of China was maintained, but in reality its doors would stand wide open to the Western states and their interests.[156] Well into the first decades of the twentieth century, the open door policy influenced the politics of the West with regard to China. The rationale on which it was based, as Max Weber noted, was characteristic of the general nature of imperialism, which must continually open new doors and thus gain access to new markets and colonies abroad.[157]

It was easier, however, for Westerners to demand open doors from other countries than to offer open access to their own. It was not even seen as contradictory to advocate an open door policy in foreign markets while simultaneously demanding protectionism for one's own economy.[158] The one-sidedness of the open door metaphor is also evident in other political contexts. Now and then, for instance, European nationalists have claimed that the doors of their countries are unprotected and open to foreigners. This figure of speech existed before the age of nationalism and was already common in early modernity, where it was not used to warn of the danger to nation-states, but to the whole of Christianity. In his famous *Ship of Fools* (1494), the humanist Sebastian Brant used precisely this

metaphor of the open door to warn his Christian contemporaries about the danger of Europe being conquered by the
Turks:

> None realize how close it be,
> They fancy they'll come off scot-free,
> Until misfortune hounds their gate,
> And then they stir and crane their pate.
> For Europe's gates are open wide,
> The foe encircles every side,
> With sleep or rest he's not content,
> On Christian blood alone he's bent.[159]

Keys and locks are not a European invention, nor are they
specific to Western culture. Yet even where they have been
known for centuries—as in premodern Japan and Iran—
they did not have the same symbolic importance as in Europe,
where the key was a prime symbol of security, control, and
power. And this tradition still lives on today. On a metaphoric
level, we even speak of *keywords* and *key ideas*, referring to
terms and concepts with which we try to bring order and priorities to an ever more complex world. On the literal level,
keys remain an indispensable and omnipresent technology.
True, some of their earlier functions have disappeared: cities
no longer have gates, and thus no keys. Our houses, by contrast,
still cannot do without keys, and the thought that doors might
stay open against our will still causes anxiety. Consequently,
the keys with which we lock our houses and protect our possessions have become ever more sophisticated: highly complex
chip cards now give access to places with strict security measures. Their primary advantage over traditional metal keys is

that, in case of loss, the lock need not be replaced but simply recoded.[160] Not just in real life, but also in the virtual world, keys are continually becoming more complex. The electronic "access keys" and passwords of today, without which we cannot open the "portals" and "gateways" to the digital world, are part of a long tradition, even if we are not aware of it. The number of keys, both real and digital, that we use every day seems to increase all the time. And at this point in time, it is not at all clear whether we still have the power of the keys or whether the keys now have power over us.

CHAPTER THREE

"Whence Is That Knocking?"
Precarious Passages

O N A TYPICAL DAY, EACH one of us passes through doorways four or five hundred times.[1] At first this may seem an entirely trivial activity, marked by routine and lack of conscious attention. A closer look, however, reveals that this routine hinges on both a complex set of social conventions and a deeply rooted sense of etiquette. Consider the threshold of a house, for instance: precisely because it constitutes a crucial boundary in Western culture, crossing it is permissible only under certain conditions and when accompanied by the necessary formalities. We may at times wish to peek beyond or through our neighbors' doors, but in reality we are bound by a strict code of conduct. Even when we find a door open, we do not simply enter; we knock, even when the person we are visiting is clearly visible through the door.[2] If, by contrast, we are standing in front of a closed door, the procedure generally consists of several steps. In many apartment buildings, visitors must first pass a doorkeeper or concierge. Upon reaching the actual apartment door, they knock or ring a doorbell. The door is then opened, usually by an adult, as it is still considered unacceptable in many places for children to answer the door. Hosts and guests shake hands, coats are taken, and shoes stowed. Not until this moment has one truly arrived in the house or apartment. When guests later take their leave, a host accompanies them back to the threshold, where the ceremony is repeated in reverse.[3]

As this sketch illustrates, crossing the threshold of a home is often quite a formalized procedure. And in crisis situations it becomes even more complicated: in fact, there are specific manuals—for police, for example—detailing the circumstances in which a door may be opened by force, and how this should be done.[4] In short, it is fair to say that Western culture is characterized by a deeply rooted "hesitancy to enter."[5] Still, it would be wrong to claim that this hesitancy is an invention of modernity, for it was very much alive in premodern times.[6] In fact, the various social practices associated with the act of entering were even more complex then than they are today, and many of them—some still in existence—cannot be fully explained from a rational perspective. Rather, they reflect an interplay of rational and irrational ideas. Clearly, many Western practices, as routine as they seem to most of us, are neither universal nor anthropological constants, and as sociological studies show, immigrants from non-Western countries sometimes find these entrance rules exaggerated and even bewildering.[7] What people do at (and associate with) doors in everyday life varies from society to society—and precisely these differences can provide us with deeper insight into how people in a given society make sense of that ubiquitous yet amorphous phenomenon that we call "space." This chapter focuses on three specific practices: knocking on, passing through, and touching doors, all of which are related in different ways to fears of contamination and unwanted entry.

The history of *knocking* is also a history of individual and collective hopes and fears. For the person inside the house, a knock might be an eagerly awaited signal, but it can also signify imminent danger and intrusion. Outside the door may stand an expected guest — or an unexpected criminal. Indeed, in the Western imagination, knocking has often been associated with danger — for instance, Death knocking on the door, a subject depicted in European art in countless variations over the centuries. Destiny, too, can knock on the door, and just as eerily: the four most famous notes in Western music, the opening motif of Beethoven's Fifth Symphony, were born in this imaginative space.

Yet knocking also could inspire a sense of hope. In Christian tradition it was believed that Christ himself might appear at the door and wish to enter: "Behold, I stand at the door, and knock," he announces in the Book of Revelation. And for anyone who opens the door to him, "I will come in to him, and will sup with him, and he with me."[8] People in premodern times knew these lines very well.[9] But they also knew that Christ would not open the doors to his own "house" — the kingdom of heaven — to everyone. One of his parables warns sinners in no uncertain terms: "When once the master of the house is risen up, and hath shut to the door, and ye begin to stand without, and to knock at the door, saying, Lord, Lord, open unto us; and he shall answer and say unto you, I know you not whence ye are."[10]

Medieval and early modern Europeans were also familiar with Old Testament passages in which knocking on a door is associated with danger.[11] The almost archetypal potential of the unexpected knock is evoked in thrillers and horror movies to this day, but arguably no one has captured it as powerfully as Shakespeare did with Macbeth's terrified exclamation: "Whence is that knocking? How is't with me, when every noise appals me?"[12] Of course, Macbeth is easily startled in this particular situation because he has just committed a murder, but the fear that he is experiencing was not unknown to people in Shakespeare's time. Premodern Europeans were certainly not inclined to rush to the door and open it whenever they heard a knock. As we have seen, keeping one's door closed was a widely followed convention, and just as we rely today on peepholes and intercoms, people in the past had their own ways of finding out who was waiting outside the closed door. Technical devices, such as small hatches that could be opened and peered through, were one option. Some private houses had them, but they were particularly common at the entrances to castles. In an account from 1466, a frustrated Basel notary who was denied access to the nearby castle of the counts of Thierstein described the "small window of the aforementioned castle doors through which the guards have the duty to see who is standing there."[13] What is more, castle ordinance often stipulated that the inner gate should be opened only in the presence of three guards on horseback. If the guards had even the slightest doubt as to the intentions of the entering individual or party, they were not to open the gate at all.[14] Urban residents, too, took great precautions. As we see in Boccaccio, it was already common in the fourteenth century for residents to go to the window before opening the door.[15] And this explains why people standing outside were advised to show patience and respect. As late as the 1730s, a pedagogical treatise recommended: "Being to enter & to goe into a house, for feare thou shouldst misse the dore, stand still & stop at the entrance, & behold and looke on the forefront: then knock at the gate or at the doore. If any looke thorow the windowes, or lattices, pray him to open."[16]

In upper-class residences, of course, the master of the house would rarely open the door himself—that task fell to servants. Among the aristocracy, the rules were particularly elaborate: barring exceptional cases, aristocratic hosts would await their guests in a specially appointed reception room, or standing at the top of a staircase.[17] Guests, in turn, had various ways of announcing their presence at the door. In ancient Rome, for example, it was quite common to use one's foot to rap at the door instead of knocking with the hand.[18] It is not clear when knocking with one's hand became the prevailing practice in Europe, but we do know that this development occurred only gradually. The French poet and *trouvère* Robert de Blois, living in the second half of the thirteenth century, recommended yet another means of announcing oneself at the door: "When you are about to enter the house, cough a little upon entering to alert those within to your arrival, either by this cough or by a word."[19] In a religious setting, by contrast, knocking with one's hand became the preferred method over the course of the Middle Ages, perhaps because it was associated with the New Testament image of Christ knocking. Aspiring monks, for example, had to wait a long time outside monastery doors and knock repeatedly in order to prove their steadfastness and determination. Tellingly, monks who were accepted into a monastery in this manner were called *pulsantes* ("those who knock"), in contrast to the *oblati* (those who, as children, had been "offered" to the monastery by their parents).[20]

The historical process by which knocking with the hand became predominant throughout Europe simultaneously gave rise to more nuanced and differentiated knocking techniques than had been possible when the foot was used. Knocking with one's hand balled into a fist was one option, of course, but not the only one. In premodern society certain groups developed specific knocking practices to announce themselves in distinctive ways. Among beggars, who went from door to door asking for alms, it was not uncommon to carry a wooden knocker to rap on the door, and this sound was well known to people at the time.[21] Court messengers, by contrast, knocked on the door with a judge's staff.[22] And even when the bare hand was used, there were still different registers for knocking. Many dignitaries—the early modern mayors of Cologne, for example, when they made visits in the city—had servants knock for them. The diarist Hermann Weinsberg, himself a respected councilman, reports that he would "rush hurriedly to the door" upon hearing the mayor's servant knock.[23] In other contexts, the actual number of knocks could have a specific meaning: among freemasons, admission to the lodge was permitted only to those who knew the specific way, and number of times, to knock.[24] The strength of the knocks, too, could be a statement about the person standing outside. In early modern Italy it seems to have been customary for prostitutes' clients to knock in a particularly brutal manner in order to intimidate the women inside; as one contemporary described it, the clients would "give [the doors] such a furious knocking as to make themselves appear uncouth," almost to the point of "breaking the doors in pieces."[25]

Those inside the house had their own preferences as to how visitors should knock. Among the upper classes, raw blows of the fist were considered inappropriate or even rude; for reasons of exclusivity and social distinction, aristocrats expected visitors to announce themselves in much more re-fined ways. This was particularly important at royal courts. Writing about Versailles and other royal French palaces, an eighteenth-century German nobleman reported, "Knocking on doors is not allowed in royal houses; instead, if they are closed and one knows that there are people inside, one is supposed to scratch lightly at them with one's nails."[26] In cit-ies, affluent homeowners installed sophisticated doorknockers on their front doors. Here, too, a variety of technical options were available. Installing a movable metal hammer (fittingly called *marteau de porte* in French) was one possibility; other options included a mallet or a ring made of iron or brass.[27] In fact, the function of ring-shaped doorknockers often went beyond knocking: they could also serve as rotating handles for opening and closing doors from the outside.[28] But quite apart from technological considerations, aesthetic ones also were at play in the decision to install such devices. In this context, we recall that in premodernity the terms "family" and "house" were often used synonymously. The front door therefore was not only a prominent part of the house from an architectural point of view, but also a marker of the family's honor and status. In early modern Venice, where belonging to a respected family was crucial for political status, citizens invested time and thought to ensure that their front doors adequately displayed their station and Venetian identity. Since bronze was quite expensive, doorknockers also played an important role in impressing guests and passersby as yet another ornament on the lavishly designed doors of the time.[29] In the imperial city of Nuremberg, even less affluent burghers did their best to install knockers on their front doors, and here, too, it was more than pure function driving the trend.[30]

Since door rings made a statement about the respectability of a house and its residents, it is no surprise that they also found their way into a number of legal practices related to the entire house. In real estate transactions, for example, grasping the door ring could seal the purchase of a property or, in more contentious situations, signify the right to seize the house. Neither haphazard nor spontaneous, these rituals were highly formalized and generally performed in the presence of a judge (as we know from illustrations to medieval law codes) (Figure 21).[31] It is also possible that these rituals were influenced by, or modeled on, religious precedents. In the Catholic tradition, door rings traditionally fulfilled a symbolic as well as a legally binding function: the act of grasping a church door ring allowed a fugitive to secure asylum in the sanctuary, and this in turn led to the installation of elaborate sanctuary

Figure 21. A man taking possession of a house by grasping the
door handle in the presence of a judge. Miniature from the
Görlitz Saxon Mirror, 1386. Biblioteka Jagiellońska, Kraków.

knocker like the famous one at the northern door of Durham
Cathedral (today a World Heritage Site).[32]

The custom of attaching door rings to holders shaped
like animal heads certainly had a religious origin. Of course,
it is often hard to distinguish between pagan and Christian
influences: knockers in the shape of cats' heads, for example,
may have originated in the pagan tradition of "construction
sacrifices"—that is, sacrifices involving the burial of domestic
animals, dead or alive, under the threshold of doors or gates.
These sacrifices were thought to have a magically protective
function and to avert evil.[33] Knockers shaped like lions' heads,

by contrast, were more closely related to Christian iconography and symbolism (Figure 22). When attached to church doors, they symbolized Christ the Redeemer; in secular architecture, by extension, they conveyed the righteous and godly governance of the master of the house.[34] Only in the course of secularization did the originally religious-mythical connotations of these animal-shaped doorknockers slowly disappear: today they are no more than decorative accessories.

The installation of door rings, however, often involved more than just aesthetic and symbolic considerations. In line with these objects' religious and legal functions, considerable attention was given not only to their design, but also to their position on the door. Thus at the Abbey of St. Geneviève in Paris, in an effort to stem the tide of asylum seekers, the door ring was eventually placed so high that it was almost unreachable.[35]

But let us return to the close connection between "house" and "honor," for it manifested itself in both positive and negative contexts. As we have seen, when a householder's moral integrity was in doubt, his or her house—and specifically the front door—often became a site for mocking rituals and extrajudicial forms of punishment. In these situations, knocking on the door could quickly change from a gesture of politeness and respect to an act of harassment and even raw violence. The fifteenth-century Florentine chronicler Luca Landucci described a particularly gruesome case in his account of the Pazzi family's conspiracy against the ruling Medici in 1478. After the conspiracy failed, Medici partisans in Florence quickly turned to revenge. The Medici ordered the public execution of the

Figure 22. Replica of the twelfth-century sanctuary
knocker on the north door of Durham Cathedral.
The original is kept in the Cathedral Treasury Museum.

leaders of the Pazzi clan, in most cases by defenestration or by hanging them from the windows of public buildings. But this did not satisfy all Medici supporters. Landucci reports that a group of youths dug up the still fresh grave of Jacopo de' Pazzi and removed his body. They then dragged it by the hangman's rope, still tied around the dead man's neck, through the streets of Florence: "And when they came to the door of his house, they tied the hangman's rope to the door-ring, saying: 'Knock at the door.'"[36] The door, of course, remained shut. The youths then threw his body into the Arno.

Landucci expressed his amazement that the youths showed no sign of revulsion at the corpse during this macabre episode. Yet, like most of his contemporaries, he did not object to the actual desecration, for this was not the first time in early modern Florence—nor would it be the last—that the body of a person executed for a grave crime was exhumed and maltreated in all sorts of gruesome ways. In France, too, bodies of particularly hated criminals were sometimes exhumed and then dragged before a statue of the king, where they were mocked and ordered to perform the so-called *amende honorable,* the ritual begging for pardon.[37] The Florentine episode belongs in this context, but it has other layers of meaning as well. After all, the Pazzi conspiracy—and the ensuing revenge—was not only a conflict between *individuals* with competing political views and ambitions; it was also the escalation of a longstanding rivalry between two *Houses.* Tellingly, the de facto Florentine ruler Lorenzo de' Medici, who narrowly escaped assassination by the Pazzi, explicitly accused his enemies of waging a war "against me and my house."[38] Thus, the Medici faction's decision to defenestrate many of the conspirators from the windows of palaces and official buildings, or to hang them at the window bars, was not arbitrary: it was a graphic display of their power to eject their opponents, quite literally, from the spaces in which the strength of their House was concentrated.[39] In the same vein, the House of Pazzi no longer had a place in Florence: those family members who were spared execution were exiled from the city. And the macabre episode surrounding Jacopo de' Pazzi's corpse also fits this motif: the grisly knocking ritual made clear that the house itself had lost every shred of honor and that, toward this House, all conventions of politeness and respect—including knocking, especially with the door ring—were null and void. Significantly, this method of humiliation lived on in Florence. A few decades later, after a usurper, Giuliano Buonaccorsi, was gruesomely executed, raging Florentines dragged the corpse through the streets. An anonymous chronicler reports: "And then they went to beat on the door where a sister of his lived, and, knocking, said, 'Open, Giuliano is here.' And then they dragged him to the Arno."[40]

The contrast between legitimate knocking and its subversion is a recurring theme in early modern history, even if not always in such an extreme form. Knocking without purpose or for harassment was often a means of drawing attention to the deviant behavior of a householder or an entire House. This form of public censure and humiliation was common in many parts of Europe and was an established part of folk culture, as reflected, for example, in the rites of charivari (also known as "rough music"). In German lands, mocking rituals of this kind existed as early as the Middle Ages. Often it was male neighbors who ridiculed a head of household for failing to control his wife or who was rumored to be impotent.[41]

Religious minorities also fell victim to such mocking rituals, as described in contemporary Jewish accounts. It was not at all uncommon for Christians to throw stones at or knock forcefully on the doors of Jewish houses—and as long as these acts were committed by youths, the authorities often did not intervene.[42] Many Jews put up with these recurrent disturbances. Others chose to defend themselves. For instance, on a Saturday in 1644, a group of young Christian workers stopped outside the house of Moyse ben Lazarus, a Jewish resident of the Westphalian city of Minden. One of the youths pounded on the front door with a shovel in order to disturb the Sabbath rest. Much to the young men's surprise, Moyse came rushing out with a large broomstick and dealt a head wound to one of the youths (the wrong one, it turned out).[43]

To be sure, attacks on or against doors also occurred *within* the Jewish community. Here again, the victims tended to be outsiders or deviant individuals. The freethinker Uriel Acosta, for example, was attacked in 1623, when rabbis and other Jewish community leaders in Amsterdam turned against him because of his critique of rabbinical orthodoxy. He recounts in his autobiography:

> The next step they took was to set their children upon me in the streets, who insulted me all together as I walked along, abusing and railing at me, crying out, "There goes a Heretic, there goes an Apostate." At other times, they assembled together before my doors, flinging stones at the windows, and doing everything they could to disturb and annoy me, so that I could not live in peace in my own house.[44]

For Acosta and others like him, the fact that these attacks by fellow Jews mimicked aspects of anti-Semitic ritual was especially humiliating.

As these examples show, there were certain circumstances in which early modern authorities tolerated or even encouraged throwing stones at or forcefully knocking on doors. At the same time, there was always a risk that they might lose control of such rituals and become targets themselves.[45] In many parts of Europe, violently knocking on doors was popular among young people as a way of rebelling against societal norms and hierarchies. This was especially common during the weeks before and after Christmas, when youths customarily knocked on the doors of neighbors to commemorate the birth of the Lord and wish the families a happy new year. In return, they often received small gifts, such as fruit or baked goods. Though a benign custom on the surface, in practice these "knocking nights" (*Klöpfleinsnächte*) became problematic, because they gave rise to begging and even extortion of "gifts." What is more, unruly youths subverted the kindly intentions of the tradition, plaguing their neighbors with vile curses and incessant knocking. The boundary between pranks and outright violence in such cases could easily become blurred, as a seventeenth-century Nuremberg chronicle reports:

> Here in this city of Nuremburg there is an old but very evil custom, in which numerous young people—girls as well as boys—run rampant once a year on *Oberstnacht* [the night of 5 January], which they like to call *Bergnacht*, and they beat heavily and viciously upon the residents' house doors and window shutters with hammers, mallets, and clubs. Afterwards they run quickly away, and one can neither see nor know who

the knockers were . . . Thus on 6 January of this year, 1616, it happened that, when the knocking and pounding did not cease, one head servant came out of his house in a rage in the middle of the night. At that moment he saw a young girl passing by in the street, and, thinking her responsible for the knocking, he beat her with a club, whereupon she spewed blood and fell dead to the ground.[46]

Such episodes remind us that knocking on a door—a cultural practice that today almost always signifies politeness—fulfilled various other social functions in the past.[47] True, this form of harassment still occurs in our time, but the concepts of "house" and "honor" are no longer as closely entwined as in the premodern period. Today, a person who pounds on a door or rings the bell in order to harass can be punished for disturbing domestic peace, or even for vandalism. But these acts rarely have the power to insult residents' *honor*, and certainly do not lead to violent conflicts. At the same time, knocking has lost most of its social meaning because of technological progress: in many Western societies the existence of electric doorbells has entirely eliminated the need for it. In premodern times, some houses had bells near *internal* doors, but these served an entirely different function: they were used to summon servants and staff *within* the house rather than to announce the arrival of guests outside. The modern concept of the doorbell, by contrast, took centuries to spread throughout Europe. In southern German-speaking regions, especially in large cities like Vienna and Munich, some front doors were equipped with bells as early as the seventeenth century. But in northern Germany they mostly appeared only in the late eighteenth century and gradually acquired a shape that is still familiar to us today, consisting of a mechanical trigger, a metal bell, and a nameplate next to the trigger. Until the age of electricity, however, such bells were just one method—and not the most common one—by which visitors announced themselves at the door.[48] Doorbells did not become a standard feature until the nineteenth century; but when they did become popular, they quickly replaced manual knocking.

From a purely practical perspective, of course, there is much to be said for the efficiency of electric doorbells. But we should also bear in mind that, with their identical and often shrill tone, they do not allow for differentiated signals to the same extent that manual knocking does, with its varied patterns and intensities. As Walter Benjamin once remarked, the sound of the electric doorbell can unfurl a "despotic terror"— and at least in this vacillation between terror and curiosity to know who is at the door, there remains a trace of the ambiguity and fear that was for centuries so strongly bound to the act of knocking.[49]

Announcing oneself at a door was (and still is) merely a prelude to a much more complex procedure: the act of *passing through* a door, or entering. There are, of course, many ways of crossing thresholds, but not all of them are socially acceptable. Even today, in Western culture, stumbling over a threshold is often seen as a bad omen—and the risk of injury alone does not explain this. In fact, in the Greco-Roman world, stumbling over the threshold was believed to bring misfortune to the house and its inhabitants. By the same token, it is not just a matter of courtesy when a groom carries his bride over the threshold, as has been done since antiquity.[50] The early modern period was no exception in this respect. In northern Germany, for example, it was customary for the groom and wedding guests to go to the house following the marriage ceremony and to wait there for the bride. When her coach arrived, accompanied by music, she would approach the front door, where the groom awaited her with bare head. He would then ask the assembled guests three times, "May I in honor bring in my bride?" And each time the group would answer, "Bring her in, in God's name!" After the final refrain, the groom would lift the bride and swing her gently over the threshold into the house, saying, "In honor I bring in my bride."[51]

This ritual was not just a matter of gentlemanly courtesy: if the bride were to cross the threshold on her own and stumble, people would suspect that something was amiss—specifically, that malicious spirits had tampered with the threshold. And if the threshold were compromised, the home (in German, *Heim*) could quickly become *unheimlich* (uncanny). The threshold, then, was more than a physical barrier separating the house from its surroundings: it also marked the entrance to a space that was seen as a shelter for the living. This notion that the house was a space for the living, at the exclusion of the dead, is not as self-evident as it may seem today. We know from anthropological studies that in some non-European societies it was customary to bury the dead inside the house, which was not felt to be dangerous from a sanitary point of view (though European explorers and colonists promptly forbade it).[52] In Europe, house burials were common in the

Neolithic period, as archaeological excavations have shown.[53] Slowly, however, it became more common to bury people outside the house, although for quite some time it was still acceptable to bury the dead immediately in front of or under the threshold.[54] In excavated Celtic settlements dating from the fifth to the second century BCE, for example, archaeologists have found numerous skeletons of children buried under the thresholds of houses.[55] And as late as the Middle Ages, Paulus Diaconus (c. 720 – c. 799) reported that Alboin, the king of the Lombards and a devout Christian, was buried under the steps leading to the royal palace.[56] As these examples suggest, the threshold of a house was the closest that death was allowed to approach the shelter of the living. And this, in turn, came from the belief that the threshold was the ultimate boundary "to ban the dead from the world of the living."[57]

The fear that death, as well as other natural and supernatural threats, might find a way to enter the house has led many societies to devise special, often magical, rituals of protection for doorways and thresholds.[58] Among these is the idea that one has to prevent the threshold from being contaminated with any trace of evil. In this vein, Germanic law stipulated that when apprehending the culprit behind a serious crime, the authorities should drag him or her out, dead or alive, through a hole dug *under* the threshold.[59] In ordinary situations, by contrast, the dead were always carefully carried *over* the threshold so that they would not come in contact with it. In Mediterranean countries, the fear of contaminating the threshold led to a still more extreme practice: those who died inside the house could be carried out only through a window or a smaller side door (tellingly named the *porta dei morti* in Italian).[60]

Throughout the Middle Ages and well into the early modern period, the most common method of trying to ward off death and prevent other evil from entering was the burial of so-called construction sacrifices under the threshold of a new building.[61] This practice reflected an old superstition that the first person to enter a new house would also be the first to die. Additionally, these sacrifices were believed to give long-term protection against evil spirits, fires, and plagues. Such measures were especially popular in rural areas, where they could also be taken retroactively, for example, during dangerous epidemics among livestock. Throughout German lands, it was common to bury a sick horse or calf alive under the door. In some areas, people used young, blind dogs or other small domestic animals such as chickens and cats, and sometimes even bees and beetles (Figure 23). Archaeologists excavating medieval and early modern towns have also found various other material objects and texts under the thresholds of houses, all of which are thought to have been buried there for their apotropaic effect. These include coins, talismans, and religious cult objects, as well as agricultural products such as grains, flowers, and eggs. Sometimes an animal skull was placed over the door, either as an additional preventive measure or to commemorate a previous construction sacrifice.

Construction sacrifices, like many other customs of pagan origin, never received official approval by the church. Of course, what people did in their everyday lives was frequently

Figure 23. This mummified dog, along with a metal key, was
found in a leather-lined casket in the wall above the entrance of
Burgk Castle in Thuringia, Germany. A forensic examination
revealed that the dog was buried alive as a construction
sacrifice, probably in the fourteenth or fifteenth century.

at odds with religious doctrine, and the custom of making
construction sacrifices is just one example of this. In fact, archaeologists have even found a construction sacrifice—more
precisely, an entire sheep—under a Protestant church entrance of that period.[62] The persistence of such pagan customs
in Christian Europe owed partly to the fact that, at least in
popular culture, they were bolstered with Christian meaning.

Eggs buried under a threshold, for example, were often eggs that had been laid on Maundy Thursday. And the sharp pike teeth that were sometimes placed above doors could be seen as analogous to Christ's crown of thorns.[63] Even so, it is important to stress that church doctrine considered only the pagan ritual itself illegitimate, while acknowledging the hope for the apotropaic effect that lay at the heart of such sacrifices.

Indeed, the Catholic Church had its own protective rituals for doors and thresholds. Some were reserved for church buildings, as seen in the elaborate consecration ceremonies of Catholic churches, where special attention was paid to doors and thresholds. The bishop, after walking around the new building, would strike the door with the base of his crosier and say, "Lift up your gates, ye princes, and be ye lifted up, ye everlasting doors, and the King of Glory shall come in." Later in the ceremony he would again touch the main entrance with his crosier, while tracing "a cross on the upper part and another on the lower part of the door inside." This cross was intended to prevent all "malignant influences from without."[64] For private homes, the church offered a range of protective measures, including various apotropaic symbols and inscriptions. Perhaps the best known is the epiphany custom, still practiced today, in which a member of the clergy chalks C + M + B above the door—an acronym for the names of the three biblical Magi as well as for the Latin benediction *Christus mansionem benedicat* ("May Christ bless the house"). By the same token, people placed crucifixes or monograms (such as J.M. for "Jesus Mary") on the door, a custom that went back to the earliest Christian communities. To ward off the plague,

it was common to write eighteen letters of the alphabet, separated by seven crosses, above the door—specifically, the initial
letters of the verses of a plague prayer supposedly composed by
Pope Zachary (r. 741–752).[65]

Many of these once-popular rituals and symbols are now
forgotten, and therefore it is difficult for us to imagine just
how common and visible they were on premodern houses. We
get a glimpse, however, from the photograph of a home in a
village near Salzburg, taken by an anthropologist around 1900
(Figure 24). There is nothing special in the architecture of this
house, and the anthropologist chose to photograph it solely because it had an array of well-preserved protective inscriptions
and objects on the door. Nailed to the center of the lintel is a
small metal plate showing an image of the Madonna of Ötting.
Next to that, the monograms of Jesus and Mary are carved into
the wood, accompanied by additional religious symbols drawn
with chalk. On the door panel itself, in chalk, appear the first
letters of the names of the Magi (here spelled K + M + B), and
beneath that hangs a small wreath of St. John's wort, which
was blessed at the local church. As the residents of the house
confirmed, all of this paraphernalia served to ward off magic,
lightning, and witches. From the residents' account, we know
that there were further protective devices at this doorway, not
all of them visible in the photograph. For instance, a small
glass tube had been buried beneath the threshold, containing
salt and a *Benediktuspfennig* (a medallion printed with the
cross and blessing of St. Benedict).[66]

Doors of this sort, heavily armed against evil forces threatening to enter, were not at all unusual in premodernity, and the

Figure 24. Door of a house in the Salzach Valley (Austria) displaying a wide range of apotropaic signs and objects. Photograph, c. 1900.

willingness of the church to supply protective devices for doors and thresholds was certainly connected to a popular demand that could not be ignored. Since pagan traditions persisted even centuries after the Christianization of Europe, the church simply could not afford to deny these remedies. Indeed, most pagan beliefs offered a wide range of remedies for residents concerned about the integrity of their doors and houses, and the polytheistic religions of the ancient world even assigned multiple deities to the threshold. Thus, ancient Romans not only had a god of thresholds (Limentinus), but also a goddess of hinges (Cardea) and even a god of doorposts (Forculus).

Yet the church also faced the challenge of distinguishing itself from Judaism, a religion practiced all over Europe, which similarly engaged with doors and their protection. Christians knew from the Old Testament that on the night that God killed the firstborn children of the Egyptians, the Israelites were spared death because they had marked their doors with the blood of lambs and goats. This "passing over" (*passach*) of death is the source of the Hebrew word *Pesach*, which has been used since antiquity to designate the annual festival commemorating the exodus from Egypt.[67]

Among Jews, the story of the blood-marked doorposts was passed down from one generation to the next, but it was never enacted in postbiblical times. Still, one feature visibly distinguished the doors of Jewish houses from those of their non-Jewish neighbors, namely the mezuzah. The word "mezuzah" originally meant "doorpost," but it came to designate a particular kind of small container enclosing a piece of parchment with two passages from the Old Testament. Jewish custom, then as now, is to fix this container to the right doorpost of every door in the home, as well as in other spaces used for residential purposes.[68] The two biblical passages enshrined within the mezuzah contain the lines from Deuteronomy on which the custom is based: "And thou shalt write them [the words of God] upon the posts of thy house, and on thy gates."[69]

The mezuzah was originally intended as a mnemotechnical "boundary marker" that "explicitly codes the inside space as Jewish."[70] In everyday life, however, it soon took on a broader meaning: as early as talmudic times, the mezuzah was thought to have the powers of an amulet. Later on, beginning in the Middle Ages and under the influence of Kabbalistic teachings, it became increasingly popular to write the names of angels, mystical verses, and symbols on and inside the mezuzah, as they were believed to have a magical and apotropaic effect. Renowned rabbinical authorities such as Maimonides criticized such superstitious notions—but only with limited success.

Among Christians, the mezuzah raised suspicions of sorcery, though this was primarily due to prejudice or lack of knowledge. Many Christians were inclined to draw a connection between Judaism and magic, and certain customs related to the mezuzah—for example, touching the mezuzah and then kissing one's fingertips—must have seemed quite mysterious to them at the time.[71] What heightened suspicions further were reports from converts who claimed that, thanks to the mezuzot, Jews could always sleep peacefully, because "God watched over their houses from outside."[72] Christian theologians often picked out these accounts to support their claims that behind these Jewish customs lay not the intention to conform to God's Word, but rather to abuse it with superstition. While John Calvin acknowledged that the mnemotechnical function of the mezuzah was an "excellent . . . lesson" for reflecting on the Holy Scriptures, he vehemently argued in his sermons that Jews had turned it "into a charme and sorcerie."[73] As Juliet Fleming has noted, Calvin claimed that "to believe in the efficacy of words in their material dimension [was] to commit precisely the idolatry that the passage warns against."[74] Even Enlightenment scholars, such as the German Orientalist Johann Ernst Faber (1745–1774), voiced similar views. Thus Faber asserted that "the Jews' mistake was not that they took God's word literally from the beginning, but that they later coupled it with new forms of superstition."[75]

Nonetheless, some Christians, especially Protestants, retained an ambivalent fascination with Jewish mezuzot. The Anglican cleric Samuel Purchas (c. 1577–1626) remarked that "he which hath his Phylacteries on his head and arms, and his knots on his garment, and his Schedule on his doore, is so fenced he cannot easily sinne."[76] We also know that some Christian homes in early modern England prominently displayed on their walls the very lines from Deuteronomy contained in the mezuzah. Even though the lines were not posted on the door, the desired effect seems to have been similar.[77]

We find a similar Christian fascination with mezuzot in an episode that occurred in Salzburg around the year 1400, as documented in the correspondence between a Jewish man named Salman and the famous rabbi Jacob ben Moses Moelin (also known as the Maharil).[78] Salman was consulting the rabbi as to whether it was permitted to supply a mezuzah to a non-Jew who requested one, or whether one should refuse, given the danger that the recipient might treat the religious object disrespectfully. In this particular case, the non-Jew in question was the lord of the city of Salzburg—none other than the archbishop himself—who had asked Salman for a mezuzah and promised him great kindness for the rest of his life in return. Salman feared that refusal might provoke the archbishop, but the Maharil's reply nevertheless forbade Salman to supply the mezuzah. Unfortunately, the sources do not elaborate further on this peculiar episode, and it remains unclear why the archbishop—probably Eberhard III—wanted the mezuzah in the first place. He may simply have been curious, or perhaps he hoped it would have a magical effect. In any case, it is likely that Salman's refusal did anger him, and this may have been one of the reasons behind—even the catalyst for—the Jewish pogroms of Salzburg in 1404, in which all adult Jews in the city were burned at the stake.

Yet Jews throughout Europe held fast to the mezuzah and to their customs, even if this exposed them to suspicion and danger. A poignant example is early modern Spain. In the 1490s, all Jews who rejected conversion were expelled from Spain, but Spanish cities continued to house communities of crypto-Jews. These were Jews who had been baptized under the pressure of the Inquisition but who still practiced their faith or certain Jewish customs in private. It would, of course, have been extremely dangerous for crypto-Jews to attach mezuzot to their doors, so they resorted to less conspicuous ways of showing respect for their doorposts. For example, when they swept their homes—an activity not visible to their neighbors—they would pay respect to the door by sweeping away from it, toward the center of the room.[79] The situation was similar in Portugal, where Jews were expelled in several stages from the late 1490s onward, leaving behind a community of converts, many of whom continued to practice Judaism in secret. Recent archaeological studies in Portugal have brought to light more than five hundred secret signs and Hebrew inscriptions in houses in which crypto-Jews once lived. Some of these markings, alongside hidden indentations for mezuzot, were found on the doorframes.[80]

The protection of doors and thresholds against harmful supernatural influences was a major concern to premodern Europeans. In London, even in the 1790s, one could still find horseshoes nailed to thresholds in order to keep witches away.[81] But to trust in these objects alone would have been naïve, and it was no less important to remain vigilant on a day-to-day basis. Precisely because the threshold and door were vulnerable parts of the house, they were seen as likely targets of harmful magic (*maleficium*).[82] Malicious neighbors, for example, might secretly bury harmful magical objects or inscriptions under thresholds. The respected scholar Bartholomäus Carrichter (c. 1510–1567), private physician to Emperor Maximilian II, dedicated an entire chapter to these dangerous objects and their respective remedies in his treatise *Zur Heylung der zauberischen Schäden* (On the Healing of Magical Illnesses).[83] This treatise was reprinted as late as the eighteenth century, and indeed, anxieties about door magic were still widespread at that time. In the 1770s, in the German university town of

Halle, "the thresholds of houses were relentlessly whipped with brooms and rods" when fear arose that supernatural forces or witchcraft had caused a newborn to fall ill.[84] Around the same time, a similar incident occurred in the German university town of Gießen, where the city's chief physician and all the people and animals in his house suddenly fell ill for no identifiable reason. All attempts to treat the disease failed, "until the maid discovered under the threshold a small pot containing an egg wrapped up in cloth and thread; as soon as these objects were removed, the disease resolved."[85]

Although the door was a preferred site for harmful magic, it could also be a site for love spells. In sixteenth-century Rome, at the trial of a well-known courtesan known as Lucrezia the Greek, the court discovered that she had tried to win the heart of a papal servant with supernatural aids: she had gathered clumps of earth near the doors of well-known courtesans' homes, hoping that this would bring good fortune to her own house.[86] In this case, the magic did not have any harmful intention. Nonetheless, it was based on the assumption that there is a connection—even an invisible bond—between the state of the doorway and that of the house and its residents.

As part of the special attention given to doors during this period, people were particularly attentive to the issue of cleanliness. *Touching* a door could lead to various kinds of contamination, or so people feared. Of course, a clean front door area is considered important (and even legally mandated) in many parts of Europe today, but this is clearly not a recent preoccupation. In historical studies there is an unfortunate tendency to presume that the sanitary conditions of the premodern world were inadequate in every respect. True, there was no systematic street cleaning at the time, and the presence of animals everywhere also affected the sanitary situation (and the smell) in cities. So it is all the more striking that residents cared a great deal about the cleanliness of the area immediately in front of the house, especially the door.

The early modern Dutch Republic is a case in point. There, intensive cleaning of the entryway (the so-called *stoep*) and the sidewalk in front of the house was a daily ritual—and thanks to travelogues we have vivid reports about this custom. The English traveler Samuel Patterson observed in 1782 that "the smallest filth in the streets would be decreed a reproach . . . to anyone that would suffer it to lie at his door."[87] A century earlier, another English traveler remarked that the Dutch seemed to give more attention to the clean appearance of their houses than to the purity of their bodies and souls.[88] Sarcasm aside, it is true that the Dutch scrupulously followed certain unwritten rules concerning their front doors. This often included scrubbing and polishing not only the door itself, but also the doorstep, the hinges, and the knockers. Visitors and residents alike were required to dust off their shoes on a special mat in front of the door and usually had to remove their shoes as well. Some residents provided their guests with slippers that could be worn on top of one's shoes.[89]

This fastidious attention to the cleanliness of the door area was no doubt partly motivated by genuine sanitary concerns. As the historian Simon Schama has noted, "to be filthy was to expose the population to the illicit entry of disease and the vagrant vermin that were said to be its carriers." In other words, those who failed to clean their houses and doors risked "open[ing] the gates to an army of infected marauders."[90] But a purely functionalist explanation is not sufficient. As Schama also notes, "the obligation to wash the pavement in front of the house . . . was not just a legal civic duty, that is to say, a public obligation, it was also a way to protect the threshold of the inner sanctum."[91] Thus, keeping the front door clean also had to do with preserving and displaying the respectability of the entire house—a kind of social hygiene.

Yet this was not unique to the Netherlands. As Keith Thomas has shown, English householders at the time also believed that domestic cleanliness was necessary "to avoid making a bad impression upon visitors or superiors." This was why householders swept the street in front of their dwellings every day and took care of their doors. And if early modern English householders did not always succeed, "it was because of inadequate technology for water supply and waste disposal, not because of indifference."[92] In any case, the cleanliness of English doorways was remarkable enough to deserve the praise of visitors from the Continent who noted that "even the large hammers and locks on the door are rubbed and shine brightly."[93] It also suggests that when English travelers to the Netherlands praised the cleanliness of Dutch doors, they were not writing out of a sense of inferiority, but because they shared the same attitude.

Similarly, in many other parts of Europe, it had been customary since the Middle Ages for city dwellers to be meticulous about the entrance area, particularly the door.[94] Some early modern householders even invoked magic to preserve the cleanliness of their front doors. Along these lines, the respected Flemish naturalist Johan Baptista van Helmont (1580–1644), a follower of Paracelsus, advised householders whose doorways were soiled in particularly unpleasant ways to resort to magical methods:

> Hath any one with his excrements defiled the threshold of thy door, and thou intendest to prohibit that nastiness for the future, do but lay a red-hot iron upon the excrement, and the immodest sloven shall, in a very short space, grow scabby on his buttocks; the fire torrifying the excrement, and by dorsal Magnetism driving the acrimony of the burning, into his impudent anus.[95]

By contrast, when residents did not keep their doorways clean or remove the refuse near their homes, the city authorities often stepped in and imposed punishments.[96] This does not mean that people cleaned their doorways only because of pressure from the authorities. Indeed, there is evidence from as early as the Middle Ages that cleaning the door was understood to contribute to the moral purity of the house as a social space. For instance, the popular thirteenth-century devotional text *De doctrina cordis*—also known in English as *The Doctrine of the Hert*—compared the cleansing of the heart and soul through confession with "puttyng out filthes of the hous," and in this context the door was seen as the mouth and the broom as the tongue.[97] The story of a pious Jew from late-fourteenth-century Neustadt (in Austria) who was known "to display particular devoutness within his house" is another example: Jewish sources report that every time a non-Jewish man left his house, he would instruct his wife to clean the door-ring with water.[98] Of course, this was motivated by moral rather than sanitary concerns; in other words, the Christian visitor had "contaminated" the entire house by touching the door.

During times of crisis, the concern for the cleanliness of door and threshold, and the fear of their manipulation, took on an added dimension.[99] This partly had to do with the central role of doors in the sanitary regime imposed at such times, particularly during the recurring episodes of the bubonic plague. Contemporary medicine generally explained the spread of epidemics through the so-called miasma theory: as nothing was yet known of bacteria or how to fight them, it was assumed that the plague was spread through miasma, or evil smells and sewage. Although this miasma theory rested upon false assumptions according to modern scientific standards, some of the conclusions and policies derived from it were not unreasonable. These included special regulations for urban sanitation and quarantine, and the marking and sealing of houses stricken with disease. Doors took on a particularly important sanitary and symbolic role in such situations. In many parts of Europe, all entrances to plague-stricken houses were supposed to have white or red crosses painted on them. "Oh sight fearfully significant!" lamented one seventeenth-century Englishman at the sight of such a cross.[100] In other places, a bundle of straw attached to the door served the same purpose.[101] Here again, the door was a boundary between the dead and the living. Notaries called to record the testament of a diseased, dying resident often stood outside the house while the patient, sitting in a chair placed in the doorway, dictated his or her last will.[102] Physicians and caretakers, too, were urged to avoid coming too close to the doors of infected houses, though that was not always possible.[103] After the residents died or evacuated, the authorities would have the house fumigated—with its doors shut—and then washed and swept clean.[104]

Healthy individuals, by contrast, were encouraged to write the Greek letter *tau* on their front doors or to hang a broadsheet with a *tau* and various prayers on it, because this letter resembled the shape of a cross, and was also—according to the Bible—a protection against the wrath of God.[105] In general, the authorities instructed the public to keep doors and windows tightly closed during times of plague. For healthy people, this was meant to prevent the infectious miasma from seeping into the house via any of its openings. Those infected, on the other hand, were ordered not to leave their houses and to stay away from any openings, as it was feared that their presence at windows and doors would increase the circulation of miasma in the public space. Samuel Pepys, observing the rampant plague in London in 1666, wrote with great concern in his diary about the rumor that "ill people would breathe in the faces (out of their windows) of well people going by."[106]

Fittingly, contemporary paintings of plague-ridden cities depict almost all buildings with the doors and windows shut.[107] In some cities, authorities even decreed that affected houses be locked from the outside. In Bremen, if warning signs such as the painted cross had been removed from the front door of an infected house, the authorities nailed the door shut.[108] Similar measures were taken in Bordeaux, where a specially appointed *Capitaine de la contagion* and his team sealed the doors of all plague-stricken houses with special padlocks and chains.[109] Food and other necessities were supplied via baskets lifted through windows, which were opened only for this purpose.[110] Sometimes the mere suspicion of an outbreak of disease was enough to justify these measures.[111]

In times of crisis, of course, these procedures were not always fully carried out—and it is noteworthy that people saw this disregard as a harbinger of the collapse of public and social order. Boccaccio expresses this in his account of the plague in fourteenth-century Florence—probably the most famous of all literary descriptions of the epidemic. As he tells it in the *Decameron*, the logistical impossibility of transporting the steadily rising number of corpses to the designated gravesites led Florentines to dump them in front of their doors. Boccaccio was not the only person at the time to see this as a particularly gruesome symptom of a world out of joint.[112] People were also disturbed to see doors left wide open. During the plague in Bordeaux in 1631, health officials and gravediggers left the doors of dead citizens' houses open, and instead of attending to patients or removing corpses, some of them took advantage of the situation to loot the houses. As a result, the city councilmen were left with no choice but to confiscate the keys to all plague-stricken houses and to tighten control over the entrances.[113]

Similar incidents occurred elsewhere in Europe as well, and in some places simmering anxieties escalated into mass hysteria. One widely publicized case came from the Silesian town of Frankenstein, where the spread of the plague in

1606 was directly blamed on the gravediggers and their alleged manipulation of house doors.[114] We should recall that
gravediggers at the time were also responsible for removing
the bodies, which meant that they could carry out their duties
only if they had access to the citizens' houses. As the case of
Bordeaux shows, raging epidemics could easily lead to a situation where one or more gravediggers worked in houses where
all the residents had died, or where only diseased individuals remained. This, in turn, led to continuous distrust of, and
harsh accusations against, gravediggers. In Frankenstein, the
public accused the gravediggers of eyeing houses that had not
yet been struck by disease. It was claimed that in order to burgle these houses, the gravediggers brought about the residents'
deaths by smearing a certain plague-bearing poison on stairways, door handles, and thresholds. Discovered only by chance,
this scheme was said to have led to the deaths of more than two
thousand people.

Retribution unfolded in a gruesome way. Nineteen people in all—not only the gravediggers, but also their wives
and children—were tortured with red-hot pincers and then
burned alive. While the events in Frankenstein caused a stir
throughout German lands, it was not a unique case: in Central
Europe alone, more than a dozen trials against gravediggers
took place during the sixteenth and seventeenth centuries.
The dynamic of the accusations was often very similar: plague
workers were scapegoated by a deeply unsettled community,
in which they had long been considered suspect because their
work revolved around, and in fact depended on, death. Addi-

tionally, many citizens who were embarrassed at not having personally buried their relatives projected their guilty consciences onto the gravediggers. These factors fueled the belief that gravediggers had access to special knowledge that enabled them to survive the plague despite close contact with the dead, and that they used this knowledge to bring about profitable mass deaths. While gravediggers were particularly vulnerable to unfair accusations during crises, they were not the only ones: in Silesia, for example, there were also cases of beggars being accused of smearing doors and door latches with infected matter; here, too, greed and envy were the alleged motivation. People similarly accused women and Jews of witchcraft during times of plague.[115]

In some places these beliefs united to create a phantom: the figure of the "greaser."[116] From the late Middle Ages onward, mysterious greasers were often accused of smearing doors, doorposts, and door latches with infected grease in order to spread the plague, by order of evil forces or the devil himself. Who exactly the greasers were, and where they came from, was the source of much speculation and disagreement among the population. Women and men alike, members of the upper and the lower classes—anyone could be accused of being a greaser. And despite the mystery of these greasers, several European languages had their own words for them: they were called *untori* in Italian (from Latin *unctores*) and *engraisseurs* in French. A seventeenth-century Italian chronicler described the traces of their sinister deeds as follows: "the spots were strewn about, still moist to varying degrees, as if someone had

sprayed and greased the walls with a pus-soaked sponge; everywhere one looked, one could see doors and house entrances
similarly besmeared."[117] Fear of the greasers ran high, especially in Italy, and led to the deaths of many innocent suspects.
Alessandro Manzoni later gave a vivid depiction of this hysteria in the plague chapters of his famous novel *The Betrothed* (*I
promessi sposi*, 1827).[118]

This fear of greasers was by no means limited to the poorer
strata of society. Throughout Europe, scholars, doctors, and
authorities took up the theory, lending it even greater cred-
ibility. The influential French barber-surgeon and anatomist
Ambroise Paré (1510–1590) urged city magistrates to keep
"their eies and mindes attentive upon a murderous and impi-
ous kinde of bearers and nurse-keepers, which allured with
a desire of gain (which whilest the plague reignes, they get
abundantly) anoint the walls, doors, thresholds, knockers of
gates and lockes with the filth and ointments taken from such
as have the plague."[119]

Of course, the grease was not always imagined: there is
evidence that in certain cities doors, door handles, and locks
were actually smeared.[120] Recent historical studies have tried
to explain this by pointing out that "destitute and desperate
people in horrific and desensitising circumstances are capable
of extremely bizarre and even evil behaviour." It has also been
argued that "some individuals, under the leadership of a few
medical practitioners, actually thought they could manipulate
a plague outbreak to their benefit."[121] I will not add to the
speculation about who stood to benefit from spreading grease
in this manner. Suffice it to note that a common feature of al-

most all these accusations is that the grease was said to appear not on the windows or walls of houses, but on the doors.

This brings us back to our observation that the door was a site onto which premodern Europeans projected two constant and collective fears: on one hand, the dreaded scenario of disease and death invading the house; on the other, the fear of losing control over one's house, with all of one's material possessions and honor along with it. In times of crisis, the significance of doors came fully to the fore, as did their weakness: the door was, and remains, a technology intended to impart a sense of security, but it was also particularly vulnerable to manipulation and contamination. In one of the few historical studies dealing with liminal spaces in early modern Europe, the historian Robert Scribner notes that "a very considerable part of the beliefs, practices and many minor rituals that filled up the daily life of our period were concerned with symbolic action to strengthen such ontological boundaries." Fittingly, Scribner compares these boundaries to "a bulkhead to hold back the swirling seas of the supernatural and its forces."[122] As the examples in this chapter show, of all liminal spaces in the house, the door required particular attention and safeguards. In fact, no other part of the house has embodied fears of intrusion, attack, and death more than the door.

This observation also leads to one of the many paradoxes that characterize the history of the door. In its Western design, it is clearly intended to minimize physical contact with the outside world: when closed, it stops people staring in and—unlike the sliding screens of traditional Japanese houses—

also serves as an auditory barrier to prevent our words from being heard outside.[123] Yet despite its function as a barrier to sound and sight, the door also demanded *heightened* sensory perception: one had to listen carefully to sounds at the door— such as knocking—and interpret them properly; a certain touch might be part of a religious or apotropaic ritual (as with the mezuzah); eyes and nose helped detect both visible and invisible forms of door contamination and manipulation. And as we will see in the next chapter, in addition to requiring acute sensory perception, doors literally had to be *read*.

CHAPTER FOUR

Reading Doors

P
OSSIBLY THE MOST FAMOUS DOOR in European
history is the main door of the Castle Church of
Wittenberg. Martin Luther is said to have posted
his Ninety-Five Theses here on 31 October 1517,
as a trenchant critique of the Catholic Church and in particular its practice of selling and granting indulgences as penance
for sins. Historians all agree that the dissemination of Luther's
theses, which were soon received far beyond Wittenberg, set
the Reformation in motion. Luther's act of nailing the theses
to the church door, with hammer in hand, remains the most
iconic episode in this context. It has received countless mentions in historical studies and textbooks, and many works of
visual art have depicted this scene, including, since the twentieth century, a number of films (Figure 25).[1] The historical
site has long been a popular tourist attraction, and visitors can
read the full text of the theses engraved on an imposing bronze
door donated by the Prussian king in the nineteenth century
(Figure 26).

But one problem remains: to this day it is not entirely clear whether the posting of the theses actually happened. For the past fifty years, historians have fiercely contested the historicity of the event. According to recent estimates, around three hundred publications have addressed this controversy.[2] However, the debate has not always focused on the question of "how things actually were" (to use Leopold von Ranke's famous words). Instead, it has often been waged along confessional frontlines: some of the harshest critics of the event's historicity have come from the ranks of Catholic theologians, while,

Figure 25. Martin Luther posting his Ninety-Five Theses at the door of the Castle Church in Wittenberg. Historicist wall painting by Ferdinand Pauwels, 1872. Wartburg-Stiftung Eisenach.

Figure 26. The "Theses Door" of the Castle
Church in Wittenberg in its present state.

unsurprisingly, many vocal defenders have been Protestants.[3]
One of the reasons why the controversy has attracted so much
attention is because it raises the question of how the historical
Luther should be portrayed.

Interesting as this debate may be, the purpose in this
chapter is different. I do not intend to determine whether the
Reformer literally took hammer in hand in 1517 or to assess

how this famous image has informed our understanding of Luther himself, but rather to explore what it can tell us about the actual object involved: the door. Starting with Luther, this chapter thus broadens out to investigate the significance of doors, both as places of publicity and the circulation of knowledge and as sites of controversy and conflict in early modern Europe. Although the chapter offers no answer as to whether Luther actually nailed the theses to the door, I draw on cultural history, legal history, and theology to gain a sharper view of the historical context in which the event should be situated and why such an event would have seemed quite natural to early modern people. These considerations lend further support to the observation that the door in premodern times was not simply a functional object separating inside from outside; in fact, it was also a hub of information and a particular form of material text. In other words, the door functioned as a medium on which both political events and everyday matters could literally be read. From this perspective, Luther's supposed act opens a new door on the history of publicity, the circulation of information, and the material culture of news in early modern urban spaces.

First, let us review the most important evidence surrounding Luther's posting of the theses and the different interpretations of the event. For our purposes, it will suffice to sketch the two diametrically opposed positions that have dominated the long-standing debate among scholars.

Both camps of historians accept that Luther himself never spoke of posting the theses. Those who argue that the posting occurred rely primarily on an account from Luther's fellow Reformer Philipp Melanchthon, as well as on a note written by Luther's secretary, Georg Rörer, that was "rediscovered" in 2006 and received considerable media attention. Both documents speak explicitly of the theses being posted.[4] Historians who view these sources as proof of the historicity of the event argue that the two documents report the incident with different nuances and therefore were written independently of one another. The opposing camp, by contrast, points out that although both accounts come from Luther's companions, neither account constitutes an eyewitness report. Furthermore, they argue that both were recorded many years after the event: Melanchthon's account dates from 1546, nearly thirty years later, and Rörer's note—though dating from Luther's lifetime—was written only in the early 1540s. From the skeptics' perspective, these testimonies thus represent deliberate attempts to mythologize Luther. Skeptics also argue that the reports contradict the chronology of other events in the fall of 1517 as reconstructed from Luther's own letters.[5]

A further bone of contention is whether Luther's theses were originally circulated in handwritten form or were printed from the outset. This much is certain: On the day in question, 31 October, Luther sent his theses to two bishops. He then sent the theses to other dignitaries and theologians during the course of that fall. From this, the skeptics conclude that the theses originally existed only in handwritten form and that Luther intended to circulate them only among a small group of people in order to solicit their responses.[6] They therefore consider it unlikely that Luther nailed the theses to the door in this form; rather, it was the controversy stirred up by the initial circulation that motivated Luther to publish his theses. Those who argue for the historicity of the event, however, follow a very different line of reasoning. Since the theses were long and complicated, they argue, it would have been laborious to produce multiple copies by hand. Therefore, the document must have been printed from the outset.[7] While an original print matching this description has not been found to date, these historians consider it plausible because they see the theses as a formal call for an academic disputation. Indeed, in the university city of Wittenberg at the time, such calls were commonly printed as broadsheets, which were then posted on the doors of various churches in the city (*in valvis ecclesiarum*), in accordance with the statutes of the Faculty of Theology. However, these broadsheets were usually posted by the university beadle rather than by the author.[8]

Against this backdrop, researchers have argued about whether Luther actually intended to follow the rules of academic disputation when he made the Ninety-Five Theses public. If he did, then his intention—according to the understanding of the time—was to call for a disputation *extra ordinem*, that is, without specific academic occasion. In this case, the posting would still have been a "normal internal academic procedure" according to University of Wittenberg custom, and if the account of Luther's secretary, Rörer, is credible, Luther followed the academic rules by posting his theses on the doors of several Wittenberg churches.[9] Other European universities adopted a similar procedure for the announcement of disputations, as well as for other academic news: if a student had done something to warrant expulsion from a university, the citation to appear before the rector would also be posted on the door of the (university) church.[10]

This brings us to a point not sufficiently considered in the debate so far: it was perfectly possible at the time to post an announcement or critical broadsheet on a church door—or indeed on several church doors—without calling for an academic disputation. We know that Luther's sympathizers started to post prints of his theses in various public places near Wittenberg a few weeks after he wrote and first circulated them. Whether his followers posted these prints specifically on doors remains unclear, but it is entirely plausible. Bishop Adolf von Merseburg, a critic of the sale of indulgences, noted in November 1517 "that the poor people who gathered together and sought mercy have been warned of the deception carried out by Tetzel [the notorious seller of indulgences], and the *conclusiones* composed by the Augustinian monk from Wittenberg have been posted in many places [*an vilen ortern angeslagen*]."[11] Four years later (1521), the following decree appeared in Antwerp:

> On pain of confiscation, forfeiture of goods, and personal punishment it is prohibited to read, sell, or carry around in public books by a certain friar by the name of Lutherus, for they smack of heresy. Slanderous libel, rondels, or ballads directed against those who are not followers of Luther shall not be written, distributed, or pinned and pasted to church doors or any archways.[12]

From the 1530s on, a string of reports, primarily from central Germany, mention Luther's followers posting various theses on church doors. For instance, in March 1530 in the Westphalian city of Minden, the impetuous preacher Nikolaus

Krage both wrote the new Church Order and actually posted nineteen theses on every church door in the city. With these theses, written in German, he challenged all "Papists" in the city to a "public disputation" (*apentliken disputation*)—not an academic one—within the next four weeks. That same year, his theses were also published as an appendix to the printed version of the Church Order.[13] A few months later, the Protestant preacher Gerdt Oemeken posted his own theses on the door of St. Mary's Church in Lippstadt; and in Soest, the Dominican monk Thomas Borchwede wrote twenty-two theses and posted them on the door of his church as well as on others in the city, declaring his opposition to the Dominican order and, more generally, to the doctrines of the Catholic Church. The following year (1532), in Osnabrück, the evangelical preacher Dietrich Buthmann posted forty-four theses on the door of St. Mary's Church, intending to defend them at a disputation in the city hall.[14]

All these examples demonstrate how widespread it was in the sixteenth century for German Protestants to post theses and broadsheets on church doors. This ties in with Irene Dingel's observation that, as part of the Reformation, the genre of disputation increasingly "made its impact in the non-academic, public sphere and began to make use of the vernacular along with the Latin."[15] It is possible that these Protestants were following Luther's example, but this is not an inevitable conclusion, for Luther was neither a founder nor a pioneer of this practice. In fact, posting writings on church doors had been part of everyday culture for centuries, and even in academic circles it was not limited to the announcement of disputations.

In certain cases, church authorities not only tolerated postings on their doors, but actually required them. As early as the High Middle Ages, there is evidence that summonses to appear before the Holy See were considered effective only when they had been posted on church doors of the Roman Curia.[16] Pope Boniface VIII (r. 1294–1303), one of the fiercest advocates of the church's temporal power and of papal supremacy, went so far as to claim that a summons should be considered effective as soon as it was posted on the door of the main church in whichever city was currently hosting the pope.[17] In the case of a summons to appear before a church court, prevailing opinion dictated that the writ of summons be delivered to the defendant in person. If the defendant refused it, ignored it, or simply hid, the next legitimate step was to post the summons on the church doors. The court clerk charged with this task had to record the exact time of the posting and how long he let it hang there.[18]

The secular authorities followed similar rules, although a summons from them could also be posted on the doors of city halls, city gates, or the defendant's home.[19] Admittedly, powerful defendants did not always obey. In the 1420s, the nobleman Konrad von Weinsberg realized this when King Sigismund assigned him to bring violators of the imperial feudal law before the court. As instructed, Weinsberg posted citations on the church doors of various cities but achieved nothing with the emperor's more formidable opponents; equally frustrating was the fact that he had to copy out these futile summonses by hand, or else have them produced at his own expense.[20]

The effectiveness of church-door postings of this sort thus depended on the circumstances and sometimes had its limits.

Clearly, in some situations, letters or oral communication would have been more practical. Nevertheless, the posting of legal announcements on doors, and particularly church doors, remained standard practice throughout the premodern period. It was considered a necessary procedural step and a long-standing tradition.[21] Even if the addressee was unlikely to read the posting in situ, its display on a church door documented the fact that formal action had been taken, ensuring the highest degree of public attention. In 1466, when the mayor and councilmen of Basel protested the Count of Thierstein's attempt to levy new customs duties, this was precisely their course of action. The municipal leaders stated their grievance in a lengthy *appellatio,* and while copies were sent to the emperor and the Count of Thierstein, the original version was posted on the door of Basel Minster. The notary Johann Salzmann, who was in charge of this procedure, reported:

> Between six and seven o'clock in the morning, while the mass in honor of Our Lady was being celebrated, I the undersigned notary publicly affixed the following appeal to the door of the minster. I left it hanging there for a while, so that each and every person who entered or left the minster would see and read this appeal. I then removed it and in its stead I posted a faithful copy which I left there.[22]

Church doors thus were and remained a standard location for announcing and documenting various events and decisions. We know, for instance, that announcements of excommunication were frequently publicized through a post on the church doors of the relevant parish as well as of neighboring parishes and dioceses. The earliest extant evidence we have of this is from Italy in the mid-ninth century.[23] During the Middle Ages and early modern period, we also find the posting of writs of outlawry, issued by secular authorities, on church doors.[24] These writs were called *Achtbriefe* in the Holy Roman Empire. Similarly, newly ordained Catholic priests would announce the celebration of their first mass by posting a placard on the church door, hoping to receive money offerings to mark the festive occasion. Some priests even made a habit of "earning" gifts by posting an announcement every time they visited a new city.[25] On the other hand, it was perfectly legal, albeit morally dubious, for a pope to extort money from his subjects by posting additional tax regulations on church doors (*in ostio ecclesiae*) in the Papal States.[26]

Crucially, church doors were also sites where the church could display its claim to power and autonomy, both over its flock and in relation to secular authorities. This was what the Bishop of Constance had in mind when, in 1491, he and members of his cathedral chapter posted a list of the privileges granted to them in the past by pope and emperor on the doors of various city churches (*offentlich an die kirchen türen angeschlagen*).[27] This led to great indignation among the city authorities, since the bishop was simultaneously denying the city *its* privileges. The city magistrate twice sent a delegation to the cathedral chapter to declare that the city of Constance and the rest of the diocese would no longer tolerate the ostentatious posting of clergy privileges on church doors.[28] But a representative of the cathedral chapter rejected this complaint and justified his position by pointing precisely to the privileges that had been posted on the doors.

At other times, internal conflicts in the church led to provocative postings. During the Franciscans' bitter struggle with
the pope in the 1320s, the leaders of the order held a ceremonial reading and posting of a lengthy declaration at the door of
Pisa Cathedral. Shortly thereafter, an imperial announcement
was affixed to the same door, declaring the pope deposed.[29]
Postings were also at the center of a controversy in Basel in
1482, when the city leaders rejected Rome's call to extradite
the archbishop Andrea of Crain, who was reputed to be one of
the fiercest critics of Pope Sixtus IV. Andrea had dared to post
placards throughout the streets of Basel, in which he called
the pope "a son of the devil" and accused him—with a telling metaphor—of having reached the papacy "not through
the door but through the window of simony." A high-ranking
papal loyalist countered by posting a placard on the minster
door, in which he made a scathing attack on the city authorities for tolerating the bishop's activities. This placard, in turn,
led the city leaders to issue a note of protest to the pope.[30]

While not exhaustive, this overview makes it clear that
premodern church doors saw far more activity than any
church doors do today; they were, in effect, bulletin boards
with a privileged and central role in the public sphere.[31] The
same phenomenon can be seen in Jewish communities, which
kept their distance from churches. Indeed, postings on synagogue doors held a similar significance. When Jewish individuals were banished from their communities, or when other
declarations of general interest were made, an announcement
would often be posted on the doors or gates of the local synagogue.[32] Important rabbinical decisions and even reports of

criminal activities, such as thefts, were likewise publicized on these doors.[33] As late as the eighteenth and nineteenth centuries, synagogue doors were used for publicity, especially in the widespread conflict between conservative forces and the supporters of Reform Judaism. In the 1840s, for instance, the orthodox rabbi of Hamburg posted on his synagogue door a fierce warning against any "deliberately frivolous treatment of sacred matters."[34]

Today, Jews and Christians alike tend to take offense when posters or other writings clutter the doors of their houses of worship. In fact, in our secular society, people often seek out holy spaces precisely because they do *not* want to be confronted with or distracted by worldly thoughts and mundane matters. During the premodern period, however, the religious and everyday spheres were much more closely bound together: the "house of God"—in the sanctuary proper as well as at the door—was a place not only for devotion and reverence, but also for socializing, exchanging news, and sharing conversations (which were not restricted to spiritual topics).[35] For some people, as we know from contemporary diaries and chronicles, the spacious interiors of churches were simply good places to go for a stroll (*spaciren*, as the sixteenth-century diarist Hermann Weinsberg called it).[36] For many others, especially during the Middle Ages, the entrances and narthices of churches served as forums for legal and commercial transactions. In Mainz Cathedral, the so-called Willigis Portal facing the market still features a set of imposing bronze doors, built circa 1000 CE and engraved—during the first half of the twelfth century— with the legal rights and tax privileges of the city. By the same token, a city's official units of measurement were often displayed in the portal area of its largest church. To this day, near the entrance of the cathedral of Freiburg im Breisgau, one can still see the medieval signs indicating the standard size of loaves of bread and rolls as prescribed by the city government.[37] In the 1490s, the magistrate of Frankfurt am Main even ordered that a decree be posted on church doors detailing the measures necessary for ending the city's rat infestation. In this decree, citizens were instructed to make all possible efforts to kill rats and to deliver dead ones to a specially appointed city official who would pay one *Heller* per rat.[38]

The common use of church doors for worldly announcements and displays is a reminder that premodern people passed through these doors a great deal more often than most people do today. The interiors of premodern churches were also far less ascetic than those we find in most modern churches. True, during the Reformation, radical Protestants often stripped Catholic churches of their rich artistic decorations. Yet even the walls of Protestant churches were covered with messages, drawings, inscriptions, signs, and other symbols that would seem out of place to the modern eye. These began to disappear only during the waves of purification that swept through church interiors during the nineteenth and twentieth centuries. Early modern Catholics and Protestants alike had relatively few scruples (and were rarely discouraged by the authorities) when it came to writing or carving personal prayers, thoughts, mottoes, or simply their signatures onto the walls of churches.[39]

The practice of posting announcements, broadsheets and other writings on church doors also needs to be seen in the context of the sheer quantity of objects on display inside churches of that time. Indeed, worship spaces were so crammed full with objects that premodern churches could fairly be described as "museums of premodernity."[40] Catholics encountered many relics and works of art in their churches, but also exotic objects and curiosities that were intended to fill them with reverence for the sublimity of God's creation. And since these objects were not used for worship, even zealous proponents of the Reformation by and large let them be. Stuffed exotic animals or their skeletons, strange rock formations, and specimens of bizarrely developed plants are only some of the marvels that embellished the inner and outer walls of churches. And the preferred locations for these displays were embrasures as well as the areas above church portals, for here, at the entrance to the house of God, they would be assured lasting visibility without interfering with the spatial requirements of liturgy and prayer.[41]

Sometimes, these objects even lent their names to the church portals where they were on display. In Vienna, for example, the name *Riesentor* (Giant's Gate), which to this day refers to the main entrance to St. Stephen's Cathedral, comes from an impressive mammoth bone that was unearthed during construction work in the fifteenth century and hung in a prominent place inside the portal. It remained there until the eighteenth century, when it was transferred to the natural history collection of the university.[42]

The Castle Church of Wittenberg was similar in this respect, and historians interested in Luther's posting of the theses will find it instructive to look not only at the door itself, but also *behind* it. For this church door looked very different on the inside than it does today.[43] In fact, its appearance in Luther's day would seem bizarre, if not irreverent, to modern eyes (Figure 27): two whale rib bones were chained to a pillar directly to the left of the door, and above them hung an elephant's tusk and another large rib bone, which was believed to be from a colossus or one of the sons of the biblical giant Anak. To the right of the door, by contrast, was a canvas depicting the length of Christ, as personally measured by the

Figure 27. The "Theses Door" as it appeared from inside the church in the eighteenth century. Engraving from Christian Siegismund Georgi, *Wittenbergische Klage-Geschichte* (Wittenberg, 1761).

Elector of Saxony, Frederick the Wise, at Jesus's grave in Jerusalem during a pilgrimage to the Holy Land. These objects
remained in place long after the Reformation; in fact, over the
decades, the space became even more crowded, with the addition (to the right of the door) of a portrait of Melanchthon and
an iron tablet with Latin verses in his honor. What is more, the
objects were never removed by choice; rather, everything was
destroyed by a disastrous fire in 1760, when the city was under
siege during the Seven Years' War. But for the fire, they might
have remained on display far longer.

Church doors and the portals surrounding them were
thus *showplaces* in the literal sense—places to see and marvel
at—as well as sites for communication. This was consistent
with their symbolic meaning in Christian sacred architecture
and also with their practical significance as religious "sites of
passage." But the importance of the church door for communication also reflected its particular visibility in the everyday
life of a city—a visibility that the Reformers neither questioned nor minimized. Indeed, Protestant churches continued
the same tradition in this respect: their doors, too, served as
noticeboards for clerical or government announcements, advertisements for various professional services, and *faits divers*
of everyday life, including notices for lost and found items,
which people were explicitly encouraged to post as late as the
eighteenth century.[44] In the Catholic Church, it was still permissible as late as the 1910s to call on a disobedient defendant to appear before an ecclesiastical court by posting a summons on a church door; yet by then, publishing the citation
in a newspaper had been established as a formally acceptable

and increasingly common alternative.[45] Today, the church has abandoned both of these practices. Current canon law puts much greater emphasis on the defendant's privacy than in the past and thus mandates mail delivery: "The notification of citations, decrees, sentences, and other judicial acts must be made through the public postal services or by some other very secure method according to the norms established in particular law."[46]

One might wonder whether all the posting activity of the past damaged the surfaces of doors, especially considering the iconic image of Luther using a hammer to nail the theses to the door of the Castle Church of Wittenberg. But contrary to what that image may suggest, nailing was by no means the preferred method; in fact, early modern people—and perhaps even Luther himself—also used common adhesives such as wax and glue to paste notices and posters.[47] Tellingly, the statutes of Wittenberg University make no mention of the use of hammer and nails, and those tools are also absent from the earliest visual depictions of Luther's posting—an episode that, by the way, came to be depicted only from the seventeenth century onward (perhaps precisely because the act of posting was too common a phenomenon to be considered a heroic or revolutionary event). Instead, in the earliest extant images of Luther's posting, the theses are shown hanging on the door without any nail or other fixation device visible, which suggests the use of glue or wax. Only in the nineteenth century did hammer and nail become an indispensable part of the iconography of Luther's posting (certainly in German lands), and this new motif of Luther holding the hammer was linked inextricably to the increasingly nationalistic extolment of the Reformer.[48]

Church doors, however, were not the only bulletin boards in the early modern city, although they were certainly the most important. City gates and the doors of city halls served that purpose as well, and they were used primarily for postings by secular authorities. Accordingly, warnings against violence and criminality could regularly be seen there, as well as announcements concerning important political decisions.[49] Thus the Edict of Worms of 1521, which placed Luther under imperial ban and outlawed all his writings, was posted on the door of Augsburg city hall after being read aloud in public.[50] On the doors of princely residences, by contrast, it was customary to affix a tablet reminding entrants to keep the "castle peace" (*Burgfrieden*).[51]

Throughout Europe doorways were densely filled with postings, but a particularly vivid example can be found in early modern London, where the now forgotten genre of "siquis" flourished.[52] The term derives from the Latin *si quis* ("if anyone"), the phrase with which many of these postings began. They offered and solicited a wide range of goods and services: everything from legal counsel to medical services to instruction in skills like arithmetic and shorthand. Siquises were particularly numerous on one door of St. Paul's Cathedral, the so-called siquis door. Such was the wealth of advertisements and broadsheets there that, in 1609, the English playwright and pamphletist Thomas Dekker advised one country gentleman planning to visit the cathedral that he should take care not to "cast an eye to Si-quis doore (pasted and plaistered up with serving-mens supplications)."[53] Dekker was particularly concerned that the visitor would find offensive content there. In Ben Jonson's comedy *Every Man out of His Humour* (first performed in 1599), one protagonist tacks—precisely to this door—obscene bills "wherein he has so varied himself that, if any one of 'em take, he may hull up and down i' the humorous world a little longer."[54]

The siquis door came to play a unique role in the cathedral's appearance. But although it was possibly the city's most popular location for posting announcements and miscellany, it was certainly not the only one: people frequently affixed such notices on the doors and walls of public buildings and private houses throughout the city. Indeed, doors also offered the advantage of protecting the postings, at least partially, from the weather. As Tiffany Stern has demonstrated, the English capital's "streets were inscribed with a huge variety of texts," including "playbills, title-pages of books, advertisements, plague bills and proclamations."[55] In 1581, the Lord Mayor forbade the posting of "anye papers or breifes upon anye postes, houses, or other places," but still the phenomenon persisted.[56]

In eighteenth-century Vienna, the number of postings on private doors was especially high, partly because Vienna, unlike other major European cities, did not have official information bureaus to help travelers find accommodations. As a Hessian visitor to Vienna reported in the 1780s,

> every home-owner here posts a note to his house-door, indicating in great detail which rooms are vacant. In many houses each of the five or six floors has its own proprietor, or the tenant has rented the entire apartment but can do without one

of the rooms. As a result, all of these people post their own
advertisements, especially to the house-door, which is often
half covered with such notices. One has no choice but to read
for half an hour before one is all set.[57]

Still today, we sometimes find fliers and posters on doorways
in public places, but this is very different from the early modern phenomenon. For one thing, such posters are not nearly as
common as they were then. For another, church doors are no
longer used as bulletin boards, and certainly not for the display
of political statements or commercial notices. It is quite unusual nowadays to find posters on the doors of private houses,
and door postings are usually limited to public buildings, university campuses, and shops. And here we find another difference from the early modern period. Today, door postings—
and the remnants of paper and adhesive that they tend to leave
behind—may seem unsightly, or in some cases even offend
us as defacement of public property, but they rarely have the
power to provoke targeted and specific social conflicts. In the
early modern period, by contrast, doors frequently became
sites of malicious or provocative insults, and a large number of
conflicts ensued, some of them violent.

As we have seen, the premodern concept of a building's
"honor" focused in large part on the door. As a result, doors
were often decorated with great care and functioned as highly
visible indicators of the wealth and prestige of the residents.[58]
However, in order to interpret such embellishments, one
needed to know how to "read" doors properly. That is to say,
one had to read not only the written texts that often appeared
on them, but also their nontextual signs and symbols. In

German lands, it was customary to announce important family events by displaying specific objects on the door: in some places, it was common practice after a birth to hang colored ribbons on the door to indicate the number of children and their sexes. The death of a respected male family member, by contrast, would be commemorated by displaying his coat of arms on the door for a year, or—if it was already there—by adding a marker with his date of death.[59]

Given the significance of the door for the honor of the house and the reputation of the family—the terms "family" and "House" often being interchangeable—it was only natural that a malicious act against a door constituted a serious affront. Today, we would probably dismiss an insulting door posting as a minor offense, but to early modern sensibilities it was felt to be, quite literally, a slap in the face: architectural theory of the time compared the door in the façade to the mouth on a person's face, and the very word "façade," which gained currency in the major European languages during the early modern period, derives from the Italian *faccia*, meaning face.

If we want to understand why so much conflict took place at the door in the early modern period, we must keep in mind the entwined ideas of "honor" and "house." The Dutch advocate Joos de Damhouder (1507–1581), like most jurists of his time, was all too familiar with door-related conflicts. In his *Praxis rerum criminalium* (first published 1554), an influential and widely printed handbook of criminal law, he devoted an entire chapter to what he called *iniuriae per scripta*, or the various ways of damaging a person's honor in writing.[60] Damhouder's

Figure 28. *De iniuriis per scripta* (On wrongs committed
with writing). Woodcut from Joos de Damhouder,
Praxis rerum criminalium (Antwerp, 1601).

discussion also included a vivid illustration (Figure 28). In the
background one can see a man standing on a stool, handing
out libelous documents to a gathered crowd in a public square.
Closer to the fore is a second man posting a piece of insulting
writing to the wall of a house. And in the foreground proper,
intentionally given the most prominent position, a third of-
fender is posting libel directly on the door of the house.

As Damhouder notes in another section of his book, it was
quite common to defame a people by affixing libel as well as

objects to their doors (*uspiam ad valvas*).[61] From an early modern perspective, it was a particularly grave insult. Many contemporary jurists argued that affixing libel to doors and walls should be considered injurious not only to victims' personal honor, but also to their "domestic peace" (*Hausfrieden*).[62] The specific content of the libel might affect the degree of insult, but it was the *act* of illegally affixing it that constituted the injury to the honor and peace of the house.

The spectrum of insults and accusations contained in such defamatory texts was very broad, as was the range of situations in which verbal injuries came into play.[63] Tellingly, premodernity had its own lexicon—now largely forgotten—for describing this phenomenon, and this is further evidence of the fundamental difference between the uses (and abuses) of door postings in that era and the predominantly commercial placarding that we see in ours.[64] One term that was commonly used for certain types of defamation in the early modern period was the "pasquil." In the English sphere, it dates back to 1533; in Italy, even a few decades earlier.[65] The word refers to a statue in Rome by the name of Pasquino, on which people posted insulting texts. According to popular lore, the statue's name derived from a fifteenth-century Roman known for his sharp-tongued verse. The term "pasquil" spread rapidly across early modern Europe, and, as the practice of the "pasquinade" became more widespread, its preferred showplace moved from statues to doors.[66]

Pasquils were typically motivated by various types of social transgression and deviance, proven or alleged, such as theft, perjury, personal vices (including drunkenness, miserliness, or lying), unchristian behavior, or even physical deformity. Social outsiders were often targeted, and also women. In Rome in 1559, under cover of night, the following pasquil was tacked to the door of a courtesan named Camilla: "Camilla the Sienese the thin / Has a dive for cops, for pubkeepers, / For louts to sleep in."[67] In London in 1613, an anonymous author wrote this message "at large in a peece of paper" and posted it on a woman's door: "Within this doore / Dwelleth a verie notorious whore."[68] Verses like these do not show great poetic talent, but they served their purpose—to attract public attention in the neighborhood, disseminating accusations that in some cases have survived to this day, often without enough evidence for the historian to determine their veracity. It is noteworthy that pasquils were not limited to the lower rungs of society and were especially popular among academics. Complaints about the loose living of students were very common in early modern university cities. In 1555, the administrators of the University of Ingolstadt addressed a widespread problem when they complained that "[m]any of the students show themselves to be neither studious nor decorous, but instead spend more time in taverns than in the university, and more time in the streets than with their books."[69] The degree of alcohol consumption suggested here, as well as the students' high spirits, clearly fueled students' continuous production of pasquils. Professors and government officials were frequent targets of ridicule in pasquil form, as were clerics and soldiers. Even professors occasionally stooped to defamatory writing, and some were dismissed from their universities as a result.[70]

So-called *Scheltbriefe* ("letters of insult"), which became common throughout Central Europe during the late Middle

Ages, were another genre of defamatory writing. They were most common among the upper classes and the nobility and were frequently related to money disputes and difficulty collecting debts.[71] In form and content, these were letters in which the creditor appealed to debtors' and their families' honor but deliberately insulted them at the same time. Significantly, *Scheltbriefe* were not sudden outbursts of rage, but rather a carefully calculated strategy, for if the debtors—especially aristocrats—refused to pay their debts, then an attack on their honor was one of the creditor's last means of pressuring them without going to court. In some cases, the possibility of defamation was even mentioned in the original bond indenture or contract.[72] In letter form, however, the impact of the insult was limited to its recipient; for full effect, the letter had to be made public.[73] Thus *Scheltbriefe* gradually evolved into public postings, often illustrated with offensive pictures. In Bohemia, for example, if the issue had not been resolved after fourteen days, the creditor had a legal right to post the insulting letter in public. And while the authorities in other territories forbade such activity, it nonetheless continued in practice, reaching its peak in the sixteenth century.

What pasquils and *Scheltbriefe* had in common was the intent to defame their targets, though in the case of the pasquil, malicious gossip played a larger role. This might also explain why pasquils were not only posted on houses secretly, but also often written anonymously or under a pseudonym. On the whole, early modern authorities did not object to denunciations per se—at least, as long as the informer turned directly to the authorities. The problem with pasquils was that they threatened the authorities' hard-earned monopoly on law and order—a hold on power that grew gradually starting in the late Middle Ages, especially following the ban on the right to feud and the Perpetual Public Peace decree (the *Ewiger Landfrieden*), which came into force in the Holy Roman Empire in 1495.[74]

Moreover, pasquils often took aim at secular authorities and clerics themselves. In many places, the pasquil reigned throughout the early modern period as the "the most customary form of popular protest."[75] When authorities were targeted, there was concern that the libel might give way to more drastic forms of protest or even to an uprising. In Rome, the birthplace of the pasquil, Pope Alexander VI massively increased his contingent of guards in 1498 after finding threatening verses posted on the door of his library.[76] Similar fears arose in Worms during the Diet of 1521, shortly before the emperor declared his famous imperial ban against Luther.[77] The Reformer's supporters had ventured into the streets during the night to inscribe the doors of numerous houses with the words, "Woe to that country whose king is a child." A placard then appeared on the door of the city hall, claiming that four hundred noblemen were ready to attack the imperial party. Instead of a signature, the word *Buntschuch*—a common byword at the time for an alliance or conspiracy against the authorities—appeared three times on the placard. This caused great alarm in the Catholic party, and similar fears were stoked a few years later in France during the so-called *Affaire des Placards* in 1534, when Protestant sympathizers secretly posted anti-Catholic placards throughout several French cities.

In an especially provocative feat, the Protestants even managed to post a placard on the door to the king's bedchamber in the Château d'Amboise. This affair led the French monarchy to further tighten its grip on the Protestants in the country, and several alleged perpetrators were executed as a result.[78]

Pasquils, even the more harmless ones, were always a thorn in the side of the authorities. Throughout Europe, writing and posting pasquils was illegal, and violators faced serious consequences. It was also quite common to offer a high reward for the arrest of pasquil-makers, especially if they had attacked the honor of a government official, cleric, or other respected individual.[79] Punishments for this crime were sometimes meted out in draconian fashion: under certain circumstances, jurists even considered capital punishment, and not only in political cases like the *Affaire des Placards*.[80] When high justice was not an option, such as in Jewish communities, violators nevertheless paid a heavy price. The discovery in 1640 of "certain pasquilles and libelous pamphlets on the door of the Synagogue" caused the leaders of the Jewish community in Amsterdam to ban "the person or persons who produced and posted such papers, and to consider them cursed by God and separated from the people."[81]

In practice, of course, strict enforcement of these laws was easier said than done. Pasquils could be posted without any difficulty under cover of darkness, and their texts rarely revealed any clues as to authorship. Thus, despite continuous reenactment of the prohibition on pasquils, the problem persisted throughout the early modern period. *Fehdebriefe* ("letters of feud," also called *Absagebriefe*), in which the author explicitly challenged an individual or (more frequently) a group of people to a feud, posed similar problems for the authorities. Since these were often conflicts between groups instead of individuals, posting on the door of a private house was not the preferred means of conveying the *Fehdebrief.* Also, the purpose was to intimidate not only members of the specific group, but also all those around them who might come to their aid, and to threaten them all with violence.[82] The instigators therefore would often post their *Fehdebriefe* on the doors of public buildings, including churches. They would sometimes tack other symbolic objects to the door as well. A bundle of coal, for example, signified an open threat to burn down the opponents' houses—a recognized form of vendetta according to the rules of the traditional right of feud.[83]

The history of libelous writings like pasquils, *Scheltbriefe,* and *Fehdebriefe* offers a wide array of insights into the use and abuse of written communication in premodernity.[84] Thus far, historians have primarily studied this phenomenon by examining the texts themselves; and with this focus on *what* was posted, they have tended to overlook the importance, in all these conflicts, of *where* the text was posted. Yet, as we have seen, the frequent choice of doors for this purpose was neither random nor coincidental, and it is only when we investigate the significance of doors in their everyday as well as symbolic contexts that we can understand all the practices once associated with these sites.

This leads to a basic observation: premodern people routinely "read" the doors that surrounded them—not necessarily in the literal sense, of course, since not everyone at the time was literate—but each of the texts and objects that one might find on a door had a clear meaning. For the purpose of deterrence and in order to proclaim their power, authorities sometimes used doors, especially church doors, to display proof of punishment. The resulting sight was often gruesome, as in the case of fourteenth-century Prato, where one of the cathedral's portals displayed the severed hands of a cleric who had attempted to steal relics. To this day, local lore has it that the bloodstains can be seen on the door.[85] A similar tradition existed in England. Visiting Rochester Cathedral in 1661, Samuel Pepys took considerable interest in "observing the great doors of the church, which they say was covered with the skins of the Danes." While the precise circumstances of the flaying remain unclear, this grisly demonstration of power was apparently not uncommon in medieval England. Indeed, the same was said of Worcester Cathedral and Westminster Abbey, and microscopic examinations undertaken in the nineteenth century confirmed the human origin of the fabric covering the doors.[86]

Among ordinary people, objects or signs on doors often were used to reveal situations in which traditional gender roles had been reversed. If a married man was beaten or insulted by his wife, the neighbors would ridicule him by hanging a mallet on his front door.[87] If there was evidence, or even an allegation, that a wife had cheated on her husband, it was not uncommon for the man to find a phallus or the proverbial horns of the cuckold painted on his door.[88] Prostitutes, in contrast, were accustomed to finding their doors smeared with tar, battered, turned upside down, or even set on fire.[89] Excrement, human or animal, was likewise smeared on house entrances to signify the dwellers' compromised moral integrity.[90] If residents of two different houses were reputed to be engaging in forbidden social or sexual relations, their neighbors might lay a trail of straw or other material from one door to the other.[91] And like pasquils, these "postings" involving nontextual objects could just as easily be directed against the authorities, secular and religious: indeed, in seventeenth-century Strasbourg, the authorities found it necessary to explicitly forbid throwing feces and garbage at the doors of public buildings.[92] In other places, unpopular clerics might discover dead dogs hanging on their doors, while ousted or hated leaders repeatedly found the doors of their residences destroyed or smeared with animal blood.[93] When the deposed revolutionary Robespierre was led to the guillotine through the streets of Paris in 1794, the door of his house was simultaneously smeared with animal blood.[94]

One could claim that this door-related violence, or "doorscorning," was simply vandalism of the sort that we encounter today and that there is nothing special in this particular history.[95] Although random acts of vandalism existed then, too—fueled, as today, by drunkenness or anger—in the cases under discussion more than mere property damage was at stake, especially when the acts took on a ritualized form, demonstrating a particular inner logic and strategy.[96] This is particularly clear in a once common but now largely forgotten German ritual of the early modern period, revolving around the hierarchy of "honorable" (*ehrlich*) and "dishonorable" (*unehrlich*) professions.[97] People whose work involved handling filth or other impure things were considered dishonorable, particularly gravediggers, executioners, and knackers (who earned their money by disposing of animal cadavers). Knackers were socially marginalized, but at least they had a monopoly over their "dishonorable" trade, and any man who disposed of an animal corpse by himself was encroaching on the knackers' territory. When an infringement of this sort came to light, an elaborate and ritualized form of revenge unfolded: the knacker would plunge a knife into a conspicuous place in the offending citizen's doorframe, preferably in the presence of onlookers. Far from being a random gesture of rage, this was meant to suggest the act of piercing the door with a sword, which jurists considered to be an especially harsh blow to a householder's honor.[98] As a result, the "honorable" citizen now found himself in a double bind. If he were to remove the knacker's knife by himself, it would damage his social reputation, since it was improper to accept a challenge from a person of inferior status. But if he were to leave the knife in place, then evidence of his transgression would remain visible to the public, since contemporaries knew how to "read" this sign on the door. There was only one way out of this dilemma: he would have to pay compensation to the knacker, who would then remove the knife himself.

Let us now return to Martin Luther. If he actually posted his theses on the church door in Wittenberg, he presented the church authorities with a similar challenge (even though they could not have foreseen the enormous historical repercussions of this event). No one, to be sure, would have questioned that Luther—as a professor of theology at the university—had a right to post announcements on church doors, but it was also clear that if the theses were left hanging at the door, Luther's critique would enjoy high visibility at the city's most important site for news and information. To remove them would have been to acknowledge that there was validity to the monk's argument, or at least that it had touched a nerve. In other words, the removal of the theses would in itself have sent a message, because so many other items were posted daily on the church doors and were allowed to remain there untouched.

This, of course, is not an answer to whether or not Luther posted his theses on the Wittenberg church door on 31 October 1517. However, the ideas presented in this chapter bring us closer to understanding the phenomenon of posting itself, which historians have largely neglected, in contrast to the hotly debated topic of the historicity of Luther's posting of the theses. Luther's act, whether real or legendary, needs to be seen as part of this long tradition of posting, and within the context of hundreds of such postings on doors. Historians' neglect of these issues may simply stem from how outlandish this phenomenon seems to us today; compared with our relatively pragmatic outlook on doors and doorways, the people of early modern Europe imbued their doors with a far greater variety of meanings and roles in their daily lives. Perhaps most significantly, doors served as hubs for information in early modern Europe. Some of the messages circulating in this hub were in written form, but many others comprised a complex language of images and symbols. Thus, the ability to "read" a door was not necessarily bound to conventional literacy, but rather required the skill of interpreting a variety of specific signs and practices and drawing the right conclusions. Proficiency in this skill not only helped premodern people orient themselves in a densely built-up and even bewildering urban landscape, but also enabled them to assess their social surroundings.

"Reading doors" is certainly not a skill that we cultivate today. But the study of this practice recasts the door as a palimpsest containing a forgotten chapter in the history of culture and the circulation of information in premodern Europe.

CHAPTER FIVE

The "City's Eyes"
Gates and the Urban History of Europe

W E BEGAN BY WALKING THROUGH early modern Florence, noting the considerable attention that contemporaries paid to doors and portals. The premodern city contained many such sites of passage, and city dwellers as well as visitors had to know how to read and navigate them. Of course, there were doors and portals to buildings, and—as we have seen—these entrances were often carefully designed and frequently adorned with inscriptions or symbols. But there were also other sites of passage in the premodern city that required expertise and attention. Indeed, urban space was often subdivided into different quarters using internal gates and walls—for instance, to separate ecclesiastical enclaves (such as monasteries), neighborhoods of religious communities (such as Jewish ghettos), or military installations (such as fortresses) from other parts of the city. Even larger than the entrances to these compounds were the gates of the city itself. They were by far the most striking and important sites of passage in the premodern city, and they form a natural endpoint for this book, not least because, from the premodern perspective, the differences between city gates and house doors were differences of scale, not of substance. It was common to treat the city and the house as analogues, each enclosed by proportionate walls and openings, and some authors explicitly compared the function of city gates and house doors.[1]

City gates and walls have intrigued scholars for years, especially architectural historians.[2] Yet existing studies predominantly focus on their military function, architectural features, and design. In contrast, we know relatively little about the experience of entering a walled city and the various procedures and problems related to passing through a gate. This chapter probes the lost cultural practices related to city gates, while also raising the question of what city gates meant for the way people conceptualized and experienced urban space. Indeed, city gates not only served several concrete functions in the urban space, but also had symbolic significance. As Christopher Friedrichs notes: "not every city had a wall, and not every walled community was a city. But the correlation was remarkably high."[3] Churches and marketplaces could be found in villages, but walls were, by and large, exclusive to cities.[4] As early as the Middle Ages, city walls symbolized the *civitas* as a distinct area of security, order, and law, for city dwellers enjoyed certain rights and privileges still unavailable to peasants.[5] Tellingly, in medieval France the term *bonnes villes*— "good cities"—became synonymous with the idea of the walled city.[6] In the Netherlands, civil liberties and city gates were entwined semantically: in Dutch, a burgher is a *poorter*, someone who has the right—according to popular etymological derivation—to live within the gates (*poorten*) of a city.[7] In German lands, a popular saying held that the only thing separating burghers from peasants was the city wall ("Bürger und Bauer scheidet nichts denn die Mauer").[8]

Outside of Europe, city walls and gates had similar functions and significance; in fact, in the premodern world, city walls were a universal phenomenon.[9] In Mandarin, for example, the character *cheng* signifies not only "city" but also "wall."[10] One of the world's oldest cities, Jericho, is inextricably bound to the biblical account of the destruction of its walls. In Babylon and Babylonia, the significance of gates is evident in the very name of the state: *Babel* descends from the Akkadian *Bâb-ilu* ("God's Gate").[11] Even so, it is worth paying special attention to the city walls of early modern Europe, not least from an architectural point of view. The early modern period saw substantial advances in fortification techniques, and some historians have suggested that the arrival of bastioned fortification—which was far more effective in withstanding heavy artillery than medieval city walls had been—brought about a "military revolution."[12] In any event, these advances in the sixteenth and seventeenth centuries led many cities to replace their medieval walls with more modern fortifications.[13] Some of these new defenses, built from scratch using improved methods, were even considered invulnerable.

The construction and renovation of walls during this period resulted in an ever-increasing number of gates. The Italian architect Sebastiano Serlio (1475–1554), who wrote a treatise about gates and doors, aptly observed, "If ever there was a time for inventing new styles of city and fortress gates, that time is now, given that the foremost leaders of Christians, who ought to be trying to keep peace amongst themselves, are in fact the very men who are continually causing and inciting new wars."[14]

Furthermore, during the early modern period, the already extensive practice of building city walls and gates entered theoretical consciousness and became an independent topic of discussion. Renaissance authors began to take an interest in the varied history and ancient traditions of these structures and sought to learn from them. In contrast, medieval authors mostly approached city walls and gates from an eschatological rather than an "archaeological" perspective. For them, the Revelation of St. John served as a point of reference, especially its vision of the heavenly Jerusalem, "whose gates shall not be shut at all by day: for there shall be no night there."[15] This passage exerted a powerful influence on the medieval imagination and on the construction of cities.[16] A city with twelve gates like St. John's was considered the ideal, even though it could be realized only in the largest and most prosperous cities, such as Cologne and Bologna.

This eschatological outlook continued into the early modern era, but beginning in the Renaissance, a pronounced *historical* interest in the phenomenon of the wall gained currency alongside it. Paintings by Renaissance artists such as Andrea Mantegna show a clearly archaeological view of ancient walls and their ruins.[17] Humanists, too, displayed a keen interest in the city walls of antiquity. Giovanni Pontano, for instance, proclaimed the walls of ancient Babylon one of the Wonders of the World and pointed out that the imposing appearance of the walls of ancient Naples had prevented Hannibal from conquering that city.[18] The polymath and architect Leon Battista Alberti had similar interest in the legendary city walls of Greco-Roman antiquity as well as the walls of Babylon, which he read about in Herodotus.[19] Renaissance architects took an interest in any and every ancient source available on city walls, and builders even turned to scholars of antiquity to decide questions such as whether it was better to have soldiers or special fieldworkers build the ramparts.[20] It was considered impossible to build a perfect wall without recourse to antiquity, and a perfect wall, in turn, was seen as a prerequisite for creating an ideal city and society.

It is no coincidence that the major utopias of the early modern age were located either on almost inaccessible islands (Morus, Bacon) or in artfully walled cities (Filarete, Campanella).[21] Nor is it by chance that Lucantonio degli Uberti, in his monumental woodcut from 1500, framed his depiction of the city of Florence with a chain and an iron lock (Figure 29).[22] The walls of Florence, which are also visible in this image, guarantee the safety and prosperity of a city that, as the chainlike frame suggests, can literally be "locked up." Granted, sober political observers such as Machiavelli, and even architect-humanists such as Alberti, warned not to put all of one's hopes in walls. In this vein, the bitter infighting in many Italian cities led Dante to bemoan the uselessness of city walls when "those whom one same wall and one same moat enclose gnaw at each other."[23] Indeed, city fortifications could only be as strong as the will to maintain them in peace and defend them in war.

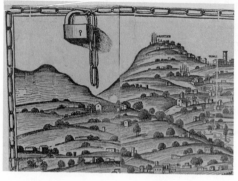

Figure 29. Lucantonio degli Uberti, *View of Florence* (so-called Catena Map), with detail showing chain and iron lock. Woodcut, c. 1500–1510. Kupferstichkabinett, Staatliche Museen, Berlin.

Machiavelli expressed admiration for the ancient Spartans, who "did not permit their cities to have walls, because they chose to rely for defense on the virtue of the individual, and wanted no other." But even he admitted that, in his own day, "the best thing he [the ruler] can do is to fortify the city where he dwells."[24] While the Spartans had mocked Athens as a city of women because of its walls, in the early modern period it was the wall-less city that looked helpless and effeminate, or in Alberti's words, "naked."[25] Nor was Alberti's expression a rhetorical cliché: an engraving by the Italian artist Giovanni Battista Braccelli from the early seventeenth century depicts a city without walls as a defenseless woman, who—lying on her back with legs spread—is constantly at risk of "penetration" (Figure 30).[26] Reality may have justified these notions, because in medieval and early modern Europe very few large, wall-less cities were not conquered at some point. The most famous exception is Venice, but Venice's saving grace was its unusual location in a lagoon, as well as a great deal of luck in times of crisis.

The dichotomy between walled and wall-less cities is, however, imperfect, as many city walls were constructed in phases over long periods of time, and some remained perpetually unfinished.[27] Contemporaries were also aware that even in an otherwise perfect wall, gates would always be a weak point, especially considering advances in military technology. Early modern discourse on gates reflects a fundamental tension between this inherent weakness of gates on one hand and

Figure 30. Giovanni Battista Braccelli, untitled engraving, from *Bizzarie di varie figure* (Livorno, 1624).

the considerable symbolic and practical significance of them on the other, which found expression in ornamentation and imposing exteriors.[28]

The combination of military and symbolic purposes ensured that gates tended to be far more lavishly appointed than the rest of the city wall.[29] Protruding considerably from the walls around them, gates often were decked with flags and, in the words of an eighteenth-century author, adorned with "sententiae, insignia, and images."[30] Throughout Europe, one can sometimes find cannonballs lodged in the outer sides of gates. These are rarely relics of battle; rather, they were embedded intentionally in the stonework to attest to the sturdiness of the gate and for apotropaic power.[31]

In many places, approaching parties also faced the challenge of crossing ditches and bridges in order to reach the city gate (Figure 31). The gate itself was almost always stationed with armed sentinels, whose presence transformed the gate into what Shakespeare called the "city's eyes."[32] The travelogues of early modern Europeans visiting the Middle East provide a valuable glimpse of European gates, as these travelers found different customs abroad. As a sixteenth-century German noted on his travels in the Levant: "gates are not always guarded by soldiers like those in our own cities—especially our important ones. Instead, at the main gates—those through which the streets pass—there stand at most two or three men, who do not so much guard the gate as just collect the toll, and one can also see that, unlike our guards, they are not armed."[33] Another difference was that many European gates were subdivided into several smaller gate systems and underpasses.[34]

Figure 31. The sixteenth-century Sint-Jorispoort (St. George Gate) in Antwerp. This gate was also known as the Keizerspoort (Imperial Gate). The ramparts, the water-filled moat, and the stone bridge leading to the gate are all visible in this photograph, which was taken in 1860, shortly before the city's defortification.

The fact that many gates functioned as bulwarks, however, says relatively little about their actual military significance, for although these gates grandly proclaimed their defensive features, they were not always defensible.[35]

In short, despite significant advances in structural design from the Middle Ages onward, city gates generally remained the weakest links in city security. In order to minimize this risk, it would have been necessary to convert the gate itself into a continuously guarded mini-fortress, exactly as the German architect Joseph Furttenbach (1591–1667) suggested in a now scarcely remembered treatise.[36] Furttenbach, whose reputation extended far beyond his native southern Germany, argued for a monumental "labyrinth" of a gate surrounded by a complex system of ditches and underpasses (Figure 32).[37] His plan boasted several stories, so that intruders trapped in the courtyard could be attacked from above with "hand grenades, a rain of fire, tar, stones," or firearms.[38] Of course, multistory gates of this kind would also require living quarters for the permanently stationed guards and their families. When under no immediate threat of danger, the families would pursue handiwork in designated workspaces, helping to keep personnel costs low.[39] We may find it difficult to imagine anyone being drawn to the lifestyle of this kind of garrison, which in modern terms has many of the features of a "total institution"—a structure, moreover, where the guards would be expected to prioritize the defense of the gate over that of their own "wives, children, and worldly goods."[40] For Furttenbach, the garrisoned families were merely cogs in the machinery of this supersized gate. In times of great danger, thought Furttenbach, the women and children ought to rush to help the men in battle.[41] Furttenbach's plans were never realized. Aside from the significant cost of constructing and operating such a gate, the difficulties it would create for everyday travel and commerce must also have spoken against it. And as Simon Pepper notes, "in a surprising number of cases, security was compromised by the design of magnificent formal gateways prominently placed in ways that owed much more to urban design than to the practical exigencies of fortification."[42]

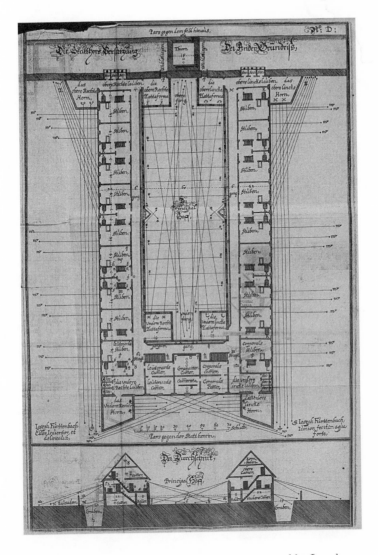

Figure 32. Blueprint of the elaborate gate proposed by Joseph Furttenbach in his *Paß-Verwahrung* (Augsburg, 1651).

Any gate's design had to reflect the different functions of the two natural sides: the country-facing side (*Feldseite*) and the city-facing side (*Stadtseite*) (Figures 33 and 34). The city-facing side, which was often partly blocked from view by dense rows of buildings, gave the inhabitants a sense of security, while the country-facing side proclaimed the identity of the city to the world and projected the fortifications as "icon[s] of power and permanence."[43] Moreover, gates and city walls served as fiscal boundaries, limiting entry to those who could afford to pay a toll or duty. In addition, they functioned as so-

Figure 33. The imposing country-facing side (*Feldseite*) of the Rothenburg Gate (c. 1390) in the imperial city of Dinkelsbühl, southern Germany. The projecting gateway (barbican) in front of the actual entrance dates from the sixteenth century.

Figure 34. The city-facing side (*Stadtseite*) of the medieval Rothenburg Gate in Dinkelsbühl. The second floor of the gate tower housed prison cells and the city's torture chamber.

cial boundaries, and last but not least, as lines of demarcation defining zones of religious freedom and restriction. Next, we take a closer look at these four functions and their effect on those who wished, for whatever reason, to enter a city.

We can trace the symbolic significance of the city gate back to antiquity and the Middle Ages, when a gate stood as a *pars pro toto* for its city, as illustrated on coins, coats of arms, and seals.[44] This does not mean that all the gates of a given city were identical. Quite the contrary, gates were highly individualized "faces of the city" and often bore individual names indicating their specific function: the name of the city's patron saint, of the adjacent city quarter, or of another city to which the gate's outbound road would lead.[45] Europeans in early modern times had a strong sense of the variations among city gates, and they often devoted extensive space in their travelogues and accounts of cities to describing the gates they encountered. In some cases, gates even served to define property beyond the city walls. In Italy, for instance, notarial documents often referred to rural properties, such as vineyards or estates, as "extra portam" and then added the name of the nearest gate. Thus, gates served not only as crucial reference points, but also as extensions of the city's political and judicial authority into the rural geography for miles and miles.[46]

In addition to being emblems of municipal identity, city gates sometimes also functioned as loci of municipal politics. In medieval England, for example, local officials held meetings in special chambers built above city gates.[47] In most of Europe, however, the primary ceremonial function of the city gate was its use as a space for receiving important dignitaries, especially—if the city was not independent—the city's overlord, who held the *jus intradae* (the right of entrance). Such ceremonies were organized in detail and at great expense. Sometimes the city would even expand an existing gate, create an entirely new gate, or install imposing pillars or "gates of honor" (*Ehrenpforten*) inside or outside the city.[48] A widely read German manual for ceremonies explains that gates of honor were typically "adorned by columns, paintings, statues, and emblems, and they were made of wood, alabaster, porphyry, as well as gold and silver." On such occasions, the population was called upon to stand by the wayside and greet the visiting dignitary—and it went without saying that "no one may appear in ragged, old, or loose clothes."[49]

When the arriving dignitary was the ruler of the city or region, the gate was not only where he officially entered the city, but also where local officials acknowledged his superior status. Sometimes, the wooden doors were taken off their hinges and laid on the ground as a supreme gesture of deference.[50] Most often, however, city officials would hand over the keys to the city in a solemn ceremony; usually, the ruler would accept and then return them with equal ceremony.[51] The question of how the keys, and which ones exactly, should be handed over to the ruler was often a subject of intense deliberations among city officials, as was the case when Charles VIII of France "liberated" Florence in 1494.[52] Through these lavish ceremonies, city leaders concealed the considerable risk they were taking in literally handing over their most important privilege: the right to determine who could enter and leave the city.[53] As Edward Muir has observed, "the dangers inherent in opening the city to a powerful outsider were thus met with ceremony."[54] In La Rochelle, for instance, during the king's visit, city officials customarily opened a certain gate for him while stretching a silk ribbon across it as a symbolic barrier. They would cut the ribbon only after the king solemnly confirmed the privileges of the city in a speech outside the gate.[55]

Given the enormous significance of city walls and gates for the self-image and "honor" of a city, their destruction was not only a military disaster but also a humiliation and a trauma—a blow to the "face of the city."[56] Shakespeare used anthropomorphic metaphors of this sort and wrote of the need in wartime "to save unscratched your city's threatened cheeks."[57] Familiar biblical narratives such as Joshua's trumpeters destroying the walls of Jericho or Samson's attack on the city gates of Gaza show that the idea of equating breached fortifications with humiliation was hardly unique to medieval Europe.[58] In the premodern age, of course, large battering rams, and then more efficient gunpowder-based technologies, proved more reliable than trumpets and divine intervention in bringing down city walls. Irrespective of the technologies at play, the purpose of razing fortifications was almost never purely military. Indeed, all it took to make a city vulnerable to future attacks was to demolish its *walls*, yet as a rule the *gates* were razed as well, underscoring that these were often gestures of humiliation.[59] In some cases, gates were the sole locus of destruction, clearly as a form of punishment. In the fourteenth century, for example, certain cities in the Margraviate of Brandenburg endorsed a false pretender to the throne, the "False Waldemar." When the reigning Wittelsbachs regained the scepter of sovereignty, all the gates through which Waldemar had ridden were walled up and replaced by new ones. Some of these *Waldemartore*, sealed up to impose eternal shame on the cities, were not reopened until the nineteenth century.[60] In the medieval and early modern Low Countries, too, it was not uncommon for counts to punish rebellious city corporations by demolishing the city gates that customarily were used for ceremonial entries.[61]

Control of the gates, moreover, was a crucial tool with which the city's leadership could exert influence over the social life and demographic composition of the city. In this context, the gate functioned as a kind of social filter.[62] As Maria Boes has noted, beginning in the fifteenth century, city gates were "increasingly used . . . not so much to admit, but to prevent people from coming to town, especially those whom they had expelled previously."[63] It was not unusual to encounter the heads of executed criminals on display at the city gates, put there in hopes of deterring potential emulators.[64] Exiles and other banned persons were ordered, under pain of severe punishment or death, to stay outside of a certain radius around the city, or in some cases not to come closer than the city gates. In her remarkable collection of private letters, Alessandra Macinghi Strozzi, whose son had been exiled from Florence by the Medici for political reasons, describes how she was "very shaken up" by her brief and emotional reunion with him in 1465, when he was allowed to meet her at one of the city gates for a few hours.[65]

Apart from those under exile or ban, two other types of people were vigorously repelled by most cities: vagabonds and beggars.[66] Even so, this did not deter them from trying to enter the gates. Members of religious minorities, particularly Jews, were also barred from passing through the gates of many cities. Sometimes, gate guards and clerks kept lists of names of authorized and unauthorized Jews.[67]

Similarly strict regulations applied to the sick, although there were finer distinctions in these cases. Someone who came to town for a conventional doctor's visit or procedure could count on being admitted, but those who suffered from infectious diseases or gave the impression of being contagious were usually turned away at the gate, especially during epidemics of the plague. Gatekeepers, along with clergy and physicians, played a key role in managing health crises and received special instructions at such times.[68] In general, Italian city-states had particularly strict health regulations, such that beginning in the late Middle Ages, one usually could gain entry only by showing a health certificate from one's previous place of residence.[69] From the sixteenth century onward, the requirement of a health certificate became more common north of the Alps as well.[70]

City gates also functioned as a fiscal boundary, as excise taxes or customs duties were levied on many goods and wares passing through the gates. At the gates of Berlin in the eighteenth century, these taxes applied to almost forty different wares, for which reason a 107-page-long *Akzise-Buch* ("excise book") came into use.[71] In Brussels, every gate had its own small office with the city's coat of arms, in which the list of taxable goods was kept ready for use.[72] In some cities, travelers paid directly at the gate, while in others (such as Berlin), they would be given a document to take with them to the tax authority in the city center.[73] Certain goods, such as cattle for slaughter, typically underwent a simpler inspection and were brought in only through a specific gate designated for this purpose.[74]

In Renaissance Florence, tolls (*gabelle*), collected at no fewer than eleven gates, were one of the city's most important

sources of income.[75] Even cities that were part of a larger territory, and which therefore had to remit part of this income
to their overlord, still retained considerable sums from these
tolls with which to line municipal coffers. For instance, in
Brandenburg-Prussia, a large territorial state, income from
border taxes and gate customs constituted half of the state's
total tax revenue well into the eighteenth century.[76] For Brussels, too, excise tax was a major source of income.[77] Thus, if a
city were to relinquish or lose control of its gates, it would also
lose one of its most important sources of revenue.[78]

Finally, city gates had important religious significance,
a topic that has been discussed relatively little in research to
date. Indeed, a comprehensive study would require in-depth
treatment spanning many periods, since pre-Christian influences intermingle here with Christian traditions.[79] Already
in biblical times, city gates were often sites of religious cult
and law.[80] In ancient Greece, the sacred dimensions of the city
walls served "as an extension of the sacredness of the polis
itself."[81] In Roman culture, too, city walls were fundamentally
res sacrae.[82] The Romans even gave the boundary stone its own
god, Terminus, and revered dual-faced Janus for his protection
of sites of passage such as gates.

Some of the sacred rituals connected to gates in Christian
culture were related to the gate itself. In light of the military,
legal, and political significance of city walls and gates described above, it is not surprising that divine assistance was
invoked for their safety. The custom of painting images of the
Virgin Mary on gates for this purpose was practiced in Constantinople and in late-medieval Italy.[83] Moreover, it was not

unusual in Italy to decorate gates with representations, usually sculptures or frescoes, of the city's patron saint and of Saint Peter, who, as we addressed in Chapter 2, was said to hold the keys to the kingdom of heaven.[84] These images were popularly thought to exert an apotropaic effect and in particular to ward off the devil and other evil spirits, whose pernicious influence might weaken the security of the city. When suspicions of this kind arose, city authorities occasionally deemed it necessary—for instance, in Renaissance Florence—to have priests ritually purify the walls.[85] Similarly, when the Sienese suspected that the Florentines had manipulated one of their gates through certain magic spells, the city paid two fearless citizens to spend a night at the gate in order to perfect a certain magical potion.[86] Another common custom throughout Europe was to build chapels above city gates (as well as atop castle and monastery gates), which was believed to guarantee special protection for the gate, in addition to giving the gate an even more dignified appearance and inspiring donations from travelers grateful to have arrived at their destination.[87]

Aside from rituals that centered on the gates, there were many other religious and superstitious traditions for the benefit of the *people* traveling through them. In the case of Florence, Richard Trexler has shown that "processions touched the gates as part of the *via sacra*, military forces had to pass under them at propitious times, and visiting dignitaries could not traverse them without solemn preparations and ceremonies."[88] This held especially true for those gates that were considered to be per se holy sites because they had been the setting of some miraculous or religiously significant event. The best-known example is the so-called Golden Gate in Jerusalem, through which Jesus is said to have entered the city on a donkey on Palm Sunday. Medieval and early modern pilgrims were willing to spend considerable amounts of money to purchase fragments of this gate from Muslim merchants. Some Europeans risked severe punishment from the Muslim authorities by secretly breaking small stones from the gate, which were purported to protect against stroke, epilepsy, and plague.[89]

In the age of confessionalization, city gates in Europe also came to demarcate zones of religious practice. This phenomenon became particularly salient in the aftermath of the Reformation and, more specifically, the Peace of Augsburg (1555), which gave every ruler the right to determine the religion of his territory and cities. As a result, city dwellers with religious beliefs different from the official state religion had to hold their religious services and ceremonies outside the city walls—at the manors of country aristocrats, for example— where different regulations might be in place. As Benjamin Kaplan has noted, "this distinction transformed the border that divided the city's jurisdiction from the estates surrounding it into a religious frontier."[90] In Catholic Vienna, for example, Protestants had to leave the city walls in order to practice their faith. This weekly trek en masse through the city gates came to be known as *Auslauf* ("walking out"). The same phenomenon regularly occurred in other parts of Europe, for instance in the Low Countries under Spanish rule, where thousands of city dwellers streamed into the forests and fields outside their city walls in order to attend the sermons of Protestant or Calvinist ministers. Consequently, the seemingly pastoral sixteenth-century Dutch paintings of the biblical Sermon on the Mount, with the gates of early modern cities in the background, were actually poignant social commentaries on contemporary religious oppression. Indeed, the reality was not as idyllic as it might seem from these paintings. This was also true for cities like Paris, where, in the early seventeenth century, a Catholic crowd attacked the Huguenots during the highly symbolic moment of their return to the city gate.[91]

We can now return to the question posed at the outset: What was it like to have the "deliberate experience" of entering an early modern walled city under normal circumstances?[92] To answer this question in a systematic and pan-European way, we must consider the situation in various European cities; but at the same time, we will pay particularly close attention to Brussels and Antwerp, two of the largest European cities of the period, so as to illustrate the entire gamut of gate-related policies and problems that could arise in a given place. While early modern Brussels in its heyday counted almost eighty thousand residents, Antwerp's population surged well past one hundred thousand in the middle of the sixteenth century.[93] There are, however, other reasons for focusing on these two cites: both were admired throughout Europe for their lavish walls and fortifications, and in both, "the linking of certain city gates with civic political prowess" was a deeply rooted tradition that stretched back centuries and was reflected in recurring and elaborate processions.[94] Above all, both were major centers of commerce. Few other cities saw so many or so var-

Figure 35. The stately exterior side of Antwerp's St. George
Gate (Imperial Gate) with a group of guards. According to a
Latin inscription above the entrance, Emperor Charles V, ruler
of Spain and the Holy Roman Empire, was the first mortal to
have entered through this gate in 1545. Photograph, 1860.

ied a set of travelers and merchandise pass through their gates
daily (Figure 35).

When foreigners wished to enter a walled city in early
modern Europe, they usually had to undergo inspection.[95] The
only variable at play was how intensively the inspection was
carried out. In many places, inhabitants of the city had the
right to leave and enter at will, though they had to prove their

citizenship.[96] The exact manner in which this was accomplished remains unclear.[97] Most citizens used the same gate every time—the one intended for their part of the city. We therefore can presume that, especially in smaller towns, the gatekeepers recognized most of the citizens coming and going. As a result, most citizens could avoid inspection as long as they had no goods to declare, although in theory it was still officially required. A telling record of this informal flexibility can be found in Goethe's *Werther*: "[Werther] came to the city gate. The watchmen, who knew him, let him go out without a word."[98]

When it came to people who were unknown or foreign, the situation was far more complicated. In Brussels, so-called *commissaires* at the gate would ask foreigners at least eight questions, apparently in the following order: (1) where were you born? (2) where did you most recently live? (3) when did you leave that place and why? (4) where did you most recently stop on your journey? (5) what is your full name? (6) what is your occupation or other distinguishing trait (*qualité*)? (7) why are you here and how long do you expect to stay? and (8) where will you be lodging in the city?[99] Even if travelers could answer these questions, however, they still might not gain entry to the city. The *commissaires* had strict instructions not to let in any foreign beggars or vagabonds. Furthermore, anyone who gave the impression of being ill had to produce a health certificate (*certificat de santé*). If a traveler had not yet arranged for accommodations in the city, the *commissaire* had to call the gate guards, who would then lead the visitor to a city official—in some cities, directly to the mayor—where the case would be given further scrutiny.[100]

If the *commissaire* found no reason to forbid entry, the traveler would pay the necessary toll and customs duties, receive a pass to the city, and enter through the gate. He or she would then have to produce this pass in order to get accommodation in any hostelry and also to leave the city at the end of the stay.[101] But the gatekeepers' duties did not end with issuing this document. At the end of every workday, after closing the gate, the staff of each gate had to submit a list to the municipal authorities (in Brussels, the *trésorerie*) documenting the full names and the intended accommodations of all noncitizens who had been admitted that day. The gate clerks, who worked from the time the gate opened until it was closed, were responsible for drafting these lists.[102] In Antwerp, these gate clerks also had to keep records of any suspicious moments and irregularities.[103] Lists of foreign arrivals were common in many European cities, but comparatively few have been preserved in the archives; and while they may seem monotonous now, for their contemporaries they were a prized source of news and novelty.[104] Indeed, in premodern times, the arrival of foreign visitors was always an interesting piece of news. In Berlin, for example, even in the eighteenth century, the king would have the list of foreign arrivals brought to him every evening. In Augsburg, which was not a royal seat, the mayor was responsible for reviewing this list.[105] In the nineteenth century, although city gates were beginning to disappear, it became common to publish in the local papers the names of foreigners staying in hostels and hotels—a practice that came to an end only with the rise of mass tourism.[106]

Entering through a city gate was a complex and often multistage process. Specific gate ordinances described in great detail the various inspections that guards had to perform on foreign visitors and on people who arrived with taxable wares.[107] In some Italian cities, foreigners also had to relinquish any weapons at the gate.[108] As is often the case, it was easier for cities to announce these rules than to enforce them, for not every traveler knew the rules of each city, and not every gate commissary or guard was equally diligent.[109] The latter was partly due to the gatekeepers' working conditions: they were poorly paid, and in certain cities they were known to juggle multiple jobs in order to improve their incomes. From time to time they also eased the inspection regulations in exchange for "gifts."[110] Sometimes, respectable burghers were assigned to supervise the day-to-day operations at the gate, but this did not necessarily put an end to such abuses. In sixteenth-century Cologne, for instance, the councilman Hermann Weinsberg, in his capacity as captain of a civic guard, occasionally supervised the gatekeeping; but we also know that he was in his seventies at the time. Although he was exempt from night shifts because of his age, he still had to get up very early in the morning to retrieve the keys from the city hall at seven o'clock, and he would need to stay at the gate until closing time. Given his frail health and his occasional absentmindedness, which he mentions quite openly in his diaries, it is doubtful that he was the best man for the job.[111] That said, even when gatekeepers carried out their duties properly, they received little sympathy. One of Boccaccio's protagonists in the *Decameron* laments, "You know how those custom officers always make a nuisance of themselves and want to see everything."[112]

Despite these detailed ordinances, misunderstandings and breakdowns in communication often slowed activities at the gate. Not every traveler who arrived at the city gate had a sufficient command of the local language, and this made the inspection and interview far more complicated. In regions with two or more common languages, misunderstandings were a daily affair; it is no coincidence that in Brussels, candidates for gatekeeper positions who had both French and Flemish language skills explicitly indicated their bilingualism in their applications.[113] But overall, language barriers were a comparatively minor problem. A far heavier burden resulted from the arguments and brawls that arose out of the customs inspections. Quite a few travelers felt that they were being unjustly taxed and protested vociferously. At times, brawls that began at the gates led to protests or riots that spread to the entire city.[114] In addition, there were always a few travelers who would try to falsify their declarations or smuggle their wares past the authorities.[115] Smugglers tried countless (and sometimes rather ingenious) ways of avoiding these controls. In Antwerp, for instance, some women hid food under their clothes, pretending to be pregnant. And one butcher was even said to have used coffins to conceal his meat products.[116] If the gatekeeper suspected a person of smuggling, tensions could escalate quickly: in 1696, a miller attacked an inspector with a knife because the inspector wanted to search his wagonload.[117]

Disputes of honor constituted a further problem, because the gate—perhaps more than any other public urban space— was a great leveler: every person had to pass through it, and very few foreigners were spared inspection. (High dignitaries with special privileges and letters of safe conduct were the major exception.) Many aristocrats and upper-class travelers found inspection by low-ranking officials insufferable. In 1755, for example, when a gatekeeper in Brussels tried to inspect the passengers of a stagecoach arriving from Ghent, a nobleman emerged from the coach, furiously refused to be inspected, struck the guard three times, and pulled out his dagger. The guard managed to subdue the nobleman only with the help of a courageous bystander and several sentinels who were called for backup.[118] Such episodes were particularly common in university cities because students, many of whom had aristocratic or upper-class backgrounds, often cultivated an exaggerated sense of honor. As a result, they were ready to pick a fight with anyone who would get in their way, and gatekeepers were bound to do so. Further aggravating the situation, it was not uncommon for brothels and taverns to be located outside the city, not least because alcohol could be sold at cheaper prices there than in the city. Thus, city residents—especially students—returning from such outings were often boisterous or intoxicated on their arrival at the gate.[119] The resulting violence affected not only the gatekeepers, but sometimes bystanders. In 1561, for instance, students reentering the city of Freiburg began a brawl with a group of baker apprentices who happened to be at the gate. In an act of provocation, the students shouted, "Where are the barley-munchers [*gerstenfreßer*], they should be beaten here and there!" The bakers responded, "We are bakers, and we do not deny ourselves," which in turn prompted the students' rejoinder, "We are students, and we, too, do not deny ourselves." Soon enough, a fight ensued.[120]

Soldiers were another group whose arrival at city gates often led to violence. Not only were they armed, but they also tended to travel in large groups—two factors that could easily ignite a dangerous situation. The authorities in Antwerp tried at least to contain the problem, if not to solve it, by designating two gates for soldiers.[121] Yet their services were sometimes needed at other gates: as some in Brussels argued, soldiers could come to the aid of the guards during disputes.[122] It was expensive, however, for the city (or overlord) to employ soldiers from a standing army, and in places where this was the case, the financial burden was often passed on to the citizens in the form of a special "guard tax."[123]

Finally, one other factor could lead to conflict: the crowds that thronged at the gate. The number of people and vehicles seeking entry to the city was particularly high in the run-up to important religious or civic festivities. Thanks to the meticulous records of Endres Tucher, Nuremberg's chief building official, we know that no fewer than 1,874 carriages and coaches entered through the city's five main gates to attend the annual *Heiltumsweisung* (a major religious event) in 1463.[124] But even on ordinary days, the constant traffic of people, wagons, and animals on their way in and out of the city caused frustrating and even dangerous congestion. In the eighteenth century, Kassel experienced repeated misfortunes of this kind: an ox impaled a woman, and a herd of cows trampled an officer to death.[125] Aggravating the situation in many places, bystanders, beggars, and children tended to congregate near the gates, not least because the adjacent residential areas usually contained the living quarters of the social underclasses. Indeed, in some cities the authorities deliberately expelled certain marginal groups, especially prostitutes, from the city's center and consigned them to designated areas such as the neighborhoods along the city walls.[126] As the architect Sebastiano Serlio lamented: "The habitations of the poorest men in cities are far from the piazzas and noble places and are near the gate. These men are the humblest sort of craftsmen who work in various lowly trades."[127] The urban area directly behind the gate was also a favorite place for traveling merchants, who enjoyed the access to new arrivals. City officials continually issued decrees banning assembly and disturbance of traffic near the city gate. They also banned loitering near the gate and hawking wares.[128] But we can infer from the frequency of these decrees that these problems persisted.

Furthermore, urban development tended to flank the city walls, and in some places, houses were actually fused into the walls, often in violation of building regulations. Perhaps more importantly, this also intensified the chaos in these parts of the city.[129] To make matters worse, the gatekeepers generally stood facing outward toward the city's surroundings, such that what happened inside the city, in the shadow of the wall, was beyond their field of vision. As a result, it was quite common for walls to be covered with graffiti and inscriptions, some of which were very obscene. It is also telling that in Italian cities, crucifixes were often painted on or affixed to the city-facing sides of the walls in order to dissuade the unruly or drunk from urinating on them.[130]

A person who wished to pass through a city gate also had to be aware of logistical considerations—perhaps most importantly, the gate's hours of operation, which could vary significantly depending on the month and season.[131] In Brussels, the opening and closing times were adjusted every two weeks. During the second half of April, for example, the gates were open from 4:00 in the morning until 8:00 in the evening. In December, however, the gates did not open until 6:30 and closed as early as 5:00 in the afternoon.[132] In many places, gate bells were used in the evening to signal closing time. Later in the evening, these same bells also sounded the curfew for hostels and taverns.[133]

The gates' opening times were often posted publicly, though people in the surrounding boroughs also knew the operating hours from daily experience. Still, closing times posed a constant problem, and authorities had to intervene regularly.[134] For one thing, the gatekeepers were not always punctual. Not uncommonly, they would arrive a bit late or end their workday early, disregarding the inconvenience this caused to merchants and travelers. In Brussels, the magistrate deplored the fact that despite the detailed regulations, "the city's gates were not opened and closed according to the appointed hours."[135] Similar complaints were made in other large European cities.[136] The situation was especially complex on Sundays and holidays, when it was customary in some places to close the city gates, or at least some of them, during Mass.[137] In Calais, much to the chagrin of travelers, authorities sometimes closed the gates in the middle of workdays, especially at midday.[138]

For those unfamiliar with a given city, the situation was particularly difficult and confusing. Travelers, especially those traveling long distances, generally had to plan their journeys in advance so that they would be sure to arrive before sundown.[139] Arriving on time or early was more than just a virtue — it was a necessity. Locals and foreigners alike sought to avoid the dreaded situation of standing in front of a locked gate. The colloquial term *Torschlußpanik* ("panic of gate closure"), now used in German in a figurative sense, still resounds with the anxiety that premodern people felt at the prospect of being locked out of a city.[140] A person approaching a city after closing time could only hope that at least one of the gates was staffed by a night watchman. If so, the traveler would either have to pay a considerable sum of money (if the gate regulations provided for this circumstance) or try to bribe the gatekeeper. In many places, however, the gatekeepers first needed to consult the mayor, as he was the one who kept the keys to the gates at night.[141] Travelers who could produce a special permit were generally more successful in this situation.[142] Some cities made exceptions for sick and infirm travelers who required medical help, as well as for doctors, surgeons, midwives, nurses, and others who could provide emergency aid.[143] Even then, however, much was left to chance, for night watchmen were notoriously unreliable: sometimes they were engrossed in conversation or gambling with fellow guards; at other times, they got drunk on the job or simply fell asleep. Tellingly, in Antwerp, gatekeepers were expressly forbidden to drink beer or to provoke one another with "defamatory, scandalous words."[144] Similar stipulations existed in numerous other places.[145] The authorities in Strasbourg opted for a more pragmatic approach, realizing that the best they could do was to choose the lesser of two evils: the risk, on one hand, that the guards would fall asleep, or on the other, that they would pass their time with gambling and conversation. From the perspective of the authorities, the latter was the lesser danger—on condition that alcohol was strictly prohibited. As a result, Strasbourgeois guards were permitted to gamble (as long as the stakes were not too high) and converse with one another (provided that they did not talk about religion or lapse into insulting one another). They were even allowed to read, as long as this did not lead to conflicts of any sort.[146]

Those who arrived at the gate too late and who were neither rich nor privileged had no choice but to spend the night outside the walls. In 1570, this happened to Cologne councilman Hermann Weinsberg after he spent a summer day with his family in his vineyard outside the city. On their trek back along the Rhine, they were delayed and eventually found the city gates closed. Weinsberg decided that it would be safest for him and his family to spend the night on one of the boats along the Rhine.[147] Not all people who found themselves in this situation acted with such resignation: some would throw tantrums or even try to open the gates by force. Sometimes, they even succeeded in getting the night watchman to open the gate—if only to lead them directly to the city jail.[148] Few travelers were as unconcerned at the prospect of spending the night outside the gates as the Quaker William Penn (1644–1718), who later became the founder and namesake of the American Province of Pennsylvania. On one evening in 1677, during his travels as a missionary through Holland and the Holy Roman Empire, he arrived in Duisburg, where he and his companions found the gates already locked. Through his unwavering trust in God, Penn managed to find a silver lining even in this situation. As he later reported: "there being no Houses without the Walls, we laid down together in a Field, receiving both natural and spiritual Refreshment, blessed be the Lord. Three in the Morning we rose, sanctifying God in our Hearts that had kept us that Night. . . . Soon after the Clock had struck Five, they opened the Gates of the City, and we had not long got to our Inn."[149]

For both city authorities and travelers, nighttime entry was a serious problem throughout the premodern period. The security concerns of city officials are easy to understand, but magistrates also feared that a lax approach to nighttime entry would aggravate two other problems: intrusion by vagrants and beggars, and avoidance of excise taxes. Few cities handled nighttime entry as efficiently as Augsburg. Starting in the sixteenth century, the city maintained a special night gate—the *Alter Einlaß* ("old entrance")—which was constructed and equipped specifically for this purpose. The gate comprised several underpasses, which opened and closed by means of a sophisticated mechanism, without putting the gatekeepers in danger.[150] A gate equipped with such complex machinery was exceptional in Europe at the time, as we can see from Michel de Montaigne's travel diary. During a visit to Augsburg in 1580, he marveled at the *Alter Einlaß* and was even given a tour of it. Full of admiration, he wrote: "It is one of the most ingenious things that can be seen. The queen of England sent an ambassador expressly to ask the city government to reveal the working of these machines; it is said that they refused."[151]

In light of the difficulty of entering a walled city after sundown, it is no wonder that crowds frequently mobbed the gate near closing time, sometimes leading to tumultuous scenes. Such throngs provided an easy target for pickpockets, and the bottlenecking of traffic could also quickly ignite social tensions. In 1589 in Antwerp, where the populace was hostile to Spanish rule, a group of unidentified individuals—likely anti-Spanish locals—attacked a Spanish soldier at gate closing and stole his cloak, hat, and dagger.[152] In Freiburg, a few decades earlier, students refused to comply with the order to leave the gate area at closing time and instead attacked the gatekeepers.[153] Similar incidents, some of which even led to fatalities, appear again and again in urban sources.[154]

In short, no magistrate in the early modern age would have relinquished control of the city gates willingly, not only because of their many crucial functions, but also because of the importance of mitigating the daily problems that arose in connection with them. There were, however, situations in which this control slipped, or threatened to slip. The most frequent cause was the capture of the city by enemies or its annexation to a territory governed by another ruler. Neither situation necessarily led to a politics of laissez-faire at the gates or even to their removal; however, the result was often a transfer of authority over the gates (as well as a portion of the income they generated) to powers outside the city. Other, lesser factors could also undermine a city's control of its gates. One constant threat was the creation of alternative ways of entering or leaving the city. It is true that city walls often looked imposing, but they were also expensive to maintain and required constant repair.[155] Holes developed due to natural circumstances like inclement weather, but also as a result of sabotage.[156] In any case, walls were rarely insurmountable: under cover of darkness, a person could often find a safe place to climb over the walls or fortifications and thus get in or out of the city. Statistically speaking, this was probably not a great danger: most citizens and travelers still passed through the gates as prescribed. The problem was therefore more a qualitative one, as scalable city walls or walls with holes in them tended to inspire the very people whose entry the city was most keen on barring, namely vagabonds, beggars, and smugglers. It is hardly surprising, then, that cities brought out the heavy artillery—both figuratively and literally—to deal with this problem. Almost everywhere in Europe, climbing the city walls after dark was strictly prohibited.[157] In Brussels, it was forbidden to climb the walls by night or by day, or to avoid the gates by any other means (such as by damaging the fortifications). Violators of these laws faced punishments ranging from severe fines or jail sentences to banishment or even the death penalty. The guards were also permitted, after issuing a warning, to open fire on a transgressor caught trying to enter the city by cover of night. In some places in Europe, it was even forbidden to go near the walls at nighttime.[158]

Nonetheless, incidents, conflicts, and transgressions of this kind were not what ultimately led to the downfall of city walls and gates. Their disappearance, doubtless one of the most radical transformations in the long history of European cities, came about for other reasons.

The disappearance of city walls and gates opened a new chapter in the history of urban space. Recent research has shown that there were various reasons for the process of de-fortification, which intensified in many European cities during the nineteenth century (Figure 36).[159] In some places, its ideological roots can be traced back to the early modern period. This is especially true of France, where the development of a strong central state in the seventeenth century led to a

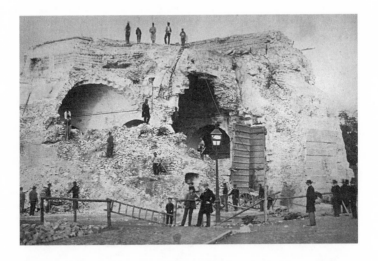

Figure 36. The demolition of Antwerp's St. George Gate (Imperial Gate), once the most imposing of Antwerp's seven city gates. At the order of the city council, all city gates, along with the ramparts, were razed in the 1860s and 1870s. Photograph, c. 1865.

discourse that advocated the demolition of city walls and fortifications in the country's heartland in favor of building stronger fortifications at its outer borders.[160] On a symbolic level,
this signaled that the country was internally at peace. However, it could also be seen as a demonstration of the monarch's
absolute power: in times of crisis, formerly fortified cities were
no longer able to present any meaningful resistance or protest
against the monarch. Even in France, however, defortification
proved long and arduous and was not always the result of an
official decision. As Michael Wolfe notes: "Few towns in the
interior actually saw their walls completely razed. More often,
the loss of the urban edge's military function was a piecemeal
process of private appropriation or benign neglect."[161]

The swift growth of cities during industrialization was another important factor in defortification: for city authorities,
walls and gates began to be seen as hindrances to urban expan-
sion and rapidly increasing traffic. But these pragmatic considerations were not the only factors at work: attitudes toward the
function and aesthetics of urban space were also undergoing
radical change.[162] As early as the eighteenth century, a writer
in the English press, for example, characterized the city gate
as a "monument of Gothic barbarism."[163] It is important to
note that this criticism was not aimed at medieval architecture in general, but at city gates and walls specifically. In the
nineteenth century, many castles and fortresses were built in
the "neo-Gothic" style, but this architectural revival did not
extend to walls and gates.[164]

Today, the cultural practice and experience of entering a
city through a gate has become foreign to us, or even faded

completely from memory.[165] In essence, we do not really enter cities anymore; in most cases, we do not even know where
a city begins or ends. By and large, there are no longer any
legal, fiscal, or religious boundaries between cities and their
environs. Granted, the categories of "city" and "country" con-
tinue to exist in our vocabulary, and they still refer to different
landscapes and distinct ways of life.[166] But the boundary between city and country is no longer concrete. Of course, even
in premodern times, some cities sprawled out into suburbs,
and not every city had a wall.[167] On the whole, however, it remains true that since the nineteenth century, throughout Europe, "urban space [has] become essentially defined by its very
borderlessness."[168] Nowadays, the "open city" has become the
paradigm of our understanding of urban space.[169]

In the premodern era, by contrast, the lay of the land was
different. The differences in the urban experience are particularly apparent when we look at early modern travel guides,
which show that gates played a very prominent role in the
structure and perception of urban space; and what is more, the
tours described in these guides often began at one of the city's
gates, for these were not only the places where foreign travelers first entered the city, but also landmarks that merited attention in their own right.[170] Along the same lines, Francis Bacon, in his *Essays,* explicitly advised travelers to devote special
attention to the individual forms and characteristics of walls
and fortifications when visiting a city.[171] Indeed, premodern
travelers, unlike travelers today, paid much less attention to
the size of a city's population than to the scope of its perim-
eter or walls.[172] The size of a city was not necessarily expressed

through the number of inhabitants, but far more frequently through the physical experience of the size of the wall and gates.

Today, where they still exist, city walls and gates are primarily viewed as historical points of interest, but they no longer have a practical or symbolic meaning (Figure 37). We

Figure 37. View through one of the two gates of the medieval walled town of Monteriggioni, near Siena. In the Middle Ages, the city enceinte, with its mighty gates and towers, evoked Dante's awe (*Inferno*, canto 31) and secured the survival of the small town. Today, the gates stand always open, offering picturesque views of the Tuscan countryside but no longer serving any practical or defensive purpose.

should not, however, idealize their past, because this would be to overlook the ambivalence with which they were viewed in premodern times. On one hand, they formed part of a city's promise of security and civic pride. On the other, the system of taxation and inspection that travelers endured at the gate was a source of nuisance to most. When we view city gates as historical monuments, we do not see the difficulties and potential conflicts that were once associated with them. We also overlook the fact that inspection and identification, which we often classify as part of the modern "security state," were already being explored and tested during the premodern era, especially at the city gate. We still find these practices all around us today, though in different settings. The transition to modernity involved a radical shift of priorities: as Lewis Mumford notes, "the territorial state itself became the 'City' that was to be defended."[173] Granted, the shift was gradual and not always the consequence of a governmental decision; rather, as case studies have shown, it was the outcome of a "dialectic of local and national interests which produced the boundaries of national territory."[174] For travelers today, the result is that the borders of countries have become the kind of barrier that they rarely were in the early modern age.[175] On political and legal levels, this development marks a deep and unmistakable caesura.[176] But on a day-to-day level, there is actually significant continuity between the gate inspections of that time and the practices at border crossings in our time.

Today, travelers entering a foreign country must first go through passport control. At U.S. airports, for the past several years, foreigners encounter a sign showing border officials, accompanied by the words, "We Are the Face of the Nation." While in the past, the gates—each individually crafted and with its own name—constituted the "faces of the *city*," nowadays border officials, stationed in glass cubicles as uniform as they are sterile, have become the faces of the *nation*. The city has become irrelevant in modern border crossings. Although airports are often named after cities, they are usually quite far from urban centers; and even when travelers land at an airport situated in a city, the experience of arriving, particularly in terms of security and customs, has less to do with the city and more to do with the country or state in which the airport is located. Train travel is an altogether different experience, as those who arrive at a train station are immediately in the city and do not have to undergo any sort of inspection; yet even in this case, the actual transition is not when they enter the city, but when they disembark from the train. In short, for modern travelers, the experience of entering a city is no longer connected to any particular threshold. Richard Sennett has argued that urban space "has become a means to the end of pure motion—we now measure urban spaces in terms of how easy it is to drive through them and to get out of them."[177] Sennett is certainly correct in observing that we recognize the feeling of leaving a city behind us—of "getting out"—but in most cities this experience is no longer connected to passing through a specific location. The city no longer ends at a wall; instead, the transition between city and country is stretched and fragmented in a thousand ways, blurred across the belts of "*sub*urbs" that now circumscribe most of our large cities. Yet it is precisely here in the suburbs—and not only in the United

States, but also in South Africa, Asia, and the Arab world—
that we encounter the walls of today: the walls of "gated communities," behind which more than eight million people
live in the United States alone.[178] One need not go as far as
Lewis Mumford, who—with his nostalgia for antiquity and
the Middle Ages—spoke of "Mass Suburbia as Anti-City."[179]
The clear demarcation lines of the premodern age cannot be
brought back with such polemics, nor would anyone seriously
contemplate building new city walls. However, we do not have
to restore city walls and gates in order to draw some lessons
from their long history. As Walter Benjamin once remarked
in passing, gates were part of the *character* of a city.[180] In the
transition to modernity, gates have vanished just as irrevocably
as the once clear borders of a city; but what we can learn from
their history is the art of granting a city its character. The
mega-cities of our modern age threaten to separate us from
this legacy. Indeed, for most modern cities, it is difficult to find
a geographical and conceptual center where such a character
could crystallize. But it is not impossible.

"God is in the midst of the city," the psalm tells us (46:5)
—although we modern citizens will see very little in this ancient verse at first glance. It is true that few of us seek the
sacred in the modern city; but more importantly, the assurance with which premodern people spoke of the center (and
borders) of a city is now lost to us. Cities have remained with
us, and they are growing more rapidly than ever before. But
maintaining their special character, or defining it anew, has
become no easier. Quite the opposite, in fact: this task is now
more critical than ever.

EPILOGUE

IN 2011, A GROUP OF American psychologists published a study on the effects of walking through doorways, based on a sample group of sixty participants. The psychologists observed that when people "pass through a doorway to move from one location to another, they forget more information than if they do not make such a shift." They concluded that "walking through doorways serves as an event boundary" that "can reduce the availability in memory for objects associated with the prior event."[1]

Yet doors are not just sites of forgetting (or of "updating one's event model," to use scientific terminology). In fact, when we look at doors and other technologies of enclosure from historical and anthropological perspectives, it becomes clear that they have also always required people to remember—in particular, to remember the many daily conventions and norms associated with doorways: we must remember to lock our doors, to wait before passing through someone else's door, and to pay attention to the message signaled by the door's position (open, closed, or perhaps just ajar). As this book has shown, the situation was in certain ways even more complex during premodern times, and three reasons for this stand out.

First of all, security concerns were more pressing then. Today, most of us deposit our financial assets and savings in the bank, but the vast majority of premodern people had no choice but to store these at home, not least because private banking, in the modern sense, did not exist. The resulting anxiety was reflected in deep-rooted suspicion and sometimes outright fear of open doors, as amply documented in sources from that period and in the draconian punishments imposed for the unlawful duplication of keys. Throughout the premodern era, male householders carefully guarded what they claimed was their natural and exclusive right to carry the keys to the house and its rooms. To extend this right to one's wife, or to rescind it, had concrete ramifications not only for the day-to-day operation of the household, but also for the wife's legal status. Of course, the concept of *potestas clavium* also played a crucial role in the political and religious realms, but despite obvious differences, we observe a common thread running through all: that behind the "power of the keys" lay the implication that "keys mean power" (to recall Dürer's words). Charged as they were with ideas of power and control, technologies such as keys and locks were a source of great pride among Europeans. There was, in fact, a long tradition of imagining and describing non-European societies as clueless—or careless—about the use of keys and locks. What is more, Europeans derived a sense of civilizing superiority from their own expertise with these technologies. Tellingly, keys and locks were among the objects that early modern Europeans took along on their global voyages of discovery, not least to impress the foreign societies they would encounter.

The second reason why doors and gateways received more attention than today is because they were often designed in a highly individualized fashion reflecting the purpose, and aspirations, of the building as a whole. Unlike today, the doors of private residences were not standardized or mass produced. To the contrary, people paid a great deal of care and attention to the design and general appearance of front doors and portals. Entrances were decorated with ornaments and inscriptions to indicate the social status and honor of the residents, to extol the "honor" of the house, or to proclaim the residents' religious views. Religious symbolism was even more prominent at the entrances of sacred buildings, especially churches, and it is impossible to understand their lavish design and decoration without knowing the theological significance and the manifold religious rituals and rites of passage associated with these parts of the "house of God."

Third, doorways and gateways were omnipresent in the premodern city in a way that is no longer the case in modern urban spaces. This included, for instance "gates of honor," erected for special political or religious occasions both within and outside the city; gates enclosing religious and social enclaves and minorities inside the city; and finally, the gates to the city itself. As we have seen, the imposing city gates were prime emblems of civic identity and city power, while also serving as fiscal arteries and social filters. Despite differences of scale, each of these sites of passage called for special attention, and ego-documents such as travelogues and diaries make it clear that early modern people paid a great deal of attention to them. As we have seen, people knew how to *read* doors. This involved both the ability to draw conclusions from the design and decoration of a particular door, and to read the signs that were temporarily affixed to it—whether written texts, such as an announcement or a pasquil, or defamatory objects. Indeed, it is no exaggeration to say that doors, especially those of public and religious buildings, were among the most important signboards of the early modern city. Against this backdrop, it is perfectly plausible that one of the most famous episodes of early modern history—namely, Luther's posting (or, as I have suggested, *pasting*) of the Ninety-Five Theses on the church doors of Wittenberg—did in fact occur. Ironically, the more circumstantial evidence emerges to support the truth of this iconic episode, the less revolutionary the event appears. Indeed, such postings were a perfectly common sight on city doors at the time.

Today, many of the cultural, legal, and political practices that were once associated with doors have fallen into oblivion, even among historians. In the same vein, some of the sites of passage discussed in this book have entirely disappeared from the world we live in, while others that still exist have lost their importance and meaning. In twentieth-century religious architecture, for instance, there is a tendency to deemphasize the prominence of the entrance, which may be "emblematic of the fact that in the modern era, there is no clear path dictated by society towards God and salvation."[2] City gates are another case in point. Where premodern city gates have survived, they have become historic monuments, devoid of any function in the urban spaces that we now prefer to envision and design as borderless. Wherever they have been preserved, city gates—like most other doorways—have long ceased to function as the signboards and hubs of information that they were in the premodern period. This partly has to do with changing attitudes toward the aesthetics of urban space, but also, in the case of churches, with a much less osmotic relation between sacred and secular space than existed in premodernity.

The fact that we pay less attention today—or, at least, less *conscious* attention—to doors also has to do with technological factors. Indeed, on the whole, the entrances that capture our attention—the windows and portals of the digital world—tend to be virtual. Virtual, too, are the keys that unlock these entrances: the ever-multiplying passwords that we need but sometimes fail to memorize. In other words, forgetting and remembering at doors remains a challenge, and in this new virtual world there are also many other challenges—especially regarding issues of access, privacy, and security—that recast and, as it were, transpose the dialectics of openness and closure that runs through the history of the material world we live in. Whether their historical precedents are always recognized is a different question, not least because technology has made it a lot easier for us to block out or overlook the challenges presented by actual, physical doors. In a certain way, opening doors has become too easy. Many public buildings, where large numbers of people enter and leave daily, now have automated doors that open and close almost miraculously, without any need to push, pull, or even touch them. As a result, the precarious and multistage moment of passage—formerly associated with countless superstitious beliefs—is diminished and defused, at least on the surface, by the convenience of automation.

Technological progress has also affected our relation to doors in other ways. Writing in the 1940s, Theodor W. Adorno criticized the way in which technology makes "gestures precise and brutal, and with them men." Significantly, Adorno cites doors as an example: "Technology expels from movements all hesitation, deliberation, civility. It subjects them to the implacable, as it were ahistorical demands of objects. Thus the ability is lost, for example, to close a door quietly and discreetly, yet firmly. Those of cars and refrigerators have to be slammed, others have the tendency to snap shut by themselves, imposing on those entering the bad manners of not looking behind them."[3]

Of course, not everyone would go as far as Adorno, who saw a "violent, hard-hitting, resting jerkiness of Fascist maltreatment" in the kinds of movements that modern technologies demand of us.[4] Yet it is certainly true that the technologization and automation of our everyday lives has led to the disappearance of a wide range of cultural practices that existed for centuries. More specifically, it has leveled the fine nuances that, in the past, accompanied the act of passage. Suffice it to mention the electric buzzer and its shrill monotone, which has replaced the highly differentiated spectrum of knocking practices that existed in premodern Europe.

Still, doors matter. The opening episode of this book ought to remind us of this: when, toward the end of World War I, the

German and Austrian governments ordered the removal of all door knobs, handles, and bolts, the public cried out. In other words, in modern everyday life, doors may be easy to ignore— until we lose control of them. Then it becomes clear that doors have not lost their potential to epitomize individual fears and collective anxieties. On the most immediate level, we speak of the fear of losing our valuables and our privacy; on a more general level, doors have been connected to anxieties of powerlessness, entrapment, and exclusion since time immemorial. And these anxieties extend to the metaphysical. As we have seen, in Western culture, the spiritual drama of salvation and damnation was, for centuries, imagined to unfold at two particular doorways, namely those of heaven and hell.

Today, the number of people aspiring to gain entry to the gates of heaven has shrunk dramatically. According to recent surveys, only 35 percent of Europeans believe in a life after death.[5] Probably even fewer people believe in the centuries-old idea of a guardian standing at the gates of heaven endowed with a special "power of the keys" to grant admission. By contrast, the story of the gate of hell has taken a different, and darker, turn in our modern secular age. For centuries, theologians, writers, and painters imagined the unspeakable suffering taking place behind the gate of damnation. But it was only in the twentieth century that these horrific visions became reality, giving the gate of hell a very concrete form. Above it was written: *Arbeit macht frei.*

ACKNOWLEDGMENTS

While I was researching and writing this book, many people and institutions opened doors for me. The Frontier Fund at the University of Heidelberg and the William F. Milton Fund at Harvard University generously supported my research. Bernard Bailyn, Joseph Connors, Christopher Friedrichs, Deborah Guth, and Daniel Merzel read earlier versions of chapters, and I am much indebted to them — and to the two anonymous reviewers for Yale University Press — for their invaluable suggestions and comments. Thomas Maissen, who also read early drafts, has been an unwavering believer in this project. I am deeply grateful for his support and encouragement.

For advice, leads, and support, I also thank Aysegül Argit, David Armitage, Julien Ayroles, Mario Biagioli, Ann Blair, Jochen Bußmann, Joyce Chaplin, Tom Cohen, Theodor Dunkelgrün, Anthony Grafton, Emily Hauze, Florian Klinger, Joseph Koerner, Samuel Krug, Jeanette Malkin, Charles Marcrum, Lucie Martin, Marc Mudrak, Rohan Murty, Karen Rosenberg, Daniel Smail, Giora Sternberg, Anton Tantner,

Martin Treu, Kerry Wallach, Lina Weber, and Winnie Wong. My thanks also go to the staffs of the libraries and archives on both sides of the Atlantic that allowed me to use their collections, especially the Herzog August Bibliothek Wolfenbüttel and Houghton Library at Harvard.

The Harvard Society of Fellows provided me with an ingenious setting for writing this book. I express my gratitude to the Senior and Junior Fellows, and especially to the Society's chairman, Walter Gilbert, and to its administrators, Kelly Katz and Diana Morse.

Jennifer Banks, my editor at Yale University Press, supported this project with great enthusiasm from the outset. Together with Heather Gold, she expertly shepherded it through the publication process. Sincere thanks also to Jessie Dolch for her meticulous copyediting of the final draft.

This book is dedicated, with love, to my parents, staunch supporters and indefatigable readers.

NOTES

Unless otherwise noted, all translations are my own. All Bible quotations are taken from the King James Version.

Abbreviations

AVB   Archives de la Ville de Bruxelles

CE   *Catholic Encyclopedia.* 15 vols. New York: Appleton, 1907–1912.

DRW   *Deutsches Rechtswörterbuch* (available online: http://www.rzuser.uni-heidelberg.de/~cd2/drw/)

HdA   *Handwörterbuch des deutschen Aberglaubens.* 3rd ed. 10 vols. Berlin: De Gruyter, 2000.

HRG   Handwörterbuch zur deutschen Rechtsgeschichte. 5 vols. Berlin: Schmidt, 1971–1998.

IG   See bibliography, under *Index der Gebodboeken.*

Jurade   See bibliography, under *Inventaire sommaire.*

LexIkon   *Lexikon der christlichen Ikonographie.* 8 vols. Rome: Herder, 1968–1976.

LexMA   *Lexikon des Mittelalters.* 10 vols. Munich: Artemis, 1977–1999.

LexThK   *Lexikon für Theologie und Kirche.* 11 vols. Freiburg im
         Breisgau: Herder, 1993–2001.

NP   New Pauly: Encyclopaedia of the Ancient World/Der
         neue Pauly: Enzyklopädie der Antike. Stuttgart: J. B.
         Metzler, 1996–2003 (online).

SAA   Stadsarchief Antwerpen

TPMA   *Thesaurus proverbiorum medii aevi.* 13 vols. Berlin: De
         Gruyter, 1995–2002.

Introduction

1. For an account by one of the initiators of these measures: Koeth, "Rohstoffbewirtschaftung." See also Wegs, *Österreichische Kriegswirtschaft,* esp. 69–73.

2. Wegs, *Österreichische Kriegswirtschaft,* 73.

3. *Die Enteignung der Türklinken,* 3, 8.

4. *Berliner Lokal-Anzeiger* of 5 July 1918, quoted in ibid., 16. Italics mine.

5. Ibid., 12.

6. Ibid., 14.

7. Wegs, *Österreichische Kriegswirtschaft,* 73.

8. Kafka, *Complete Stories,* 3–4. I have slightly modified the translation.

9. Seligmann, "What Is a Door?," 64, 73. In a similar vein, see also Latour, "Mixing Humans."

10. Kaufmann, "Portes, verrous et clés," 281.

11. Febvre, "Pour l'histoire d'un sentiment."

12. Keane, "Architectural Criteria," 3. In the United States, the earliest emergency-exit regulation dates to the nineteenth century and was a response to the Great Fire of Boston (1872). See Bukowski, *Emergency Egress,* 1. The Triangle Shirtwaist Factory fire in New York (1911) prompted further regulation. I am indebted to the anonymous reviewer for pointing this out.

13. Luke 13:22–30.

14. Bachelard, *Poetics of Space*, 222.

15. Seligmann, "What Is a Door?," 74.

16. Simmel, "Brücke und Tür," 58.

17. Cassirer, *Essay on Man*, 32; Cassirer, "Begriff der symbolischen Form," 79. The English translation is from Krois, *Cassirer*, 50.

18. Unwin, *Doorway*, 25; Lefebvre, *Production of Space*, 209.

19. Le Goff, *Birth of Purgatory*, 4. On door symbolism, see, e.g., Biraghi, *Porta multifrons*; Siegert, "Türen."

20. Seligmann, "What Is a Door?," 55.

21. Ibid., 63.

22. Bourdieu, "Family Spirit," esp. 65. See also Cassirer, *Philosophy of Symbolic Forms*, 2:103.

23. Gennep, *Rites of Passage*, 20.

24. Turner, "Passages, Margins, and Poverty," 232.

25. Gennep, *Rites of Passage*, 20.

26. Gaidoz, *Vieux rite médical*, esp. 78–79.

27. Gennep, *Rites of Passage*, 20.

28. See esp. Trumbull, *Threshold Covenant*; Turner, "Passages, Margins, and Poverty"; Frake, "How to Enter a Yakan House." See also Heidemann's study of the so-called *Akka Bakka*, the small ritual gates that to this day play an important role in the religious and political life of different ethnic groups in southern India: Heidemann, *Akka Bakka*.

29. Benjamin, *Passagen-Werk*, O2a, 1.

30. On Benjamin's fascination with threshold experiences and threshold sites, see Menninghaus, *Schwellenkunde*, 26–58.

31. Benjamin, *Passagen-Werk*, O2a, 1.

32. Selle, *Eigenen vier Wände*, 34; de Botton, *Architecture of Happiness*, 247.

33. Benjamin, *Passagen-Werk*, C5a, 2.

34. Bachelard, *Poetics of Space*, 17.

35. Simmel, *Brücke und Tür,* 58. I have slightly modified the translation.

36. Lefebvre, *Production of Space,* 209.

37. Camesasca, *History of the House,* 401; Goitein, *Mediterranean Society,* 4:118.

38. Thébert, "Private Life," 387–389

39. Seligmann, "What Is a Door?," 69.

40. Schmitt, "Schwelle," 340.

41. Kant, *Theoretical Philosophy,* 103. The essay is titled "The False Subtlety of the Four Syllogistic Figures Demonstrated by M. Immanuel Kant." Italics in the original.

42. Leucht, *Tractatus novus,* 5.

43. Ibid.

44. Seligmann, "What Is a Door?," 55.

45. Selle, *Eigenen vier Wände,* 33; Selbmann, *Kulturgeschichte,* 11.

46. Oxford English Dictionary online, s.v. "window."

47. Siegert, "Türen," 167.

48. Keane, "Architectural Criteria," 4. On problems caused by revolving doors, see also Weilenmann, Normark, and Laurier, "Managing Walking Together."

49. A considerable corpus of studies now exists on this theory, and it would be beyond the scope of this book to give a comprehensive review of the literature. Suffice it to point to the essay in which the broken windows theory made its first appearance: Wilson and Kelling, "Broken Windows."

Chapter 1. "I Am the Door"

1. See, e.g., Steward and Cowan, Introduction, 15–17; Sennett, *Flesh and Stone,* esp. 15.

2. Bocchi, *Beauties.* See also the editors' introduction, 3.

3. Ibid., 28, 187, 192, 103, 127, 234, 239, 33.

NOTES TO PAGES 26–34

4. Deuchler, "Offene Türen," 80; Cahn, *Romanesque Wooden Doors*, 2–3.

5. Guldan, "Monster-Portal."

6. See esp. in the biblical account of Jacob's dream (Gen 28:17). For further biblical references to this topos, see LexIkon, s.v. "Himmelstor." For other precedents from the literature of the ancient Middle East and Greece, see also Goldman, *Sacred Portal*, esp. 78.

7. Luke 13:22–30. See also Matt 7:12–14.

8. Isidor, *Etymologies*, III.40.

9. Wildvogel and von Calm, *Janus patulcius*, 14.

10. On the Christian iconography of the gates of heaven, see esp. LexIkon, s.v. "Himmelstor."

11. Delumeau, *History of Paradise*, esp. 29–32.

12. Luke 23:43. For the linking of this verse to the "earthly paradise," see Delumeau, *History of Paradise*, 29.

13. See esp. Le Goff, *Birth of Purgatory*. Cf. also LexMA, s.v. "Fegfeuer."

14. Le Goff, *Birth of Purgatory*, 32.

15. *Purgatory*, 9.130.

16. *Inferno*, 3.1–3; 9.

17. Köhler, "Schlüssel des Petrus," 222.

18. On this idea, see esp. Guldan, "Monster-Portal."

19. Quoted in Schmidt, *Iconography of the Mouth of Hell*, 34.

20. Mazur, *Hinges*, chap. 1.

21. Luther, *Werke*, 37:65–66 (sermons of 1533/34).

22. Le Goff, *Birth of Purgatory*, 44–45.

23. For the following, see esp. *New Catholic Encyclopedia*, s.vv. "Limbo," "Descent of Christ into Hell."

24. Mazur, *Hinges*, chap. 1; Schmidt, *Iconography of the Mouth of Hell*, 153.

25. "Nicht allein Natürlichen sondern auch mitgetheilten göttlichen Eigenschafften," says the seventeenth-century Lutheran theologian David Auerbach in his *Falscher Calvinischer Schlüssel*, M ii.

26. Quoted in Le Goff, *Birth of Purgatory*, 162.

27. "Duae enim sunt portae, porta paradisi, et porta Ecclesiae: per portam Ecclesiae intramus in portam paradisi." (Pseudo-)Augustine, *Sermo CLIX: De Pascha (1), Patrologia Latina*, vol. 39, col. 2059.

28. Abegg, "Symbolik und Nutzung"; Götz, "Bildprogramme," esp. 24–25; LexIkon, s.v. "Tor—Tür." For an overview of the technical execution, see the contributions to Kasarska, *Mise en œuvre*. With respect to Byzantine architecture: Frazer, "Church Doors," esp. 162.

29. Similarly in John 10:7: "Verily, verily, I say unto you, I am the door of the sheep."

30. Bucer, *Deutsche Schriften*, 4:170.

31. Reinle, *Zeichensprache der Architektur*, 246, 253; Sauer, *Symbolik des Kirchengebäudes*, 119, 296–297; Schwarz, *Sachgüter und Lebensformen*, 76.

32. Klappheck, "Vom Sinn des Tores," 110.

33. Frazer, "Church Doors," 162.

34. Ezek 44:1–3.

35. Reinle, *Zeichensprache der Architektur*, 247, 254–255; Abegg, "Symbolik und Nutzung," 154; Pouchelle, *Body and Surgery*, 148.

36. Sauer, *Symbolik des Kirchengebäudes*, 4.

37. Fassler, "Adventus at Chartres"; Cahn, *Romanesque Wooden Doors*, esp. 2–3.

38. Jung-Inglessis, "Porta Santa."

39. "[In die Kapelle] gen czway türlein. Wer da hin kumpt mi warer rew und andacht und get durch die czwey türlein, der ist ledig aller seiner sünd." Quoted in Hippler, *Reise nach Jerusalem*, 262.

40. Laube, *Reliquie zum Ding*, 88; Schmitt, "Schwelle," 343.

41. Teut, "Türen," 91.

42. Simson, *Gothic Cathedral*, 113, 155.

43. Simmel, "Brücke und Tür," 59.

44. The Latin original reads: "Portarum quisquis attollere quaeris honorem, / Aurum nec sumptus, operis mirare laborem, / Nobile claret opus, sed opus quod nobile claret / Clarificet mentes, ut eant

per lumina vera / Ad verum lumen, ubi Christus janua vera." Suger, *Abbot Suger*, 46–49.

45. Deuchler, "Offene Türen," 80; Schütte, "Stadttor und Hausschwelle," 317.

46. Ni caveas crimen caveas contingere limen / nam regina coeli vult sine sorde coli." Cahn, *Romanesque Wooden Doors*, 156.

47. Abegg, "Symbolik und Nutzen," 154.

48. Isidore of Seville, *Etymologies*, VII.12.32–33.

49. For the following: Dibie, *Ethnologie de la porte*, 74–76; Vikan and Nesbitt, *Security in Byzantium*, 8; LexThK, s.v. "Ostiarier"; CE, s.v. "Porter."

50. Benedict of Nursia, *Rule of Saint Benedict*, no. 66. See also Zur Nieden, *Alltag der Mönche*, 260, 385.

51. See also Isidore of Seville's attempt to trace them back to biblical times: *Etymologies*, VII.12.32–33.

52. Erler, *Straßburger Münster*; Reinle, *Zeichensprache der Architektur*, esp. 278; Deimling, "Mittelalterliche Kirchenportal"; Abegg, "Symbolik und Nutzung"; Verzar, "Medieval Passageways."

53. Erler, *Straßburger Münster*, 44–45.

54. Theophilus, *On Divers Arts*, I.20; Deimling, "Ad Rufam Ianuam," esp. 507.

55. Deimling, "Mittelalterliche Kirchenportal," 325–326.

56. Sander, "Urban Elites," 248–250. I would like to thank the author for sending me a copy of his dissertation.

57. See esp. Wildvogel and von Calm, *Janus patulcius*.

58. Chaucer, *Canterbury Tales*, 1:24. My thanks to the anonymous reviewer who pointed to this line.

59. Reinle, *Zeichensprache der Architektur*, 279, Deimling, "Mittelalterliche Kirchenportal," 326.

60. Muir, *Ritual in Early Modern Europe*, 48.

61. My description of this rite follows the tenth-century account of Regino of Prüm, *Sendhandbuch*, 2.418. There were variations in the way that this rite was carried out elsewhere and in later periods, but

the door almost always played an essential role. See Turner, "Passages, Margins, and Poverty," 232.

62. Thus Regino in his *Libri duo de synodalibus causis et disciplinis ecclesiasticis.* See Regino of Prüm, *Sendhandbuch,* 1.295.

63. Deimling, "Mittelalterliche Kirchenportal," 324. On similar rites of repentance in front of church portals: Abegg, "Symbolik und Nutzung," 155–156; these rituals took place even when it was clear that the penitent could not avoid capital punishment. See, e.g., Davis, *Return of Martin Guerre,* 91, 93.

64. Hahnloser, "Urkunden," 135.

65. Machiavelli, *Florentine Histories,* 328.

66. Cox, *Sanctuaries and Sanctuary Seekers,* 107, 282–283.

67. Härter, "Kirchenasyl"; Smail, "Hatred," 97.

68. "[I]psius ecclesie januis et anulo inherentem inde avulserunt, ipsius ecclesie immunitatem frangendo multipliciter, et violando inpudenter." Quoted in Hahnloser, "Urkunden," doc. 9. For further cases, see ibid., 135–140.

69. Cox, *Sanctuaries and Sanctuary Seekers,* 211–212. A number of similar cases are documented in Hahnloser, "Urkunden," 135–140.

70. Keil, "Orte," 177.

71. Grimm, *Deutsche Rechtsalterthümer,* 1:242–243.

72. Wiesner, *Bann,* 89.

73. Acosta, *Exemplar humanae vitae,* 26–27. I have slightly modified the English translation.

74. Heyne, *Deutsche Wohnungswesen,* 78; Cahn, *Romanesque Wooden Doors,* 145.

75. Alberti, *Art of Building,* 29, 293.

76. Burke, *European Renaissance,* 181–182; Goldthwaite, *Building of Renaissance Florence,* 14; D'Evelyn, *Venice and Vitruvius,* chap. 3.

77. Serlio, *On Architecture,* 2:459–512.

78. Editors' introduction to Serlio, *On Architecture,* 2:xxxvii.

79. Scamozzi, *L'idea della architettura,* 1:318.

80. Pouchelle, *Body and Surgery,* 147.

81. Schwemmer, *Tore und Türen*, 106.

82. Sandrart, *Teutsche Academie*, 1:18; see also more generally Schwemmer, *Tore und Türen*, 108, as well as Burroughs, *Italian Renaissance Palace Facade*, esp. 13.

83. Cohen and Cohen, "Open and Shut," esp. 70.

84. Decembrio, *Vita Philippi Mariae Tertij*, chap. 49.

85. Völkel, *Schloßbesichtigungen*, 37. On the public accessibility of early modern castles, ibid., esp. 8, 15.

86. Quoted in Thornton, *Italian Renaissance Interior*, 30.

87. Sandrart, *Teutsche Academie*, 1:17–18.

88. Montaigne, *Travel Journal*, 1138.

89. A detailed discussion, much in the taste of baroque classicism, of how to design a stairway to complement the particular effect of a given door can be found in *Untersuchungen über den Charakter der Gebäude*, 71–76. "Dramaturgy of the stairway": Schütte, "Stadttor und Hausschwelle," 311; Müller, *Fürstenhof*, 70.

90. See, e.g., Rohr, *Einleitung zur Ceremoniel-Wissenschaft*, 72–73; also: Druffner, "Gehen und Sehen bei Hofe," esp. 544, 546; Müller, *Fürstenhof*, 40.

91. Bernardino da Siena, *Sermons*, 146.

92. Hall, *Art of divine meditation*, 102–103.

93. Rossi, *Studio d'architettura civile*.

94. *Untersuchungen über den Charakter der Gebäude*, 65–66: "Das erste, worauf wir bey der Thür sehen wollen, soll ihre Größe seyn . . . , weil sich aus der Größe der Thür ihre Bestimmung, und hieraus der Charakter des Gebäudes am leichtesten beurtheilen läßt."

95. Dibie, *Ethnologie de la porte*, 94, 129.

96. Schwemmer, *Tore und Türen*, 117.

97. Wolf, *Albrecht Dürer*, 13; see also Neuner, *Signatur bei Albrecht Dürer*, 12, 15, 104. I would like to thank Dr. Neuner for making his unpublished study available to me.

98. Wotton, *Elements of Architecture*, 119. See also Peck, "Building, Buying, and Collecting," 269.

99. Brown, *Private Lives,* 54; Schwarz, *Sachgüter und Lebensformen,* 39; Angermann, *Volksleben,* 242.

100. Schmidt and Dirlmeier, "Geschichte des Wohnens," 291; Mare, "Domestic Boundary," 125.

101. Angermann, *Volksleben,* 239–241.

102. Ibid., 242. For rural areas, see also Montaigne's observations from his journey through Bavaria and Tyrol: *Travel Journal,* 1093, 1111. See also Roche, *History of Everyday Things,* 85.

103. Rohr, *Einleitung zur Ceremoniel-Wissenschaft,* 395.

104. Tantner, *Ordnung der Häuser;* Tantner, *Hausnummer.*

105. Sturm, *Erste Ausübung,* 30.

106. Comenius, *Porta linguarum,* 109.

107. Füssel, "Umstrittene Grenzen," 177.

108. Herte, *Lutherkommentare,* 317.

109. Angermann, *Volksleben,* 126–128.

110. Ibid., 241–242, 253. The quotation is on p. 241; the original reads: "Ach Godt, wo gheit et ihmer zo, das sie mich hassen und ich Ihnen nichtes thu, und mir vergönnen und doch nicht geben!"

111. Wildvogel and von Calm, *Janus patulcius,* 14, 80.

112. The literature on this subject is vast. Suffice it to mention the following important contributions: Ariès and Duby, *History of Private Life*; Webb, *Privacy and Solitude;* Melville and von Moos, *Öffentliche und Private;* Shaw, "Construction." The question of privacy and its historical development is also an important aspect of the discussion on whether or not there was a "civilizing process" in the transition from early modernity to modernity. On this see esp. Elias, *Civilizing Process,* and the rebuttal in Duerr, *Mythos.*

113. On the concept of domestic peace in antiquity, see esp. Trabandt, "Kriminalrechtliche Schutz."

114. See esp. Osenbrüggen, *Hausfrieden;* Schmidt-Voges, "'Si domus in pace sunt . . .'"; Mohrmann, *Volksleben in Wilster,* 269–282.

115. Carpzov, *Practica,* I.39 (p. 167); Beyer and von Ende, *Dissertatio Iuris Gentium et Germanici,* chap. 43; Osenbrüggen, *Hausfrieden,* 59.

116. Osenbrüggen, *Hausfrieden,* 11–12.

117. Schmidt-Voges, "Nachbarn," 414; Kramer, "Herausfordern," 126.

118. Zedler, *Grosses vollständiges Universal-Lexicon,* s.v. "Tür," col. 1845. Similarly: Krünitz, *Oekonomische Encyklopädie,* s.v. "Thür," 590.

119. Dülmen, *Kultur und Alltag,* 1:12.

120. Carpzov, *Practica,* III.109 (p. 99); *Die Goslarischen Statuten,* 315.

121. Blackstone, *Commentaries,* 4:223.

122. For civil cases: Damhouder, *Praxis rerum civilium,* chap. 59, esp. p. 97; on the greater extent of authorities' right of entry in criminal cases: ibid., chap. 15 ("De citatione reali, id est captura"); Blackstone, *Commentaries,* 4:223 (quotation). See also Osenbrüggen, *Hausfrieden,* 37; on precedents in medieval common law, see also *Die Goslarischen Statuten,* 387–388.

123. Wildvogel and von Calm, *Janus patulcius,* 80; Krünitz, *Oekonomische Encyklopädie,* s.v. "Thür," 590.

124. Weinsberg, *Buch Weinsberg,* 5:67–68.

125. Beyer and von Ende, *Dissertatio Iuris Gentium et Germanici,* chap. 36.

126. Osenbrüggen, *Hausfrieden,* 60–96.

127. Schütte, "Stadttor und Hausschwelle," 315.

128. Osenbrüggen, *Hausfrieden,* 87.

129. Ibid., 81–96.

130. For Italy: Cohen and Cohen, "Open and Shut"; Burkart, *Stadt der Bilder,* 38, 71; for Germany: Schmidt-Voges, "Nachbarn im Haus," 422; for England: Vickery, *Behind Closed Doors,* 29.

131. Klapisch-Zuber, *Maison et le nom;* Brunner, "'Ganze Haus.'"

132. "[D]ictam domum coeperunt illamque de residuo quod ibi erat disrobaverunt atque distruxerunt, vastantes et distruentes mazis ferreis portas et fenestras marmoreas, . . . prout de praesenti videri potest, quod nullum ei ostium sive fenestra relicta est." Infessura, *Diario*, 161.

133. Bertelli, *King's Body*, 57; Ginzburg, "Saccheggi rituali."

134. IG (1592), 290.

135. Schudt, *Jüdische Merckwürdigkeiten*, bk. 5, 351–352. See also Stern, *Hoffude*, 34.

136. *Hebräische Berichte*, esp. 409 [Hebrew section].

137. For instance, during the 1548 revolt of the citizens of Bordeaux against King Henri II, as reported by the contemporary Kirchhof, *Wendunmuth*, 2:86.

138. On the house as an "actor": D'Evelyn, *Venice and Vitruvius*, 22; see also Burkart, *Stadt der Bilder*, 38, 71.

139. Wildvogel and von Calm, *Janus patulcius*, 82–83.

140. Zedler, *Grosses vollständiges Universal-Lexicon*, s.v. "Siegelwachs." For instances of seal-breaking in late medieval Marseilles: Smail, "Enmity," 28–29.

141. Zedler, *Grosses vollständiges Universal-Lexicon*, s.v. "Tür," col. 1846; Wildvogel and von Calm, *Janus patulcius*, 113–114.

142. Pinto, *Traité de la circulation*, 314. My thanks to Lina Weber for this reference.

143. Grimm, *Deutsche Rechtsalterthümer*, 1:239–240, 282; Amira and von Schwerin, *Rechtsarchäologie*, 88; Hahnloser, "Urkunden," 131–135.

144. See, e.g., the sixteenth-century chronicle of Hermann Weinsberg, *Buch Weinsberg*, 5:24.

145. My thanks to Tom Cohen for sharing with me his unpublished translation of this source. This legal procedure of seizing control of a village by opening its gates is depicted in a fresco in the Sala del Mappamondo of Siena's Palazzo Pubblico that dates to the first decades of the fourteenth century. This fresco, thought to show the

taking of the Castle of Giuncarico, was rediscovered only in 1980 and is now attributed to Duccio.

146. This summary is based on contemporary accounts published by both parties: *Kurtzer Bericht,* esp. C^{i-iv}; and *Begründeter Gegen-Bericht,* esp. E^{iv-v}, F^i.

147. Wildvogel and von Calm, *Janus patulcius,* 82; Grimm, *Deutsche Rechtsalterthümer,* 1:239–240; Spohn, "Herein!," 138; HdA, s.v. "Tür," col. 1187; Krünitz, *Oekonomische Encyklopädie,* s.v. "Tür," S. 591–592; and on the aspect of *Fraisch,* esp. Oelze, "Fraischpfänder" (with an illustration of a surviving wood chipping from eighteenth-century Hohenlohe).

148. Mercier, *Contributions directes;* Wagner, *Specielle Steuer-lehre,* esp. 462–465.

149. Fiamma, *Chronica Mediolani,* 711.

150. Bacon, *Works,* 4:8.

151. For a general discussion of analogies between Gothic architecture and Scholastic theology, see esp. Panofsky, *Gothic Archi-tecture.*

152. Sherman, "On the Threshold."

153. Comenius, *Porta linguarum,* n.p.

154. Reference is to the first English edition (1617): Bathe, *Ianua linguarum.*

155. Blount, *Janua scientiarum.*

156. Hall, *Art of divine meditation,* 102–103.

157. On this phenomenon, see esp. Schramm, Schwarte, and La-zardzig, *Collection;* Friedrich, *Buch als Theater.*

158. Sherman, "On the Threshold"; Burke, *European Renais-sance,* 179. With an emphasis on books printed in France: Dibie, *Eth-nologie de la porte,* 139–143.

159. Comenius, *Porta linguarum,* n.p.

160. Blair, *Too Much to Know.*

161. Wellisch, "'Index,'" 149; Wellisch, "Oldest Printed Indexes." See also Blair, *Too Much to Know,* 53, 137–144.

162. In the case of Comenius's *Porta linguarum*, "a key fitted to open the gate of tongues" (i.e., an index) was published separately by Wye Saltonstall in 1634: Saltonstall, *Clavis ad portam*. Buyers would often bind the *Clavis* together with the *Porta*. For other instances of early modern authors (and readers) organizing their books by adding "keys," see, e.g., Brayman Hackel, *Reading Material*, 173–174. Other terms used to designate indexes were the Latin terms *tabula* and *repertorium* (and their vernacular counterparts). Wellisch, "Oldest Printed Indexes," 80–81.

Chapter 2. The Power of the Keys

1. Boyle, *The Usefulness of Natural Philosophy* (1671), in *Works*, 6:522. See also Chaplin, *Subject Matter*, 307.

2. Humboldt, *Wiederentdeckung*, 46. See also Eibach, "Offene Haus," 622.

3. Eibach, "Offene Haus," 624, 649. For a similar take on open doors (and on keys and their emergence): Dibie, *Ethnologie de la porte*, 93, 96.

4. A fine study of the history of keys and locks is Eras, *Locks and Keys;* on antiquity, esp. 20–21, 34. However, it focuses primarily on their technological history and does not seek to explore their cultural history. For pictures of keys from Ancient Egypt and Rome, see ibid., tables 26, 30.

5. Ibid., 29; Camesasca, *History of the House*, 402.

6. Artemidorus, *Interpretation of Dreams*, 236.

7. Thébert, "Private Life," 354.

8. NP, s.v. "Lock; Key (Celtic-Germanic World)."

9. Eras, *Locks and Keys*, table 28.

10. Ibid., 59, also 51–52; Schwarz, *Sachgüter und Lebensformen*, 39.

11. Gude, *Deutsche Schlosserhandwerk*, 3.

12. Krafft, *Reisen und Gefangenschaft,* 116; Rauwolf, *Aigentliche beschreibung,* 27. Documents found in the Cairo Genizah also indicate that traditionally "locks of the doors were made of wood": Goitein, *Mediterranean Society,* 4:61.

13. Kilian, "Wohnen im frühen Mittelalter," 52.

14. Vikan and Nesbitt, *Security in Byzantium,* 8.

15. Vickery, *Behind Closed Doors,* 38.

16. Eibach, "Offene Haus," 652–653; Vickery, *Behind Closed Doors,* 30.

17. Contamine, "Peasant Hearth," 499; La Roncière, "Tuscan Notables," 189; Allen, *Locksmith Craft,* 111.

18. Montaigne, *Travel Journal,* 1138.

19. The quotation is from an Englishman's account of his travels in the county of Essex (1765). Quoted in Vickery, *Behind Closed Doors,* 42. See also Roche, *History of Everyday Things,* 85.

20. "Il fait bon fermer son huys Quant la nuyt est venue." TPMA, 10:183.

21. "Mi puerta cerrada, mi cabeza guardada." Ibid.

22. Ibid., 12:58. Similar complaints about beggars and other poor people "who come to the doors in large numbers" are recorded in the sixteenth-century diaries of Hermann Weinsberg: *Buch Weinsberg,* e.g., 4:142. In Jewish sources, too, the house door is frequently mentioned as a place where one meets beggars. Neuman, "Motif-Index," 830, 836.

23. Quoted in Contamine, "Peasant Hearth," 499.

24. Eibach, "Offene Haus," 623.

25. Ekirch, *At Day's Close,* 36–38.

26. La Roncière, "Tuscan Notables," 191.

27. Quoted in Bonfil, *Jewish Life,* 90.

28. Certaldo, *Libro di buoni costumi,* 86.

29. Ibid., 114.

30. Comenius, *Porta linguarum,* 110.

31. Ekirch, *At Day's Close*, 91.

32. Boccaccio, *Decameron*, VII.5.

33. In a sense, this is similar to a situation well known to modern airplane travelers: nearly all passengers know that their seatbelts have to be buckled at takeoff and do so without being prompted. Yet the back of every seat has a pocket that contains detailed instructions for fastening the seatbelt, and crewmembers instruct the passengers orally as well.

34. Pepys, *Diary*, 1 September 1662.

35. Ibid., 24 July 1661; 8 September 1661; 12 April 1667; 11 May 1667.

36. Weinsberg, *Buch Weinsberg*, 5:186. On Weinsberg and his difficult relations with his relatives, see also Lundin, *Paper Memory*.

37. Pope, *Selected Poetry*, 167.

38. HdA, s.v. "Tür," col. 1193, 1206.

39. Ibid., col., 1201. See also Ginzburg, *Night Battles;* and Ekirch, *At Day's Close*, 98–100; Mandrou, *Introduction à la France moderne*, 83–84; Davis, *Society and Culture*, 158.

40. Wildvogel and von Calm, *Janus patulcius*, 27; see also Schivelbusch, *Disenchanted Night*, 81 (with respect to major cities like Paris and Vienna).

41. IG (1625), 41.

42. Tlusty, "'Privat' oder 'öffentlich'?," 66–67; Hanawalt, "Contested Streets," 152; Roche, *History of Everyday Things*, 113.

43. Frugoni, *Day*, 6, 183.

44. Ekirch, *At Day's Close*, 79.

45. Pepys, *Diary*, 11 September 1663.

46. Yaari, *Zichronot Eretz Yisra'el*, 1:121–127.

47. Crete under Venetian rule: Jacoby, "Agent juif," 86; Lyon: Zeller, *Relations de cohabitation*, 15, 36, 75; Paris: Trébuchet, "Recherches sur l'éclairage," 6.

48. *Jurade*, 5:303–304.

49. Hale, *Renaissance Europe*, 41; La Roncière, "Tuscan Notables," 189; Mandrou, *Introduction à la France moderne*, 83, Hanawalt, "Contested Streets," 152.

50. With respect to the Ancien Régime in France: Fabre, "Families," 550.

51. See the excerpt from Laukhard's autobiography in Lahnstein, *Report einer "guten alten Zeit,"* 49.

52. Silesia: *Sammlung der wichtigsten*, 2:38; Nördlingen: Friedrichs, *Urban Society*, 200.

53. Kilian, "Wohnen im frühen Mittelalter," 52; Blastenbrei, *Kriminalität in Rom*, 181 n58.

54. Vickery, *Behind Closed Doors*, 32; Coke, *Third Part*, 3:64.

55. DRW, s.v. "Schlüssel."

56. Vickery, *Behind Closed Doors*, 31.

57. Trabandt, "Kriminalrechtliche Schutz," 77–79.

58. DRW, s.v. "Schlüssel."

59. Eras, *Locks and Keys*, 101.

60. *Jurade*, 3:318.

61. Holy Roman Empire: Gude, *Deutsche Schlosserhandwerk*, 9; Spain: Tintó Sala, *Història;* Scotland and England: Allen, *Locksmith Craft.* For the case of Nuremberg: Tucher, *Baumeisterbuch*, 96–101.

62. Eibach, "Offene Haus," esp. 626–628.

63. TPMA, 10:183; for the case of medieval London, see Shaw, "Construction."

64. Alberti, *On the Art of Building*, 119–120.

65. Blastenbrei, *Kriminalität in Rom*, 187.

66. In a legal ordinance from the Nördlingen region (1448), quoted in Heidrich, "Grenzübergänge," 17.

67. Vickery, *Behind Closed Doors*, 37; Gläntzer, "Nord-Süd-Unterschiede," 82.

68. This is comparable to the topos of open city gates. As F. Ratté has shown, the fact that gates were often depicted as open in late

medieval art must be seen in a symbolic context and should not be taken as historical evidence. Ratté, "Images of City Gates."

69. Cieraad, "Dutch Windows," 43; Hollander, *Entrance,* esp. 2.

70. Vickery, *Behind Closed Doors,* 30.

71. Brown, *Private Lives,* 24, 265.

72. Quoted in Mare, "Domestic Boundary," 110.

73. Ibid., 117.

74. Hollander, *Entrance,* esp. 163. The symbolic reading of such portrayals of everyday scenes and, more broadly, of Dutch genre paintings has been highlighted by the Dutch art historian Eddy de Jongh. See, e.g., Jongh, "Inleiding." For an overview of this discussion, see also Hecht, "Dutch Seventeenth-Century Genre Painting." For a similar meaning of open doors in southern Europe: Cohen and Cohen, "Open and Shut," 64.

75. Artemidorus, *Interpretation of Dreams,* 99.

76. Song 8:9. On comparison of women with houses (and doors) in rabbinical literature, see Labovitz, *Marriage and Metaphor,* chap. 3, esp. 116, 123.

77. On this idea (along with the midrashic and talmudic references), see Labovitz, *Marriage and Metaphor,* 125.

78. Classen, *Medieval Chastity Belt.*

79. Cohen and Cohen, "Open and Shut," 80; Blastenbrei, *Kriminalität in Rom,* 185.

80. "[W]olle ihm die Hintertür offen stehen lassen." Wildvogel and von Calm, *Janus patulcius,* 133–134.

81. TPMA, 12:58. On the "rhetoric of fortification of chastity" in Baroque convent architecture, see Hills, *Invisible City,* 167.

82. Prov 5:8.

83. Gen 4:7 (Jewish Publication Society translation). On the Christian tradition of seeing doors as "dangerous parts of the house" for women, see also Schroeder, "Rape of Dinah," 783.

84. Boccaccio, *Decameron,* III.10.

85. Gentzkow, *Tagebuch,* 232.

86. *Sammlung der wichtigsten*, 2:38.

87. Quoted in Baskin, "Women and Ritual Immersion," 142.

88. Bernardino da Siena, *Sermons*, 139.

89. Boccaccio, *Decameron*, VII.5; VII.2.

90. Ibid., IV.2; VII.1; VII.7; VII.8; VIII.7; Aretino, *Ragionamento*, 220.

91. Cowan, "Seeing Is Believing."

92. Cervantes, *Don Quixote*, 63. I have slightly modified the translation.

93. Montaigne, *Travel Journal*, 1230; in the early modern Low Countries the situation was similar: Pol, *Burgher and the Whore*, 183.

94. Zedler, *Grosses vollständiges Universal-Lexicon*, s.v. "Tür," col. 1844.

95. "Welche nicht will eine Hure seyn, die gebe nicht den Hurenschein." Quoted in *Sammlung der wichtigsten*, 2:38.

96. La Roncière, "Tuscan Notables," 287.

97. Alberti, *Libri della famiglia*, 257.

98. Schama, *Embarrassment of Riches*, 570–575; Mare, "Domestic Boundary," 117; Hollander, *Entrance*, 180–185. It was only in the eighteenth century that the rooms for domestic work were moved to the rear or side of the house, which in turn led to a "gradual transformation of the *voorhuis* from a multipurpose front room to a mere vestibule." Hollander, *Entrance*, 185.

99. Beckham, "American Front Porch," esp. 74.

100. Ibid., 76.

101. Vickery, *Behind Closed Doors*, 42–43; autobiographical accounts confirm the custom of not giving keys to children and teenagers: Lahnstein, *Report einer "guten alten Zeit,"* 49; Dietz, *Lebenslauf*, 31–32, 91.

102. HRG, s.v. "Schlüsselgewalt (eherechtlich)," cols. 1446–1448. It should be noted that the German term *Schlüsselgewalt* was coined by legal scholars in the nineteenth century, but it is completely in line with premodern legal discourse and its metaphors.

103. HRG, s.v. "Schlüssel," col. 1443.

104. Vickery, *Behind Closed Doors,* 43, 200.

105. As noted, in passing, by Ranum, who does not provide a fuller explanation: Ranum, "Refuges of Intimacy," 217.

106. Vickery, *Behind Closed Doors,* 44.

107. Bodin, *Six Books of the Commonwealth,* 10.

108. Quoted in ibid.

109. One such depiction is Hans Baldung's *Holy Family with five angels* (c. 1507) from the Kisters Collection, Kreuzlingen.

110. See also Schrader, "Master M.Z.'s Embrace," 19.

111. In a sketch for his famous engraving *Melencolia I.* See Winkler, *Zeichnungen Albrecht Dürers,* vol. 3, table XV. In the final version of the engraving one can see a number of keys on a ring attached to the belt of the female figure.

112. For the following: Duwe, *Erzkämmerer,* esp. 21. See also Heinig, "Türhüter."

113. Masters, *Chamberlain,* esp. 11, 67.

114. Alberti, *Art of Building,* 265.

115. HRG, s.v. "Schlüssel," col. 1444.

116. Schütte, "Stadttor und Hausschwelle," 306–307; Trexler, *Public Life,* 310; Hillebrand, *Öffnungsrecht,* 6, 66.

117. HRG, s.v. "Schlüssel," col. 1444.

118. "[D]ie schlüßel in ihre verwaltung und die personen, so sich ihnen die schlüßel zu geben geweigert haben, gewaltiglich darnieder geschlagen und die schlüßel eigens gewalt zu ihren händen genommen." Zorn, *Wormser Chronik,* 234–235.

119. Machiavelli, *Florentine Histories,* VII.26. In Bonn in 1586, a group of dissatisfied citizens requested the keys to the city from the prince-elector-archbishop. This raised the suspicions of the authorities, who ordered the citizens to surrender all their guns. Weinsberg, *Buch Weinsberg,* 3:327.

120. Matt 16:18–19.

121. For the following: Hödl, *Geschichte;* HRG, s.v. "Schlüsselgewalt (kirchlich)."

122. HRG, s.v. "Schlüsselgewalt," col. 1450.

123. Rittgers, *Reformation,* 2.

124. Hödl, *Geschichte,* 1. The use of this metaphor in Matthew can be fully understood only in the context of pre-Christian religious imagery, especially in light of Jewish and Greco-Roman sources. See the various theories presented in Köhler, "Schlüssel des Petrus." On ancient Middle Eastern precedents, see also Goldman, *Sacred Portal,* 78.

125. "Clavis est specialis potestas ligandi et solvendi qua judex ecclesiasticus dignos recipere et indignos excludere debet a regno." Quoted in CE, s.v. "Power of the Keys." See also Hödl, *Geschichte,* 40, 380–382.

126. LexIkon, s.vv. "Schlüssel," "Schlüsselübergabe an Petrus."

127. The connection of these keys to St. Peter was further emphasized by the fact that they were modeled on the key that opened the *confessio* of his tomb in Rome. Vikan and Nesbitt, *Security in Byzantium,* 8.

128. Erasmus, *Julius Excluded.* All quotations are on p. 169.

129. On Luther's familiarity with the dialogue, see the editor's introduction to Erasmus, *Julius Excluded,* 162.

130. Luther, *Von den Schlüsseln,* in *Werke,* 30/2:474.

131. "[N]icht die schlussel der kirchen züm himel, davon Christus redet, sondern Es sind schlussel des Bapsts zum abgrund der hellen." Ibid., 439 (from a first draft of Luther's treatise).

132. "[Z]u zween Dietrichen zu aller Könige Kasten und Kronen [gemacht]." Luther, *Von den Konziliis und Kirchen,* in *Werke,* 50:632.

133. The broadsheet is reproduced in Paas, *German Political Broadsheet,* 2:108.

134. Rittgers, *Reformation,* 218.

135. HRG, s.v. "Schlüsselgewalt," col. 1450.

136. For instance, in a treatise by the Lutheran theologian David Auerbach against the Calvinists (1642): Auerbach, *Falscher Calvinischer Schlüssel*. His starting point is not Matt 16:18–19, but rather Luke 11:52 ("Woe unto you, lawyers! for ye have taken away the key of knowledge: ye entered not in yourselves, and them that were entering in ye hindered"). Evidently indebted to Luther's treatise *Von den Schlüsseln*, Auerbach equates the proper "key of knowledge" with the key to heaven. See esp. his preface (n.p.).

137. Imhof, *Gewonnenen Jahre*, esp. 27.

138. According to the international *Religion Monitor 2008*. For a summary, see Höllinger, "Experience of Divine Presence," table 1. More specific figures can be found on the CD-ROM that accompanies this volume: e.g., the percentage is 33 percent for Germany, 29 percent for France, and 31 percent for Great Britain.

139. Shestov, *Potestas clavium*, 50.

140. Ibid.

141. Ibid.

142. Richard Hakluyt's instructions to the members of the Cathay expedition (1580), in Hakluyt, *Principal Navigations*, 4:147.

143. Forster, *Voyage round the World*, 1:221.

144. The following discussion on Japan draws on Sand, *House and Home*, 341–342; Daniels, *Japanese House*, esp. 61–62; Ueda, *Inner Harmony*, 193–195; Kōichi Isoda, "Dilemma des Wohnbewußtseins," esp. 113; Michiko Meid, "Einfluß westlicher Architektur," 73–79.

145. My thanks to Michael Thornton for detailing the etymology of the word.

146. Sand, *House and Home*, 341–342.

147. Ueda, *Inner Harmony*, 194.

148. Eibach, "Offene Haus," 199.

149. Tanavoli and Wertime, *Locks*.

150. Ibid., 13

151. Ibid., 13, 20.

152. Plato, *Republic*, 3.416d.

153. "Quin bifores quoque facili tractu manus apertiles ac dein sua sponte coeuntes quemvis intromittunt; it nihil usquam privati est." More, *Utopia*, 118.

154. Cited in *Sources of Swiss Anabaptism*, 345.

155. *Japan Opened*, v, and passim.

156. Rowe, *Comparative Analysis*.

157. Weber, *Wirtschaft und Gesellschaft*, 526.

158. Fordham, "Protectionist Empire."

159. In the original, the lines about Europe's gates read: "Die porten Europe offen syndt, / Zu allen sitten ist der vyndt." Brant, *Narrenschiff*, chap. 99.

160. Schiffhauer, "Kriegst die Tür nicht auf."

Chapter 3. "Whence Is That Knocking?"

1. "On passe une porte 400 à 500 fois par jour: Interview with Pascal Dibie," *Libération.fr*, 28 August 2012, http://www.liberation.fr/livres/2012/08/28/dialoguez-avec-l-ethnologue-pascal-dibie_842091.

2. Seligmann, "What Is a Door?," 69.

3. Perrot, "Roles and Characters," 229–231; Rosselin, "Ins and Outs," 53, 56; Selle, *Eigenen vier Wände*, 41.

4. See, e.g., Hüsch, *Türöffnung*, a German manual available in several editions.

5. Selle, *Eigenen vier Wände*, 34: De Botton speaks more broadly of an "anxiety of entering or leaving a house" in Western culture: De Botton, *Architecture of Happiness*, 247.

6. But see, e.g., Perrot, who argues that the "sacrosanct" character of the threshold emerged only in the nineteenth century. Perrot, "Roles and Characters," 231.

7. Garvey, "Domestic Boundaries," 163.

8. Rev 3:20.

9. TPMA, s.v. "Klopfen."

10. Luke 13:25.

11. E.g., Judg 19:22: "certain sons of Belial, beset the house round about, and beat at the door, and spake to the master of the house, the old man, saying, Bring forth the man that came into thine house, that we may know him."

12. *Macbeth*, II.2.

13. *Urkundenbuch der Stadt Basel*, 8:209: "das klein fenster der türen des genanten schlosses, dadurch man pflicht ze sehen, wer da sye."

14. Hillebrand, *Öffnungsrecht*, 59.

15. Boccaccio, *Decameron*, IX.6.

16. Comenius, *Porta linguarum*, 109.

17. Druffner, "Gehen und Sehen," 544.

18. Veyne, "Roman Home," 318.

19. Régnier-Bohler, "Imagining the Self," 331. I have checked the quotation against the original and slightly modified it.

20. Zur Nieden, *Der Alltag der Mönch*, 332, 336.

21. In Italian: "picchiatoio." See Aretino, *Ragionamento*, 118.

22. Damhouder, *Praxis rerum civilium*, chap. 58 (see esp. the illustration on p. 86).

23. "[Q]uam eilens hinunden." Weinsberg, *Buch Weinsberg*, 5:397.

24. *Allgemeines Handbuch der Freimaurerei*, s.v. "Schläge."

25. Aretino, *Ragionamento*, 280: "Mi par sentire sfracassarti la porta . . . dico sfracassare, perché le fanno picchiare con bravaria, per parer di esser bestiali." Translation modified.

26. Rohr, *Einleitung zur Ceremoniel-Wissenschaft*, 77.

27. Krünitz, *Oekonomische Encyklopädie*, s.v. "Klopfer," 647.

28. Spohn, "Herein!," 137.

29. Brown, *Private Lives*, 54.

30. Schwemmer, *Tore und Türen*, 48, 75–76.

31. Hahnloser, "Urkunden," 131–135.

32. See chap. 1.

33. HdA, s.v. "Tür," col. 1188.

34. Hahnloser, "Urkunden"; Spohn, "Herein!," 138.

35. Hahnloser, "Urkunden," 140.

36. "E, quando furono all'uscio della casa sua, missono el capresto nella canpanella dell'uscio, lo tirorono su dicendo: *picchia l'uscio.*" Landucci, *Diario*, 21. In the English edition, the passage is on p. 19. I have, however, slightly modified the translation, especially the rendering of the words "campanella [canpanella] dell'uscio," which was more likely a "door ring" (not a "door-bell"). See Carlo Antonio Vanzon, *Dizionario universale della lingua italiana*, Livorno: Sardi, 1828–1844, s.v. "campana."

37. Bertelli, *King's Body*, 242. For similar rituals involving the desecration of corpses of executed offenders in late medieval Italy, see Dean, *Crime and Justice*, 57–59.

38. Machiavelli, *Florentine Histories*, 329.

39. Jütte, "Defenestration."

40. Quoted in Bertelli, *King's Body*, 241.

41. On the pan-European phenomenon of charivari, or "rough music," see esp. Le Goff and Schmitt, *Charivari*; Thompson, "Rough Music"; for a local case study: Mohrmann, *Volksleben in Wilster*, 271.

42. Roth, "Eastertide Stoning of the Jews"; Nirenberg, *Communities of Violence*, esp. chap. 7.

43. Linnemeier, *Jüdisches Leben im Alten Reich*, 321.

44. Acosta, *Exemplar humanae vitae*, 17. Translation slightly modified.

45. Beik, *Urban Protest*, 96, 107.

46. Similar cases are reported in Moser, "Zur Geschichte der Klöpfelnachtbräuche," 127–128, 130. For a survey of this custom and its abuses, see ibid. as well as Lottes, "Popular Culture," 158–159. The quotation is from Heidrich, "Grenzübergänge," 27. The original reads: "Nachdem in dieser Stadt Nurmberg ein alter aber sehr böser Brauch ist, etlicher jungen Leute von Buben und Meidlein, daß sie jährlich in der Oberstnacht, welche sie Bergnacht zu nennen pflegen,

umb her laufen, und mit Hämmern, Schlegeln und Prügeln den Leuten an die Haußthüren und Läden ungestümiglich und grausam pochen und schlagen, und den geschwind wieder davon laufen und man nicht sehen noch wissen kann, wer dieselben Klopfer gewesen . . . [A]lso ist den 6. Jan. am Oberstag dieses 1616 Jahrs, alß das Klopffen und pochen nicht uffhören wollen, der Oberkellner daselbst by der nacht im unwillen heraußgegangen, und ein meidlein, welches für uber gangen, angetroffen, unnd daselb, weil er vermeint, sie habe angeklopfft, mit einen prügel geschlagen, daß sie blut außgespeiet, und vor todt da gelegen."

47. Heidrich, "Grenzübergänge," 27.

48. Spohn, "Herein!," 142, 146.

49. Benjamin, *Passagen-Werk,* C3, 5.

50. NP, s.v. "Tür," col. 890; Ogle, "House-Door," 251–254.

51. Karant Nunn, *Reformation of Ritual,* 27.

52. See, e.g., Firth's classic study of the Tikopia in the southwestern Pacific: *We, the Tikopia,* 77. For Indonesia and Taiwan: Waterson, *Living House,* 221–223, esp. 221 (colonial prohibitions).

53. Naumov, "Housing the Dead."

54. Ogle, "House-Door," 265.

55. "Reiche Ausbeute."

56. ". . . sub cuiusdam scalae ascensu, quae palatio erat contigua, sepultum est." Paulus Diaconus, *Historia Langobardorum,* II.28.

57. Scribner, "Symbolising Boundaries," 832.

58. Ogle, "House-Door"; Trumbull, *Threshold Covenant;* Gennep, *Rites of Passage;* for a survey see also HdA, s.vv. "Schwelle," "Tür"; specifically with respect to the early modern period: Scribner, "Symbolising Boundaries"; Schütte, "Stadttor und Hausschwelle."

59. Grimm, *Deutsche Rechtsalterthümer,* 1:243; Fischer, *Hauszerstörung,* 54. This seems to have been particularly common in cases of abduction and rape—maybe also a deliberate inversion of the husband's legitimate right to carry his bride over the threshold.

60. HdA, s.v. "Tür," col. 1190.

61. For the following, see Jahn, *Deutschen Opfergebräuche*, 14–18; Andree-Eysn, *Volkskundliches*, 107–108, 111; Schukowitz, "Bauopfer"; HdA, s.v. "Hausopfer"; LexMA, s.v. "Bauopfer."

62. Schütte, "Stadttor und Hausschwelle," 316.

63. Andree-Eysn, *Volkskundliches*, 107–108; Lütolf, *Sagen, Bräuche und Legenden*, 332; Crossman and Casselman, *Annotated Bibliography*, ix.

64. CE, s.v. "consecration."

65. Scribner, "Symbolising Boundaries," 833; HdA, s.v. "Tür," col. 1200; Andree-Eysn, *Volkskundliches*, 72; Cahn, *Romanesque Wooden Doors*, 103–104.

66. Andree-Eysn, *Volkskundliches*, 99–101.

67. Exod 12:11–13, 23. On Christian interest in the biblical story of the blood-marked doorposts, see Cahn, *Romanesque Wooden Doors*, 103.

68. The following from *Encyclopaedia Judaica*, s.v. "Mezuzah."

69. Deut 6:4–9 and 11:13–21.

70. Lipis, *Symbolic Houses*, 63.

71. On the idea of Jews as guardians of secret knowledge, see Jütte, *Age of Secrecy*.

72. See, e.g., Kirchner, *Jüdisches Ceremoniel*, 12–14, here 13: "Die Israeliten schlaffen innerhalb des Hausses in ihren Betten, Gott aber wacht für sie außerhalb desselbigen."

73. Calvin, *Sermons*, 276.

74. Fleming, *Graffiti*, 67.

75. Faber, *Archäologie der Hebräer*, esp. 430.

76. Purchas, *Purchas his Pilgrimage* (London 1613), quoted in Fleming, *Graffiti*, 183.

77. Fleming, *Graffiti*, 65–66 (with a picture of such a wall painting over a fireplace at Feering House in Feering, Essex).

78. For the following: Altmann, *Geschichte*, 199–201.

79. Muchnik, "Secret imposé," 28–29.

80. Cnaan Liphshiz, "Hundreds of Jewish Markings Catalogued in Portuguese Town" *Jewish Telegraphic Agency,* 21 April 2013, http://www.jta.org/2013/04/21/news-opinion/world/hundreds -of-jewish-markings-catalogued-in-portuguese-town.

81. Vickery, *Behind Closed Doors,* 29.

82. HdA, s.v. "Tür," cols. 1195–1199.

83. Included in Carrichter, *Kräuter- und Arzney-Buch,* 265–267.

84. The quotation is from a contemporary eyewitness whose account is reprinted in Lahnstein, *Report einer "guten alten Zeit,"* 64.

85. Quoted in HdA, s.v. "Schwelle," col. 1529.

86. Cohen and Cohen, *Words and Deeds,* 190.

87. Schama, *Embarrassment of Riches,* chap. 6 (quotation at p. 378); see also Mare, "Domestic Boundary," esp. 124.

88. Hollander, *Entrance,* 177.

89. Mare, "Domestic Boundary," 124–125.

90. Schama, *Embarrassment of Riches,* 378.

91. Ibid., 378, 389.

92. Thomas, "Cleanliness and Godliness," 71–72; Biow reaches a similar conclusion for Renaissance Italy: Biow, *Culture of Cleanliness,* esp. 183.

93. Quoted in Vickery, *Behind Closed Doors,* 29.

94. Frugoni, *Day,* 6; Friedman, "Palaces and the Street," 71.

95. Helmont, *Ternary of Paradoxes,* 13.

96. Kühnel, "Alltagsleben," 53; Friedman, "Palaces and the Street," 71.

97. Woolgar, *Senses,* 142.

98. Shalom of Neustadt, *Hilkhot u-minhage,* no. 148.

99. Wildvogel and von Calm, *Janus patulcius,* 68; see also Thomas, "Cleanliness and Godliness," esp. 72.

100. The quotation is from Hall, *Occasional Meditations,* chap. 72 ("Upon the Red Cross on a Door"), p. 161. See also Hale, *Renaissance Europe,* 23; Sturm, *Leben mit dem Tod,* 354.

101. Scotti, *Sammlung der Gesetze*, vol. 1, doc. 103.

102. Schwarz, *Pest in Bremen*, 141.

103. Dumas, "La fenêtre," 160; Sturm, *Leben mit dem Tod*, 354.

104. Mylius, *Corpus constitutionum*, 73–75.

105. Ezek 9:4–6: "but come not near any man upon whom is the mark" (the Hebrew original has תו for the word "mark"). See also Andree-Eysn, *Volkskundliches*, 63, 66; Cahn, *Romanesque Wooden Doors*, 103–104.

106. Pepys, *Diary*, 12 February 1666.

107. See, e.g., *The Miracle of Castel Sant'Angelo* by an anonymous Spanish painter (c. 1500), today in the Museum of Fine Arts in Philadelphia (cat. 798).

108. Schwarz, *Pest in Bremen*, 174.

109. *Jurade*, 3:528.

110. Ibid., 3:552.

111. Ibid., 3:529–530.

112. Boccaccio, Prologue to the *Decameron*. In German lands, too, early modern accounts of plague epidemics highlighted how doors and gates had been transformed into sites associated with danger and death. For a particularly vivid example, see the 1739 account in Lahnstein, *Leben im Barock*, 86–87.

113. *Jurade*, 3:552.

114. Morhard, *Haller Haus-Chronik*, 76. The Frankenstein case soon attracted considerable public attention throughout the Holy Roman Empire: see Janssen, *Geschichte des deutschen Volkes*, 8:460–461. On the specific context of this case, see especially Lambrecht, "'Jagdhunde des Teufels.'"

115. Lambrecht, "'Jagdhunde des Teufels,'" 143; Trachtenberg, *Devil and the Jews*, 107.

116. For the following: Naphy, *Plagues*; Nicolini, *Peste e untori*.

117. Ripamonti, *De peste*, 75: "Maculae erant, sparsim, inaequaliterque manantes, veluti, si quis haustam spongia saniem adspersisset,

impressissetue parieti: & ianuae passim, ostiaque aedium eadem adspergine contaminata cernebantur."

118. Manzoni, *Betrothed*, chaps. 31 and 32. On the historical background of Manzoni's description, see esp. Nicolini, *Peste e untori.*

119. Quoted in Naphy, *Plagues*, 169.

120. Ibid., 200.

121. Ibid., 201.

122. Scribner, "Symbolising Boundaries," 833.

123. Seligmann, "What Is a Door?," 69.

Chapter 4. Reading Doors

1. See esp. Wipfler, "Luthers 95 Thesen," Holsing, "Luthers Thesenanschlag."

2. Moeller, "Thesenanschläge," 9.

3. Among the most important contributions: Iserloh, *Luther zwischen Reform und Reformation;* Bornkamm, *Thesen und Thesenanschlag;* Aland, *Die 95 Thesen.* For a useful introduction to this discussion, see also Ott and Treu, *Luthers Thesenanschlag.*

4. For media coverage on the "rediscovered" Rörer note, see, e.g., Heike Schmoll, "Die Geschichte mit dem Aushang: Ein Fund zum Thesenanschlag Luthers gibt der widerlegten Legende neue Nahrung," *Frankfurter Allgemeine Zeitung*, 14 February 2007; Lothar Müller, "Vom Anschlag zum Antrag: Disputation in Jena—Hat Luther seine Thesen an die Kirchentür genagelt oder nicht?," *Süddeutsche Zeitung*, 21 February 2007.

5. A summary of this argument is in Leppin, "Monumentalisierung Luthers."

6. Ibid., 88–89.

7. Moeller, "Thesenanschläge," 25–29.

8. In the *Urkundenbuch* of the University of Wittenberg, this procedure is described as follows: "Promociones, et disputaciones intimet valvis ecclesiarum feria precedenti, specivocando nomina pro-

motoris, promovendi, presidentis et respondentis." Quoted in Moeller, "Thesenanschläge," 29.

9. Oberman, *Masters of the Reformation*, 149. See also Dingel, "Pruning the Vines," esp. 400.

10. *Epistolae obscurorum virorum*, 48. In the eighteenth century it was also common to affix such citations directly to the door of the student's abode: Wildvogel and von Calm, *Janus patulcius*, 55. See also Moeller, "Thesenanschläge," 29.

11. "Es gefil aber s.g. auch wol, das die arme leute, die also zulifen und die gnade suchten, vor dem betrig Tetzels vorwarnt wurden und die conclusiones, die der Augustinermönch zu Wittenberg gemacht, an vilen ortern angeslagen wurden." Quoted in Leppin, "Monumentalisierung Luthers," 86 n45.

12. "Boeken gemaekt door eenen geheeten broeder Lutherus niet te lesen, verkoopen of daermede om te gaen, vermits deselve de ketterye smaeken, op de confiscatie ende verbeurte van hunne goederen ende nog personelyk te worden gestraft; geene famose libellen oft rondeelen en balladen te schryven, uyt te geven en voor kerkdoren en poorten te slaen en plekken tegens degene die geene Luthersadherenten syn." See IG (1521), 172.

13. There it reads: "Dusse artikel sint . . . an alle kerckdören tho Minden dorch Nicolaum Kragen angeslagen. Hirup he alle papisten binnen efte buten Minden tho eyner apentliken disputation heft gevördert." For more on this episode, and for an edition of Krage's nineteen theses, see Krieg, "Einführung der Reformation in Minden," 49, 106–108 (quotation at p. 106).

14. Stupperich, *Westfälische Reformationsgeschichte*, 84.

15. Dingel, *Pruning the Vines*, 401.

16. Hergenröther, *Handbuch*, 2:596.

17. Kaufhold, "Öffentlichkeit im politischen Konflikt," 437.

18. *Codex Iuris Canonici*, can. 1720, 1721.

19. "[A]ffixis literis ad valvas templi, vel portae curiae, vel civitatis." Thus wrote Damhouder in the chapter "De Citatione in genere"

of his *Praxis rerum civilium*, 92; see also Wunderlich, *Protokollbuch von Mathias Alber*, 2:1305–1306. For England: Ingram, *Church Courts, Sex and Marriage*, 47.

20. Karasek, "Konrad von Weinsberg," 88–89.

21. Kaufhold, "Öffentlichkeit," 453–454.

22. "[Z]wüschen sechs und siben uren vormittag und sunderlich der zitt, als die mess von unser frowen in der stifft Basel wart gesungen, hab ich dickgenanter notarius dise hierinn geschriben appellacion an die porten und thür der erstgenanten stifft offennlich gehefftet und die also gehefftet ein zitt lassen stan in sölicher mass, das die von allen und yeglichen, so denn in oder uss dem selben munster giengen, mocht gesehen und gelesen werden, und dannenthin dieselben appellacion wider abgenomen und ein glöupliche abgeschrifft dahin gehefftet und die lassen stan." *Urkundenbuch der Stadt Basel*, 8:209. See also Abegg, "Symbolik und Nutzung," 156.

23. Hartmann, *Kirche und Kirchenrecht*, 279.

24. Lang, *Ausgrenzung und Koexistenz*, 326.

25. Aretino, *Ragionamento*, 149.

26. Namely Sixtus IV. See Infessura, *Diario*, 157

27. For the following episode: Schulthaiß, *Konstanzer Bistumschronik*, 74–75.

28. Ibid., 74: "das sy solche bullen hinfüro in unsere statt Costantz, noch ouch davernen im bistumb witer nit sollen anschlahen noch verkünden, sunder die abstellen, dan ain stat Costantz sollichs nit erliden mög."

29. A contemporary chronicler records: "appellatio fuit abbreviata et ad multas partes orbis missa, et ostiis maioris ecclesie Pisane . . . appensa et solemniter lecta." Quoted in Miethke, *Politiktheorie im Mittelalter*, 250–252 (quotation on p. 251). See also Wittneben, *Bonagratia von Bergamo*, 291.

30. According to this note, the Prior of Feldbach, a papal loyalist "quibusdam conminacionibus usus abierit, certam cedulam non

autenticam valvis ecclesie Basiliensis affixerit, cujus occasione clerus Basiliensis niteretur a divinis cessare." *Urkundenbuch der Stadt Basel,* 8:488. On the context, see also Burckhardt, *Erzbischof Andreas von Krain,* esp. 36, 48.

31. Brunner, "Inszenierung und Öffentlichkeit," 189.

32. Keil, "Orte der jüdischen Öffentlichkeit," 177.

33. Zimmer, *Jewish Synods in Germany,* 194; Keil, "Orte der jüdischen Öffentlichkeit," 177.

34. Bach, *Jacob Bernays,* 28.

35. See, e.g., the contributions to Coster and Spicer, *Sacred Space in Early Modern Europe,* esp. the chapter by Beat Kümin; see also Diedrichs, "Wahrhehmung des mittelalterlichen Kirchenraums"; also Erler, *Straßburger Münster,* esp. 1. On synagogues as a space for sociability and business, see Wiedl, "Jews and the City," 284–285.

36. Weinsberg, *Buch Weinsberg,* 4:183–184.

37. Deimling, "Das mittelalterliche Kirchenportal," 326–327 (with illustration). For similar cases from other cities, see Erler, *Straßburger Münster,* 29.

38. Kühnel, "Sachkultur," 25. Endres Tucher, the chief building official of fifteenth-century Nuremberg, describes how municipal announcements were read out from the pulpit before the church service (e.g., an announcement concerning the annual cleaning of the river). Tucher, *Baumeisterbuch,* 233.

39. Fleming, *Graffiti,* 36.

40. Sauer, *Symbolik des Kirchengebäudes,* 217; Laube, *Reliquie zum Ding,* esp. 31.

41. Sauer, *Symbolik des Kirchengebäudes,* 216–218; Laube, *Reliquie zum Ding,* 90.

42. Laube, *Reliquie zum Ding,* 91.

43. The following reconstruction is based on Georgi, *Wittenbergische Klage-Geschichte,* table 3 and p. 56. See also Köstlin, *Friedrich der Weise,* 14–15; Laube, *Reliquie zum Ding,* 97–98.

44. "Si quis rem ab aliquo amissam invenerit, publice ad valvas templorum, aut alibi proposita schedula id significare tenetur, ut redeat ad Dominum, quod fuit ante suum." Wildvogel and von Calm, *Janus patulcius*, 98.

45. *Codex Iuris Canonici* (ed. 1918), can. 1720.

46. Code of Canon Law (current edition), can. 1509 §1, available in English on the Vatican website, accessed 17 August 2014, http://www.vatican.va/archive/ENG1104/__P5R.HTM.

47. *Urkundenbuch der Stadt Basel*, 8:210. For further evidence and a more detailed discussion, see Jütte, "Schwang Luther 1517 tatsächlich den Hammer?"

48. On the changing iconography, see Holsing, "Luthers Thesenanschlag."

49. For a new ruler's accession to power announced by posting placards to the doors of churches and city halls: *Kurtzer Bericht von dem Ser^{mo} Herrn Georg Wilhelm*, esp. C^{i–iv}; and *Begründeter Gegen-Bericht*, esp. E^{iv–v}; for posters at the doors of churches, city halls, and city gates warning citizens not to attack the local Jews: Süßmann, *Judenschuldentilgungen*, 19.

50. Immenkötter and Wüst, "Augsburg," 6:15.

51. Wildvogel and von Calm, *Janus patulcius*, 124.

52. Stern, *Documents*, 53. Another interesting case is that of early modern Rome, described in Petrucci, *Public Lettering*, esp. 91–93.

53. Dekker, *Guls Horne-Booke* (1609), quoted in Stern, *Documents*, 270 n66.

54. Jonson, *Every Man out of His Humour*, III.1 (p. 216); Stern, *Documents*, 270 n66.

55. Stern, *Documents*, 62.

56. Quoted in ibid., 51. On the significance of tavern walls and doors as sites of such postings in early modern Europe, see Kümin, "Wirtshaus und Gemeinde," 85.

57. The account by Johann Kaspar Riesberg is available (in excerpts) in Lahnstein, *Report einer "guten alten Zeit,"* 72.

58. See chap. 1. See also Schmidt and Dirlmeier, "Geschichte des Wohnens im Spätmittelalter," 2:291; Schwarz, *Sachgüter und Lebensformen*, 39; Mare, "Domestic Boundary," 125.

59. Wildvogel and von Calm, *Janus patulcius*, 144; see also Mare, "Domestic Boundary," 125.

60. Damhouder, *Praxis rerum criminalium*, chap. 140.

61. Ibid., chap. 127 ("De Diffamatione per Libellos").

62. Schmidt-Voges, "Securitas domestica oder ius certum domus?"

63. For the following, esp. Schmidt, "Libelli famosi"; also HRG, s.v. "Schmähen und Schelten"; see also Fox, *Oral and Literate Culture*, chap. 6.

64. Schmidt, "Libelli famosi," 1.

65. Oxford English Dictionary online, s.v. "Pasquil."

66. Schmidt, "Libelli famosi," 108–109; Zeller, *Relations de cohabitation*, 80; Petrucci, *Public Lettering*, esp. 92–93.

67. The Italian original reads: "Camilla senese magra / Est locanda per li sbirri / per le hosti et per le poltroni." Quoted in Cohen and Cohen, *Words and Deeds*, 89.

68. Fox, *Oral and Literate Culture*, 317.

69. "Das sich vil der stundenten gantz unfleissig und ungebührlich auch dermassen halten, das sy merers in wüertsheusern als in der schul, merers auff der gassen als ob den büechern befunden werden." Quoted in Wolff, *Geschichte der Ingolstädter Juristenfakultät*, 181.

70. Ibid., 112, 179, 182.

71. For the following: Schmidt, "Libelli famosi," pt. 3; HRG, s.v. "Schmähen und Schelten," cols. 1451–1452.

72. Schmidt, "Libelli famosi," 81–83.

73. Heidrich, "Grenzübergänge," 33.

74. Schmidt, "Libelli famosi," 223–224.

75. Friedrichs, *Urban Society in an Age of War*, 202; Beik, *Urban Protest*, 42, 33.

76. The contemporary Venetian chronicler Domenico Malipiero reported that the posting of the verses, together with the Pope's fear of the powerful Orsini family, led the Pope to hire an additional eight hundred guards. See Malipiero, *Annali veneti,* 508. On this episode, and on the broader context of Rome as a "city of epigrams and inscriptions," see also Burckhardt, *Kultur der Renaissance,* esp. 251–253.

77. For the following: *Deutsche Reichstagsakten* 2:559–560; Herte, *Lutherkommentare des Johannes Cochläus,* 304–305.

78. For a recent study on these events and for further references see Kirby, "Emerging Publics of Religious Reform."

79. Nördlingen: Friedrichs, *Urban Society;* Antwerp: IG (1672), 154.

80. Damhouder, *Praxis rerum criminalium,* chap. 127 ("famosorum libellorum authores, puniendi sunt capitaliter"), 140 ("ob eam de Iure imponenda esset poena capitalis"). On the range of punishments, see also Schmidt, "Libelli famosi," pt. 4, and Petrucci, *Public Lettering,* 92. For the case of a sixteen-year-old boy in seventeenth-century Rome who was sentenced to death for spreading pasquils (later commuted to a fine): Stow, "Delitto e castigo," 191. In fifteenth-century Siena, a man was decapitated for drawing obscene signs on the door of a member of the government. Dean, *Crime and Justice,* 122–123.

81. Resolution of the Holy Community Talmud Torah, 9 February 1640, reproduced in the appendix to the English edition of Acosta's *Exemplar humanae vitae* (*A Specimen of Human Life*), 78–80. I have slightly modified the translation.

82. Wildvogel and von Calm, *Janus patulcius,* 136.

83. Kramer, "Herausfordern aus dem Haus," 127.

84. This is also the context in which they have been most commonly studied to date. See, e.g., the insightful studies by Schmidt, "Libelli famosi," and Fox, *Oral and Literate Culture.*

85. Deimling, "Ad Rufam Ianuam," 509–510.

86. See Pepys, *Diary,* 2:70 (10 April 1661) and the editor's annotation to this passage.

87. Eibach, "Haus," 205.

88. Dean, *Crime and Justice*, 122–123.

89. Aretino, *Ragionamento*, 292, 388; Cohen and Cohen, *Words and Deeds*, 51, 99–100; Pol, *Burgher and the Whore*, 66.

90. SAA, Vierschaar (Court of Justice): V 88/1665–5; Kramer, "Herausfordern aus dem Haus," 127.

91. Heidrich, "Grenzübergänge," 17.

92. *Der Statt Straßburg Wacht-Ordnungen*, 13.

93. Dead dogs: Eibach, "Haus," 205; destruction of doors: Infessura, *Diario*, 161; Bertelli, *King's Body*, 57.

94. Sanson, *Memoirs*, 2:209.

95. I borrow the term from Dean, *Crime and Justice*, 122–123.

96. On drunkeness and anger as reasons for nocturnal banging and battering against doors, see Boccaccio, *Decameron*, II.5.

97. For the following, unless otherwise indicated: Heidrich, "Grenzübergänge," 30–31.

98. Wildvogel and von Calm, *Janus patulcius*, 134; see also Kramer, "Herausfordern," 121, 126; Mohrmann, *Volksleben in Wilster*, 275–276; Siebenhüner, *Zechen, Zücken, Lärmen*, 126.

Chapter 5. The "City's Eyes"

1. Wildvogel and von Calm, *Janus patulcius*, 14, 82–83; on this analogy in medieval iconography, see Ratté, "Images of City Gates," 147. This chapter is an enlarged version of an article that was first published under the title "Entering a City: On a Lost Early Modern Practice," in *Urban History* 41, no. 2 (2014): 204–227.

2. For a general survey of early modern urban history: Friedrichs, *Early Modern City*; for the Middle Ages: Frugoni, *Distant City*; Hirschmann, *Stadt im Mittelalter*; specifically on city walls: Seta and Le Goff, *Città e le mura*; Tracy, *City Walls*; Creighton and Higham, *Medieval Town Walls*; Wolfe, *Walled Towns*; Blieck et al., *Enceintes urbaines*; Braunfels, *Mittelalterliche Stadtbaukunst*, esp. chap. 2.

3. Friedrichs, *Early Modern City*, 21.

4. Frugoni, *Distant City*, 14; Friedrichs, *Early Modern City*, 21; Mązak, *Travel in Early Modern Europe*, 118. A notable exception is Italy, where some villages were walled (and hence called *castelli*).

5. Braunfels, *Mittelalterliche Stadtbaukunst*, esp. 46 and chap. 2; Hirschmann, *Stadt im Mittelalter*, 16; see also Boes, "Unwanted Travellers," esp. 88.

6. Wolfe, *Walled Towns*, esp. 16.

7. According to Weiland, *Nederduitsch taalkundig woordenboek*, s.v. "poort." However, modern linguists derive the word *poorter* from the Latin *portus* (harbor). See also Philippa, Debrabandere, and Quak, *Etymologisch woordenboek van het Nederlands*, s.v. "poort."

8. Wildvogel and von Calm, *Janus patulcius*, 95.

9. Tracy, *City Walls*, passim.

10. Tracy, Introduction, 1.

11. Jericho: Josh 6:1–27. Babylon: Trumbull, *Threshold Covenant*, 103. A reconstruction of one of the Babylon gates, the resplendent Ishtar Gate, can today be seen in the Pergamon Museum in Berlin.

12. For a summary of this debate, see esp. Rogers, *Military Revolution Debate*.

13. Friedrichs, *Early Modern City*, 22.

14. Serlio, *On Architecture*, 2:252.

15. Rev 21:12–27, the quotation is from v. 25.

16. Ratté, "Images of City Gates"; Creighton and Higham, *Medieval Town Walls*, 167–168.

17 Esch, "Mauern bei Mantegna"; Esch, "Leon Battista Alberti."

18. Pontano, *Libri delle virtù sociali*, 188.

19. Alberti, *Art of Building*, 192, 390; and on the topic of city walls in general: 100–105. See also Syndikus, "Porta und Arcus."

20. Oestreich, "Antike Literatur," 358.

21. Selle, *Eigenen vier Wände*, 199.

22. Ibid., 130.

23. Machiavelli, *Discourses*, II.24; Alberti, *Art of Building*, 102; *Purgatory*, 6.83–85.

24. Machiavelli, *Discourses*, II.24 (pp. 358–359).

25. Ibid.; Alberti, *Art of Building*, 102.

26. See also Wildvogel and von Calm, *Janus patulcius*, 142; they refer to La Rochelle as "naked" after Richelieu razed its walls.

27. Demonstrated in several articles in Tracy, *City Walls;* see also Creighton and Higham, *Medieval Town Walls*, 26.

28. Schweizer, *Zwischen Repräsentation und Funktion*, 454.

29. Le Goff, "Costruzione e distruzione," 7; Creighton and Higham, *Medieval Town Walls*, 36; Wolfe, *Walled Towns*, 69.

30. Wildvogel and von Calm, *Janus patulcius*, 146; in Antwerp, and likely in other places as well, guard posts had to carry the banner of the city: SAA, Burgerlijke Wacht GA no. 4811: *Ordonnantie Op't stuck vande Borgherlijcke Wachte der Stadt van Antwerpen* (Antwerpen, 1607), §§72–73.

31. Liessem, "Eingemauerte Kugeln"; Hilliges, *Stadt- und Festungstor*, 174–179.

32. *King John*, II, 1.

33. Rauwolff, *Aigentliche beschreibung der Raiß*, 68–69.

34. Friedrichs, *Early Modern City*, 22; Mintzker, "Defortification of the German City," 49.

35. Creighton and Higham, *Medieval Town Walls*, 37; Seitter, "Entfestigung," 46.

36. Furttenbach, *PaßVerwahrung*.

37. Ibid., 8. The topos of the fortified gate as a labyrinth can also be found among Italian Renaissance architects: Hilliges, *Stadt- und Festungstor*, 108–110.

38. Furttenbach, *PaßVerwahrung*, 6.

39. "Fürnemblichen aber so ligt am meisten an deme umb wie gemelt viel Unkosten zuersparen das Gebäw auff das allergeschmei-

digst anzulegen jedoch also zu moderiren daß gleichwol ein Corporal-schafft recht vertrawte Burger: oder LandMänner . . . sowol bey Tag als auch Nachtszeiten gleich hinder dem Stadtthor ihre Losamenter und wol accommodirte Wohnungszimmer haben." Ibid., 3.

40. Ibid.

41. Ibid., 8.

42. Pepper, "Siege Law," 586. A similar conclusion is reached for Italy in Schweizer, *Repräsentation und Funktion.*

43. Creighton and Higham, *Medieval Town Walls,* 33; see also Kemp, "Mauern und Tore," at 246.

44. Reinle, *Zeichensprache der Architektur,* 255; Schweizer, *Repräsentation und Funktion,* esp. 25–29.

45. Schütte, "Stadttor und Hausschwelle," 309.

46. My thanks to the anonymous reviewer for sharing this piece of information.

47. Creighton and Higham, *Medieval Town Walls,* 169.

48. Kipling, "King's Advent"; esp. with respect to Florence, see Trexler, *Public Life,* 306–315. On the *jus intradae,* see Hillebrand, *Öffnungsrecht,* 5–6.

49. Rohr, *Einleitung zur Ceremoniel-Wissenschaft,* 60, 610–612; see also Wildvogel and von Calm, *Janus patulcius,* 12–13.

50. Bertelli, *King's Body,* 74; Pepper, "Siege Law," 589.

51. Schütte, "Stadttor und Hausschwelle," 306–307; Trexler, *Public Life,* 310.

52. See the English edition of Landucci's *Diario fiorentino,* (*Florentine Diary*), 66 n1.

53. On this right as a particular responsibility: Wildvogel and von Calm, *Janus patulcius,* 25.

54. Muir, "Presence and Representation," 95–96; similarly Bertelli, *King's Body,* 74–75.

55. Robbins, *City on the Ocean Sea,* 195. In the Holy Roman Empire, too, many cities went to great lengths to argue that the *jus*

intradae (right of entrance) was distinct from the seigneurial *jus aperturae* (the right to open and occupy a castle). Hillebrand, *Öffnungsrecht,* 5–6.

56. On the significance of city walls for the "honor" of the premodern city, see also Mintzker, "Defortification of the German City," chap. 1.

57. *King John,* II, 1.

58. Josh 6:1–27; Judg 16:1–3.

59. Wildvogel and von Calm, *Janus patulcius,* 142; Pepper, "Siege Law," 588.

60. E.g., in the city of Gransee: Reinle, *Zeichensprache der Architektur,* 256.

61. Thøfner, *Common Art,* 108; see also Paviot, "Destruction des enceintes."

62. I borrow this term from Creighton and Higham, who speak of the city gate as a "closely controllable filter system" (*Medieval Town Walls,* 37).

63. For Frankfurt am Main: Boes, "Unwanted Travellers," 92.

64. Creighton and Higham, *Medieval Town Walls,* 171. Deterrence of criminal behavior was probably also one of the reasons for the occasional use of gate towers as prisons. See Lohrmann and Kiessling, *Türme, Tore, Bastionen,* 113.

65. Strozzi, *Selected Letters,* 129, 137–139.

66. For a summary, see Creighton and Higham, *Medieval Town Walls,* 37.

67. As in eighteenth-century Dresden: *Quellen zur Geschichte der Juden,* 4:231.

68. E.g., as in Bordeaux in 1579: *Jurade,* 3:527.

69. Mączak, *Travel in Early Modern Europe,* 112.

70. For Brussels, see below. For southern Germany: Kinzelbach, *Gesundbleiben,* 238–240.

71. Kemp, "Mauern und Tore," 246; Zschocke, *Berliner Akzisemauer.*

72. "Qu'a cet effect ils ont a chaque porte un petit Bureau, avec les armes de la ville au dessus de la porte avec une Inscription, que les declarations des Marchandises et denrées, sujets aux droits de cette ville s'y doivent effectuer, afin que tous les Entrans en aient connaissance." AVB, Archives Anciennes (hereafter: AA), Liasse 166 (*Droits d'entrée et de sortie*).

73. Zschocke, *Berliner Akzisemauer,* 35–39.

74. Lohrmann and Kiessling, *Türme, Tore, Bastionen,* 113.

75. Castiglione, *Libro del cortegiano,* 194.

76. Kemp, "Mauern und Tore," 246.

77. AVB/AA, Liasse 501, *Memoire dans lequel on demontre que la proprieté des portes de la ville de Bruxelles appartient à la pluralité,* fols. 30, 34 (10 January 1788).

78. AVB/AA, Liasse 166, undated letter from the city magistrate of Brussels (c. 1750).

79. Gardner, "Introduction."

80. Levine, "City-Gate as Synagogue Forerunner"; Blomquist, *Gates and Gods.*

81. Scully, *Homer and the Sacred City,* 50–52; Picard, *Portes sculptées.*

82. Cassirer, *Philosophy of Symbolic Forms,* 2:103; Gardner, "Introduction," 202.

83. Constantinople: Gardner, "Introduction," 202; Tuscany: Braunfels, *Mittelalterliche Stadtbaukunst,* 84.

84. Gardner, "Introduction," 202; Frugoni, *Day in a Medieval City,* 27.

85. Florence: Trexler, *Public Life,* 48; Siena: Gardner, "Introduction," 208.

86. Gardner, "Introduction," 208.

87. Reinle, *Zeichensprache der Architektur,* 259–260 (with illustrations); Creighton and Higham, *Medieval Town Walls,* 175–176.

88. Trexler, *Public Life,* 48.

89. Fabri, *Evagatorium,* 1:368–369.

90. Kaplan, *Divided by Faith*, 145.

91. Ibid., 164–168.

92. Friedrichs, *Early Modern City*, 42; Schweizer, *Repräsentation und Funktion*, 9.

93. The numbers according to de Vries, *European Urbanization*, app. 1; see also Hirschmann, *Stadt im Mittelalter*, 18–19, and Voet, "Antwerp," 15.

94. Brussels: Sand and Rubbrecht, *Clés et défense;* Antwerp: Lombaerde, *Antwerpen versterkt.* On the symbolism of gates and their significance in urban rituals in Antwerp and Brussels, see also Thøfner, *Common Art*, 108, 129–132.

95. IG (1582), 360.

96. Wolfe, *Walled Towns*, 17.

97. Groebner, *Schein der Person*, does not explore the question of personal inspection at city gates; on France, see Nordman, "Sauf-conduits et passeports."

98. Goethe, *Sufferings of Young Werther*, 140.

99. AVB/AA, Liasse 501, *Instruction ou Reglement pour les Commissaires établis aux Portes* [c. 1720]. Travelers were confronted with nearly the same set of questions in eighteenth-century Berlin; see Zschocke, *Berliner Akzisemauer*, 59. In other European cities, this seems to have been handled in a similar way: Mączak, *Travel in Early Modern Europe*, 118.

100. Mayor: Lohrmann and Kiessling, *Türme, Tore, Bastionen*, 110.

101. For Augsburg: Ibid., 110; Kassel: Ebert, "Willkommene und ungebetene Gäste," 263.

102. AVB/AA, Liasse 501, *Instruction ou Reglement pour les Commissaires établis aux Portes* [c. 1720].

103. SAA, Burgerlijke Wacht GA no. 4812, *Instructie voor de Schrijvers aen de Poorten der Stadt van Antwerpen*, 4 February 1623.

104. Such as in the Archivio di Stato in Mantua (Archivio Gonzaga, Affari di Polizia). On the Roman customs registers (admittedly

not only those of city gates) and their potential as historical sources: Esch, *Economia.*

105. Zschocke, *Berliner Akzisemauer,* 60; Lohrmann and Kiessling, *Türme, Tore, Bastionen,* 110.

106. Kassel: Ebert, "Willkommene und ungebetene Gäste," 262.

107. Antwerp: SAA, Burgerlijke Wacht GA no. 4.811, *Ordonnantie Op't stuck vande Borgherlijcke Wachte der Stadt van Antwerpen* [1607], §§51–98. Similar legal decrees from later years can be found in Burgerlijke Wacht GA no. 4812. See also IG (1740), 259; (1753), 271; (1790), 303–304.

108. Mączak, *Travel in Early Modern Europe,* 118.

109. In early modern Frankfurt am Main, the decrees concerning gates for each quarter of the city had to be read aloud in public at least once a year. See *E. E. Raths Der Stadt Franckfurt Erneuerte Wacht-Ordnung,* 7. This practice was likely widespread in early modern Europe.

110. On low wages in Berlin, see Zschocke, *Berliner Akzisemauer,* 33. This also holds true for smaller cities; see Rüthing, *Höxter um 1500,* 212; Kroll, *Stade um 1700,* 98. On the corruptibility of gatekeepers in Bordeaux, see Dinges, *Stadtarmut in Bordeaux,* 271.

111. Weinsberg, *Buch Weinsberg,* 5:295–296.

112. Boccaccio, *Decameron,* VIII.3.

113. For reference, see some of the extant application letters in AVB/AA, Liasse 501.

114. Beik, *Urban Protest,* 13.

115. On this problem in Berlin, see Zschocke, *Berliner Akzisemauer,* esp. 29.

116. Van Goethem, *Photography and Realism,* 100,

117. IG (1696), 223. For similar instances, see also the files of the Antwerp *Vierschaar* (Court of Justice): SAA, V 85/8 (1610); V 87/1 (1617).

118. AVB/AA, Liasse 501, Letter of the gate commissary B. Martroye, 30 April 1755.

119. Brüdermann, *Göttinger Studenten*, 282–283, 393–394; for similar problems in Tübingen: Lahnstein, *Leben im Barock*, 128; and for Freiburg: Krug-Richter, "Du Bacchant," 90–91, as well as Siebenhüner, *Zechen, Zücken, Lärmen*, 73, 83, 90–94.

120. Siebenhüner, *Zechen, Zücken, Lärmen*, 82.

121. IG (1578), 340.

122. See the plea of the magistrate of Brussels to the emperor "de faire ordonner aux Gardes militaires qui se trouveront aux portes de cette ville de donner assistence et main forte aux Commis de portes de cette ville, lorsqu'ils en seront requis pour l'exercise de leurs fonctions." AVB/AA, Liasse 166, undated (c. 1750).

123. For Frankfurt, where the so-called *Wachtgeld* (literally, "guard money") had been levied for this purpose since the seventeenth century: Eibach, *Frankfurter Verhöre*, 84–85.

124. Tucher, *Baumeisterbuch*, 289–290.

125. Ebert, "Willkommene und ungebetene Gäste," 264.

126. Dean, *Crime and Justice*, 152.

127. Serlio, *On Architecture*, 2:92. Translation slightly modified. In cities north of the Alps, the problem manifested itself in a similar way. See, e.g., Rüthing, *Höxter um 1500*, 212–213; Kroll, *Stade um 1700*, 98; Siebenhüner, *Zechen, Zücken, Lärmen*, 83.

128. For Antwerp: IG (1614), 450; (1622), 8; (1727), 252.

129. Medieval Tuscany: Braunfels, *Mittelalterliche Stadtbaukunst*, 63. Late medieval German lands: Gönnenwein, "Anfänge des kommunalen Baurechts," 113–115. In some places, such as Bordeaux, the authorities allowed houses to be built propped against the wall and even windows to be cut in it (provided they were protected by grates): *Jurade*, 6:43.

130. Graffiti: Petrucci, *Public Lettering*, 92; crucifixes: Trexler, *Public Life*, 54.

131. Boes, "Unwanted Travellers," 92.

132. AVB/AA, Liasse 501, *Waerschouwinge* (decree) of 4 April 1743.

133. IG (1604), 423; (1686), 210; (1788), 299.

134. Ordinances concerning the opening and closing times of the gates in Antwerp, although only for the seventeenth and eighteenth centuries: IG (1614), 450; (1693), 220; (1695), 222; (1701), 228; (1705), 233; (1740), 259–260; (1745), 264; (1746), 266; (1758), 273; (1760), 274; (1787), 297; (1790), 303–304; (1793), 312.

135. "de Poorten deser Stadt op de gereguleerde uren niet en worden geopent en gesloten." AVB/AA, Liasse 501, *Waerschouwinge* of 4 April 1743.

136. For Frankfurt: *E. E. Raths Der Stadt Franckfurt Erneuerte Wacht-Ordnung*, 3; Strasbourg: *Der Statt Straßburg Wacht-Ordnungen*, 8–9.

137. E.g., in Augsburg: Roeck, *Stadt in Krieg und Frieden*, 2:805.

138. Hale, *Renaissance Europe*, 123. The magistrate in Frankfurt also complained about gatekeepers who went home during their shifts in order to eat: *E. E. Raths Der Stadt Franckfurt Erneuerte Wacht-Ordnung*, 4.

139. Boccaccio, *Decameron*, X.9.

140. Boes, "Unwanted Travellers," 92.

141. Tuscany: Machiavelli, *Florentine Histories*, 304; similarly in German lands: Cologne: Weinsberg, *Buch Weinsberg*, 5:295–296; Göttingen: Brüdermann, *Göttinger Studenten*, 283–284.

142. Mączak, *Travel in Early Modern Europe*, 53–54.

143. AVB/AA, Liasse 501, *Memoire dans lequel on demontre que la proprieté des portes de la ville de Bruxelles appartient à la pluralité*, fols. 2, 31 (10 January 1788).

144. IG (1628), 25–26; SAA, Burgerlijke Wacht GA no. 4811: *Ordonnantie Op't stuck vande Borgherlijcke Wachte der Stadt van Antwerpen* [1607], §77.

145. Frankfurt: *E. E. Raths Der Stadt Franckfurt Erneuerte Wacht-Ordnung*, 4. On the problem of alcoholism among gatekeepers in Brandenburg, see Zschocke, *Berliner Akzisemauer*, 33. For com-

plaints from Italy about guards falling asleep while on duty: Hilliges, *Stadt- und Festungstor,* 58–59.

146. *Der Statt Straßburg Wacht-Ordnungen,* 7–10, 12.

147. Weinsberg, *Buch Weinsberg,* 5:75–76.

148. See, e.g., the files of the Antwerp *Vierschaar* from the 1610s: SAA, V 86/7 and 12–14; V 87/5 and 7, Göttingen: Brüdermann, *Göttinger Studenten,* 284.

149. Quoted in Mączak, *Travel in Early Modern Europe,* 53–54.

150. Lohrmann and Kiessling, *Türme, Tore, Bastionen,* 57–59.

151. Montaigne, *Travel Journal,* 1099–1100.

152. IG (1589), 395.

153. Krug-Richter, "Du Bacchant," 91.

154. See, e.g.: SAA, V 86/24 (1614); IG (1658), 130; Brüdermann, *Göttinger Studenten,* 283.

155. An account of these regular controls can be found in Endres Tucher's fifteenth-century *Baumeisterbuch,* 247–249.

156. Friedrichs, *Early Modern City,* 25; Dinges, *Stadtarmut in Bordeaux,* 271.

157. See also Schweizer, *Repräsentation und Funktion,* 9.

158. AVB/AA, Liasse 501, Decrees of 9 May 1743 and 7 June 1783 (each of which refers to previous ordinances on the subject); see also Ekirch, *At Day's Close,* 62.

159. See Mintzker, "Defortification of the German City"; Blieck et al., *Forteresse à l'épreuve du temps;* Poling, "Inner Frontier." I thank Dr. Poling for sending me a copy of her dissertation.

160. Wolfe, *Walled Towns;* Mintzker, "Defortification of the German City," chap. 2.

161. Wolfe, *Walled Towns,* 159.

162. Mintzker, "Defortification of the German City."

163. Quoted in Creighton and Higham, *Medieval Town Walls,* 236.

164. Ibid., 243.

165. Reinle speaks of an "Urerlebnis des Stadttors" in the past: *Zeichensprache der Architektur,* 255.

166. Mintzker, "Defortification of the German City," vi.

167. Also, gardens and cemeteries were often located outside the city walls: Dülmen, *Kultur und Alltag,* 2:63.

168. Poling, "Inner Frontier," 2.

169. Mintzker, "Defortification of the German City," 1. Interestingly, it seems that even when used as metaphors, city walls are now considered good only on the condition of their gates being always open. Consider, for instance, the image of America as the "shining city upon a hill" that Ronald Reagan referenced in his farewell address: "And if there had to be city walls, the walls had doors and the doors were open to anyone with the will and the heart to get here." My thanks to Daniel Merzel for this lead. Ronald Reagan, "Farewell Address to the Nation" (11 January 1989), accessed 31 July 2014, http://www.reaganfoundation.org/pdf/Farewell_Address_011189.pdf.

170. Bocchi, *Beauties of the City of Florence.*

171. Bacon, *Works,* 6:417 (Essay 18, "Of Travel").

172. See, e.g., Bocchi, *Beauties of the City of Florence,* 26. On this phenomenon, see also Esch, "Anschauung und Begriff," esp. 285.

173. Mumford, *City in History,* 360.

174. Sahlins, *Boundaries,* 8.

175. Of course, early modern Europeans also needed passes or permit letters (in which one can see a prototype of the modern passport) in order to cross certain territorial boundaries. But the inspections at state borders were rarely as rigorous as those at city gates. See Mączak, *Travel in Early Modern Europe,* chap. 5 and esp. p. 118.

176. Torpey, *Invention of the Passport.*

177. Sennett, *Flesh and Stone,* 17–18.

178. Blakely, *Fortress America;* Creighton and Higham, *Medieval Town Walls,* 248.

179. Mumford, *City in History,* 9.

180. Benjamin, *Passagen-Werk,* 1:139.

Epilogue

1. Radvansky, Krawietz, and Tamplin, "Walking through Doorways," esp. 1632, 1644.

2. Wolf, *Making an Entrance*, 17.

3. Adorno, *Minima Moralia*, 40.

4. Ibid.

5. See chap. 2, n138.

BIBLIOGRAPHY

Abegg, Regine. "Symbolik und Nutzung des Hauptportals im Mit-
    telalter und in der Neuzeit." In *Himmelstür: Das Hauptportal
    des Basler Münsters,* edited by Hans-Rudolf Meier and Dorothea
    Schwinn Schürmann, 154–165. Basel: Schwabe, 2011.

Acosta, Uriel. *Exemplar humanae vitae.* Edited by Hans-Wolfgang
    Krautz. Tübingen: Stauffenburg 2001. Translated as *A Specimen
    of Human Life* (New York: Bergman, 1967).

Adorno, Theodor W. *Minima Moralia: Reflections on a Damaged Life.*
    Translated by E. F. N. Jephcott. London: Verso, 2005.

Aland, Kurt. *Die 95 Thesen Martin Luthers und die Anfänge der Refor-
    mation.* Gütersloh: Gütersloher Verlagshaus, 1983.

Alberti, Leon Battista. *I libri della famiglia.* Edited by Ruggiero Ro-
    mano, Turin: Einaudi 1994. Translated by Renée Neu Watkins
    as *The Family in Renaissance Florence* (Columbia: University of
    South Carolina Press, 1969).

———. *On the Art of Building in Ten Books.* Translated by Joseph
    Rykwert, Neil Leach, and Robert Tavernor. Cambridge, MA:
    MIT Press, 1988.

Allen, Aaron M. *The Locksmith Craft in Early Modern Edinburgh.*
    Edinburgh: Society of Antiquaries of Scotland, 2007.

Allgemeines Handbuch der Freimaurerei. 4 vols. Leipzig: Brockhaus, 1863–1879.

Altmann, Adolf. *Geschichte der Juden in Stadt und Land Salzburg von den frühesten Zeiten bis auf die Gegenwart.* Berlin: Lamm, 1913–1930. Reprint, Salzburg: Müller, 1990.

Amira, Karl von, and Claudius Freiherr von Schwerin. *Rechtsarchäologie: Gegenstände, Formen und Symbole germanischen Rechts.* Berlin: Ahnenerbe-Stiftung, 1943.

Andree-Eysn, Marie. *Volkskundliches aus dem bayrisch-österreichischen Alpengebiet.* 1910. Reprint, Hildesheim: Olms, 1978.

Angermann, Gertrud. *Volksleben im Nordosten Westfalens zu Beginn der Neuzeit: Eine wachsende Bevölkerung im Kräftefeld von Reformation und Renaissance, Obrigkeit und Wirtschaft.* Münster: Waxmann, 1995.

Aretino, Pietro. *Ragionamento.* Milan: Garzanti, 1984. Translated as *Ragionamenti or Dialogues of the Divine Pietro Aretino.* Paris: Liseux, 1889.

Ariès, Philippe, and Georges Duby, eds. *A History of Private Life.* Cambridge, MA: Harvard University Press, 1987–1991.

Artemidorus. *The Interpretation of Dreams* [*Oneirocritica*]. Translated by Robert J. White. Torrance, CA: Original Books, 1990.

Atsushi Ueda. *The Inner Harmony of the Japanese House.* Tokyo: Kodansha, 1990.

Auerbach, David. *Falscher Calvinischer Schlüssel: Mit welchen der Apostata M. Henrics Innichenhöfer von Hertzberg/der genandten Reformirten Gemeine in Moscaw Prediger: Die rechte Meynung von den verschlossenen Thüren . . . aufzuschliessen vermeynet.* Hamburg: Gutwasser, 1642.

Bach, Hans I. *Jacob Bernays: Ein Beitrag zur Emanzipationsgeschichte der Juden und zur Geschichte des deutschen Geistes im neunzehnten Jahrhundert.* Tübingen: Mohr, 1974.

Bachelard, Gaston. *The Poetics of Space.* Translated by Maria Jolas. Boston: Beacon, 1994.

Bacon, Francis. *Works*. Edited by James Spedding, Robert Leslie Ellis, and Douglas Denon Heath. 14 vols. London: Longman, 1861–1879.

Baskin, Judith. "Women and Ritual Immersion in Medieval Ashkenaz: The Sexual Politics of Piety." In *Judaism in Practice: From the Middle Ages through the Early Modern Period*, edited by Lawrence Fine, 131–142. Princeton, NJ: Princeton University Press.

Bathe, William. *Ianua linguarum, quadrilinguis. Or a Messe of Tongues: Latine, English, French, and Spanish*. London: Richard Field, 1617.

Beckham, Sue Bridwell. "The American Front Porch: Women's Liminal Space." In *Making the American Home: Middle-Class Women and Domestic Material Culture, 1840–1940*, edited by Marilyn Ferris Motz and Pat Browne, 69–89. Bowling Green, OH: Bowling Green State University Popular Press, 1988.

Begründeter Gegen-Bericht wieder einen an Seiten Serenissimi Herrn Georg Wilhelms Hertzogen zu Braunschweig und Lüneburg . . . Kurtzen Bericht gestellet und abgefasset: Darinnen Serenissimi Herrn Hertzogen Johann Friederichs zu Braunschweig und Lüneburg . . . wolfundirtes Successions-Recht zu denen eröffneten Zellischen Fürstenthumen . . . behauptet wird. Celle: Holwein, 1665.

Beik, William. *Urban Protest in Seventeenth-Century France: The Culture of Retribution*. Cambridge: Cambridge University Press, 1997.

Benedict of Nursia. *The Rule of Saint Benedict*. Edited and translated by Bruce L. Venarde. Dumbarton Oaks Medieval Library 6. Cambridge, MA: Harvard University Press, 2011.

Benjamin, Walter. *Das Passagen-Werk*. Edited by Rolf Tiedemann. 2 vols. Frankfurt am Main: Suhrkamp, 1983. Translated by Howard Eiland and Kevin McLaughlin as *The Arcades Project* (Cambridge, MA: Harvard University Press, 1999).

Bernardino da Siena. *Sermons*. Edited by Nazareno Orlandi. Translated by Helen Josephine Robins. Siena: Tipografia sociale, 1920.

Bertelli, Sergio. *The King's Body: Sacred Rituals of Power in Medieval and Early Modern Europe*. Translated by R. Burr Litchfield. University Park: Pennsylvania State University Press, 2001.

Beyer, Georg [Praeses], and Heinrich Friedrich von Ende [Respondent]. *Dissertatio Iuris Gentium et Germanici . . . de Violatione Securitatis Domesticae*. Wittenberg: Gerdes, 1717.

Biow, Douglas. *The Culture of Cleanliness in Renaissance Italy*. Ithaca, NY: Cornell University Press, 2006.

Biraghi, Marco. *Porta multifrons: Forma, immagine, simbolo*. Palermo: Sellerio, 1992.

Blackstone, William. *Commentaries on the Laws of England*. 4 vols. Dublin: Colles, 1775.

Blair, Ann M. *Too Much to Know: Managing Scholarly Information before the Modern Age*. New Haven, CT: Yale University Press, 2010.

Blakely, Edward James. *Fortress America: Gated Communities in the United States*. Washington, DC: Brookings Institution, 1997.

Blastenbrei, Peter. *Kriminalität in Rom, 1560–1585*. Tübingen: Niemeyer, 1995.

Blieck, Gilles, et al., eds. *La forteresse à l'épreuve du temps: Destruction, dissolution, dénaturation, XIᵉ–XXᵉ siècle*. Paris: Comité des travaux historiques et scientifiques, 2007.

———. *Les enceintes urbaines, XIIIe–XVIe siècle*. Paris: Éditions du CTHS, 1999.

Blomquist, Tina Haettner. *Gates and Gods: Cults in the City Gates of Iron Age Palestine: An Investigation of the Archaeological and Biblical Sources*. Stockholm: Almqvist & Wiksell, 1999.

Blount, Charles. *Janua scientiarum: Or, a Compendious Introduction to Geography, Chronology, Government, History, Phylosophy, and all Genteel Sorts of Literature*. London: Nath. Thompson, 1684.

Boccaccio, Giovanni. *Decameron.* Translated by J. G. Nichols. New York: Knopf, 2009.

Bocchi, Francesco. *The Beauties of the City of Florence: A Guidebook of 1591.* Translated and edited by Thomas Frangenberg and Robert Williams. London: Harvey Miller, 2006.

Bodin, Jean. *Six Books of the Commonwealth.* Translated by M. J. Tooley. Oxford: Blackwell, 1955.

Boes, Maria R. "Unwanted Travellers: The Tightening of City Borders in Early Modern Germany." In *Borders and Travellers in Early Modern Europe,* edited by Thomas Betteridge, 87–111. Aldershot: Ashgate, 2007.

Bonfil, Robert. *Jewish Life in Renaissance Italy.* Translated by Anthony Oldcorn. Berkeley: University of California Press, 1994.

Bornkamm, Heinrich. *Thesen und Thesenanschlag Luthers: Geschehen und Bedeutung.* Berlin: Töpelmann, 1967.

Bourdieu, Pierre. "Family Spirit." In *Practical Reason. On the Theory of Action,* 65–74. Cambridge: Polity, 1998.

Boyle, Robert. *The Works of Robert Boyle.* Edited by Michael Hunter and Edward B. Davis. 14 vols. London: Pickering & Chatto, 1999–2000.

Brant, Sebastian. *Das Narrenschiff.* Edited by Hans-Joachim Mähl. Stuttgart: Reclam, 1975.

———. *Das Narrenschiff.* Quedlinburg: Basse 1839. Translated by Edwin H. Zeydel as *The Ship of Fools* (New York: Dover, 1962).

Braunfels, Wolfgang. *Mittelalterliche Stadtbaukunst in der Toskana.* Berlin: Gebr. Mann, 1953.

Brayman Hackel, Heidi. *Reading Material in Early Modern England: Print, Gender, and Literacy.* Cambridge: Cambridge University Press, 2005.

Brown, Patricia Fortini. *Private Lives in Renaissance Venice: Art, Architecture, and the Family.* New Haven, CT: Yale University Press, 2004.

Brüdermann, Stefan. *Göttinger Studenten und akademische Gerichts-barkeit im 18. Jahrhundert.* Göttingen: Vandenhoeck & Ruprecht, 1990.

Brunner, Karl. "Inszenierung und Öffentlichkeit in und um Kirchen im Mittelalter." In *Ein Thema—zwei Perspektiven: Juden und Christen in Mittelalter und Frühneuzeit,* edited by Eveline Brugger and Birgit Wiedl, 187–194. Innsbruck: Studienverlag, 2007.

Brunner, Otto. "Das 'ganze Haus' und die alteuropäische Ökonomik." In *Neue Wege der Verfassungs- und Sozialgeschichte,* 103–127. Göttingen: Vandenhoeck & Ruprecht, 1980.

Bucer, Martin. *Deutsche Schriften.* Edited by Robert Stupperich. 17 vols. Gütersloh: Gütersloher Verlagshaus Mohn, 1960–1981.

Bukowski, Richard W. *Emergency Egress from Buildings.* NIST Technical Note 1623. Gaithersburg, MD: National Institute of Standards and Technology, 2009.

Burckhardt, Jacob. *Die Kultur der Renaissance in Italien: Ein Versuch.* Frankfurt am Main: Fischer, 2009.

———. *Erzbischof Andreas von Krain und der letzte Concilsversuch in Basel, 1482–1484.* Basel: Schweighauser, 1852.

Burkart, Lucas. *Die Stadt der Bilder. Familiale und kommnunale Bildinvestition im spätmittelalterlichen Verona.* Munich: Fink, 2000.

Burke, Peter. *The European Renaissance: Centres and Peripheries.* Oxford: Blackwell, 1998.

Burroughs, Charles. *The Italian Renaissance Palace Facade: Structures of Authority, Surfaces of Sense.* Cambridge: Cambridge University Press, 2002.

Cahn, Walter. *The Romanesque Wooden Doors of Auvergne.* New York: New York University Press, 1974.

Calvin, Jean. *The sermons of M. Iohn Calvin upon the fifth booke of Moses called Deuteronomie.* Translated by Arthur Golding. London: Middleton, 1583.

Camesasca, Ettore, ed. *History of the House.* Translated by Isabel Quigly. New York: Putnam, 1971.

Carpzov, Benedikt. *Practica nova Saxonica rerum criminalium.* Wittenberg: Heirs of Schurer, 1635. Reprint, Goldbach: Keip, 1996.

Carrichter, Bartholomäus. *Kräuter- und Arzney-Buch: Mit einigen Zusätzen und einer besonderen Vorrede von des Auctoris Leben und Schrifften.* Tübingen: Cotta, 1739.

Cassirer, Ernst. "Der Begriff der symbolischen Form im Aufbau der Geisteswissenschaften." In *Gesammelte Werke.* Edited by Birgit Recki, 16:75–104. Hamburg: Meiner, 1998–2009.

———. *An Essay on Man: An Introduction to the Philosophy of Human Culture.* New Haven, CT: Yale University Press, 1972.

———. *The Philosophy of Symbolic Forms.* Translated by Ralph Manheim and John Michael Krois. New Haven, CT: Yale University Press, 1953–1996.

Castiglione, Baldesar. *Il libro del cortegiano.* Edited by Walter Barberis. Turin: Einaudi, 1998.

Certaldo, Paolo da. *Libro di buoni costumi.* Edited by Alfredo Schiaffini. Florence: Le Monnier, 1945.

Cervantes, Miguel de. *Don Quixote of La Mancha.* Translated by Walter Starkie. New York: New American Library, 1964.

Chaplin, Joyce E. *Subject Matter: Technology, the Body, and Science on the Anglo-American Frontier, 1500–1676.* Cambridge, MA: Harvard University Press, 2001.

Chaucer, Geoffrey. *Canterbury Tales.* Edited by Alfred W. Pollard. 2 vols. London: Macmillan, 1907.

Cieraad, Irene. "Dutch Windows: Female Virtue and Female Vice." In Cieraad, *At Home,* 31–52.

———, ed. *At Home: An Anthropology of Domestic Space.* Syracuse, NY: Syracuse University Press, 1999.

Classen, Albrecht. *The Medieval Chastity Belt: A Myth-Making Process.* New York: Palgrave Macmillan, 2007.

Codex Iuris Canonici. Edited by Pietro Gasparri. Rome: Typis Polyglottis Vaticanis, 1918.

Cohen, Elizabeth S., and Thomas V. Cohen. "Open and Shut: The Social Meanings of the Cinquecento Roman House." *Studies in the Decorative Arts* 9 (2001/2002): 61–84.

Cohen, Thomas V., and Elizabeth S. Cohen. *Words and Deeds in Renaissance Rome: Trials before the Papal Magistrates.* Toronto: University of Toronto Press, 1993.

Coke, Edward. *The Third Part of the Institutes of the Laws of England.* London: Rawlins, 1680.

Comenius, Jan Amos. *Porta linguarum trilinguis reserata et aperta. Sive seminarium linguarum & scientiarum omnium* [. . .]. London: Miller, 1631.

Contamine, Philippe. "Peasant Hearth to Papal Palace: The Fourteenth and Fifteenth Centuries." In Ariès and Duby, *A History of Private Life,* 2:425–506.

Coster, Will, and Andrew Spicer, eds. *Sacred Space in Early Modern Europe.* Cambridge: Cambridge University Press, 2005.

Cowan, Alexander. "Seeing Is Believing: Urban Gossip and the Balcony in Early Modern Venice." *Gender & History* 23 (2011): 721–738.

Cox, John Charles. *The Sanctuaries and Sanctuary Seekers of Mediaeval England.* London: Allen & Sons, 1911.

Creighton, Oliver, and Robert Higham. *Medieval Town Walls: An Archaeology and Social History of Urban Defence.* Stroud: Tempus, 2005.

Crossman, E. J., and J. M. Casselman. *An Annotated Bibliography of the Pike, Esox lucius.* Toronto: Royal Ontario Museum, 1987.

Damhouder, Joos de. *Praxis rerum civilium.* Antwerp: Beller, 1596.

———. *Praxis rerum criminalium.* Antwerp: Beller, 1601. Reprint, Clark, NJ: Lawbook Exchange, 2005.

Daniels, Inge. *The Japanese House: Material Culture in the Modern Home.* Oxford: Berg, 2010.

Dante Alighieri. *The Divine Comedy.* Translated by Allen Mandelbaum. London: Campbell, 1995.

Davis, Natalie Zemon. *The Return of Martin Guerre.* Cambridge, MA: Harvard University Press, 1983.

———. *Society and Culture in Early Modern France.* Stanford, CA: Stanford University Press, 1975.

Dean, Trevor. *Crime and Justice in Late Medieval Italy.* Cambridge: Cambridge University Press, 2007.

De Botton, Alain. *The Architecture of Happiness.* London: Penguin, 2006.

Decembrio, Pietro Candido. *Vita Philippi Mariae Tertij Ligurum Ducis.* Edited by Attilio Butti et. al. Vol. 20 of *Rerum italicarumm scriptores,* edited by L. A. Muratori. Bologna: Zanichelli, 1958.

Deimling, Barbara. "Ad Rufam Ianuam: Die rechtsgeschichtliche Bedeutung von 'roten Türen' im Mittelalter." *Zeitschrift der Savigny-Stiftung für Rechtsgeschichte: Germanistische Abteilung* 115 (1998): 498–513.

———. "Das mittelalterliche Kirchenportal in seiner rechtsgeschichtlichen Bedeutung." In *Die Kunst der Romanik: Architektur, Skulptur, Malerei,* edited by Rolf Toman, 324–327. Cologne: Könemann, 1996.

Delumeau, Jean. *History of Paradise: The Garden of Eden in Myth and Tradition.* Translated by Matthew O'Connell. New York: Continuum, 1995.

Der Statt Straßburg Wacht-Ordnungen. [Strasbourg] 1672.

Deuchler, Florens. "Offene Türen: Räumliche Inszenierungen in der Malerei des Mittelalters." *Daidalos* 13 (1984): 79–86.

Deutsche Reichstagsakten: Jüngere Reihe. 4 vols. Gotha: Perthes, 1893–1905.

D'Evelyn, Margaret Muther. *Venice and Vitruvius: Reading Venice with Daniele Barbaro and Andrea Palladio.* New Haven, CT: Yale University Press, 2012.

De Vries, Jan. *European Urbanization, 1500–1800.* London: Methuen, 1984.

Dibie, Pascal. *Ethnologie de la porte: des passages et des seuils.* Paris: Métailié, 2012.

Diedrichs, Christof L. "Wahrnehmung des mittelalterlichen Kirchenraums." In *Kunst der Bewegung: Kinästhetische Wahrnehmung und Probehandeln in virtuellen Welten,* edited by Christina Lechtermann and Carsten Morsch, 267–284. Bern: Lang, 2004.

Die Enteignung der Türklinken und Fenstergriffe: Eingaben und Zeitungsstimmen. Spandau: Zentralverband der Haus- und Grundbesitzervereine Deutschlands, 1918.

Die Goslarischen Statuten: Mit einer systematischen Zusammenstellung der darin enthaltenen Rechtssätze und Vergleichung des Sachsenspiegels und vermehrten Sachsenspiegels. Edited by Otto Göschen. Berlin: Reimer, 1840.

Dietz, Johann. *Mein Lebenslauf.* Edited by Friedhelm Kemp. Munich: Kösel, 1966.

Dingel, Irene. "Pruning the Vines, Plowing Up the Vineyard: The Sixteenth-Century Culture of Controversy between Disputation and Polemic." In *The Reformation as Christianization: Essays on Scott Hendrix's Christianization Thesis,* edited by Anna Marie Johnson and John A. Maxfield, 397–408. Tübingen: Mohr Siebeck, 2012.

Dinges, Martin. *Stadtarmut in Bordeaux, 1525–1675: Alltag, Politik, Mentalitäten.* Bonn: Bouvier, 1988.

Druffner, Frank. "Gehen und Sehen bei Hofe: Weg- und Blickführungen im Barockschloß." In *Johann Conrad Schlaun, 1695–1773: Architektur des Spätbarock in Europa,* edited by Klaus Bussmann, Florian Matzner, and Ulrich Schulze, 543–551. Stuttgart: Oktagon, 1995.

Duerr, Hans Peter. *Der Mythos vom Zivilisationsprozess.* 5 vols. Frankfurt am Main: Suhrkamp, 1988–2002.

Dülmen, Richard van. *Kultur und Alltag in der Frühen Neuzeit.* Munich: C. H. Beck, 1992.

Dumas, Geneviève. "La fenêtre dans les traités de peste de la région de Montpellier aux XIVe et XVe siècles." In *Par la fenestre:*

études de littérature et de civilisation médiévales, edited by Chantal Connochie-Bourgne, 157–165. Aix-en-Provence: Publications de l'Université de Provence, 2003.

Duwe, Georg. *Erzkämmerer, Kammerherren und ihre Schlüssel: Historische Entwicklung eines der ältesten Hofämter vom Mittelalter bis 1918.* Osnabrück: Biblio, 1990.

Ebert, Jochen. "Willkommene und ungebetene Gäste: Fremde in Kassel im 18. Jahrhundert." In *Kassel im 18. Jahrhundert: Residenz und Stadt,* edited by Heide Wunder, Christina Vanja, and Karl-Hermann Wegner, 262–283. Kassel: Euregio, 2000.

E. E. Raths Der Stadt Franckfurt Erneuerte Wacht-Ordnung. Frankfurt am Main, 1711. First issued 1669.

Eibach, Joachim. "Das Haus: zwischen öffentlicher Zugänglichkeit und geschützter Privatheit (16. bis 18. Jahrhundert)." In *Zwischen Gotteshaus und Taverne: Öffentliche Räume in Spätmittelalter und Früher Neuzeit,* edited by Susanne Rau and Gerd Schwerhoff, 183–205. Cologne: Böhlau, 2004.

———. "Das offene Haus: Kommunikative Praxis im sozialen Nahraum der europäischen Frühen Neuzeit." *Zeitschrift für historische Forschung* 38 (2011): 622–664.

———. *Frankfurter Verhöre: Städtische Lebenswelten und Kriminalität im 18. Jahrhundert.* Paderborn: Schöningh, 2003.

Ekirch, A. Roger. *At Day's Close: Night in Times Past.* New York: Norton, 2006.

Elias, Norbert. *The Civilizing Process: Sociogenetic and Psychogenetic Investigations.* Edited by Eric Dunning, Johan Goudsblom, and Stephen Mennell. Translated by Edmund Jephcott. Rev. ed. Oxford: Blackwell, 2000.

Encyclopaedia Judaica. 2nd ed. 22 vols. Detroit: Macmillan, 2007.

Epistolae obscurorum virorum an Magister Ortuin Gratius aus Deventer. Edited by Karl Riha. Frankfurt am Main: Insel, 1991.

Eras, Vincent J. M. *Locks and Keys throughout the Ages.* Amsterdam: Fronczek, 1957.

Erasmus, Desiderius. *Julius Excluded from Heaven.* Translated by Michael J. Heath. In *Collected Works of Erasmus,* 27:155–197. Toronto: University of Toronto Press, 1986.

Erler, Adalbert. *Das Straßburger Münster im Rechtsleben des Mittelalters.* Frankfurt am Main: Klostermann, 1954.

Esch, Arnold. "Anschauung und Begriff: Die Bewältigung fremder Wirklichkeit durch den Vergleich in Reiseberichten des späten Mittelalters." *Historische Zeitschrift* 253 (1991): 281–312.

———. *Economia, cultura materiale ed arte nella Roma del Rinascimento: Studi sui registri doganali romani, 1445–1485.* Rome: Roma nel Rinascimento, 2007.

———. "Leon Battista Alberti, Poggio Bracciolini, Andrea Mantegna: Zur Ikonographie antiker Mauern in der Malerei des Quattrocento." In *Leon Battista Alberti: Humanist, Architekt, Kunsttheoretiker,* edited by Joachim Poeschke and Candida Syndikus, 123–164. Münster: Rhema, 2008.

———. "Mauern bei Mantegna." *Zeitschrift für Kunstgeschichte* 47 (1984): 293–319.

Faber, Johann Ernst. *Archäologie der Hebräer: Erster Theil.* Halle: Curt, 1773.

Fabre, Daniel. "Families: Privacy versus Custom." In Ariès and Duby, *A History of Private Life,* 3:531–569.

Fabri, Felix. *Evagatorium in Terrae Sanctae, Arabiae et Egypti peregrinationem.* Edited by Konrad Dietrich Hassler. 3 vols. Stuttgart: Literarischer Verein, 1843.

Fassler, Margot. "Adventus at Chartres: Ritual Models for Major Processions." In *Ceremonial Culture in Pre-modern Europe,* edited by Nicolas Howe, 13–62. Notre Dame, IN: University of Notre Dame Press, 2007.

Febvre, Lucien. "Pour l'histoire d'un sentiment: le besoin de sécurité." *Annales* 11 (1956): 244–247.

Fiamma, Galvano. *Chronica Mediolani seu Manipulus Florum.* In *Rerum italicarum scriptores,* edited by Lodovico Antonio Muratori, 11:537–740. Milan: Typographia Societatis Palatinae, 1727.

Firth, Raymond. *We, the Tikopia: A Sociological Study of Kinship in Primitive Polynesia.* 1936. Reprint, London: Routledge, 2004.

Fischer, Ernst. *Die Hauszerstörung als strafrechtliche Maßnahme im deutschen Mittelalter.* Stuttgart: Kohlhammer, 1957.

Fleming, Juliet. *Graffiti and the Writing Arts of Early Modern England.* London: Reaktion Books, 2001.

Fordham, Benjamin O. "Protectionist Empire: Trade, Tariffs, and United States Foreign Policy, 1890–1914." Working Paper, 2011. http://government.arts.cornell.edu/assets/psac/sp11/Fordham _PSAC_Mar11.pdf.

Forster, George. *A Voyage round the World.* Edited by Nicholas Thomas and Oliver Berghof. 2 vols. Honolulu: University of Hawai'i Press, 2000.

Fox, Adam. *Oral and Literate Culture in England, 1500–1700.* Oxford: Oxford University Press, 2000.

Frake, Charles O. "How to Enter a Yakan House." In *Language and Cultural Description,* selected and introduced by Anwar S. Dil, 214–232. Stanford, CA: Stanford University Press, 1980.

Frazer, Margaret English. "Church Doors and the Gates of Paradise: Byzantine Bronze Doors in Italy." *Dumbarton Oaks Papers* 27 (1973): 145–162.

Friedman, David. "Palaces and the Street in Late-Medieval and Renaissance Italy." In *Urban Landscapes: International Perspectives,* edited by J. W. R. Whitehead and P. J. Larkham, 69–113. London: Routledge, 1992.

Friedrich, Markus. "Das Buch als Theater: Überlegungen zu Signifikanz und Dimensionen der Theatrum-Metapher als frühneuzeitlichem Buchtitel." In *Wissenssicherung, Wissensordnung und Wissensverarbeitung: Das europäische Modell der Enzyklopädien,* edited by Theo Stammen and Wolfgang Weber, 205–232. Berlin: Akademie, 2004.

Friedrichs, Christopher R. *The Early Modern City, 1450–1750.* London: Longman, 1995.

———. *Urban Society in an Age of War: Nördlingen, 1580–1720.* Princeton, NJ: Princeton University Press, 1979.

Frugoni, Chiara. *A Day in a Medieval City.* Translated by William McCuaig. Chicago: University of Chicago Press, 2005.

———. *A Distant City: Images of Urban Experience in the Medieval World.* Translated by William McCuaig. Princeton, NJ: Princeton University Press, 1991.

Furttenbach, Joseph. *PaßVerwahrung [. . .] Welcher Gestalt ein Paß/ oder Stadtthor/zugleich aber auch das Zeughauß, sampt dem groben Geschütz und Gewöhr, mit sonderbaren angenehmen Commoditeten [. . .] in sichere Verwahrung zubringen.* Augsburg: Schultes, 1651.

Füssel, Marian. "Umstrittene Grenzen: Zur symbolischen Kommunikation sozialer Ordnung in einer frühneuzeitlichen Universitätsstadt am Beispiel Helmstedts." In *Machträume der frühneuzeitlichen Stadt*, edited by Christian Hochmuth and Susanne Rau, 171–191. Konstanz: UVK Verlagsgesellschaft, 2006.

Gaidoz, Henri. *Un vieux rite médical.* Paris: Rolland, 1892.

Gardner, Julian. "An Introduction to the Iconography of the Medieval Italian City Gate." *Dumbarton Oaks Papers* 41 (1987): 199–213.

Garvey, Pauline. "Domestic Boundaries: Privacy, Visibility, and the Norwegian Window." *Journal of Material Culture* 10 (2005): 157–176.

Gennep, Arnold van. *The Rites of Passage.* Translated by Monika B. Vizedom and Gabrielle L. Caffee. Chicago: University of Chicago Press, 1960.

Gentzkow, Nicolaus. *Das Tagebuch des Stralsunder Bürgermeisters Nicolaus Gentzkow (1558–1567).* Edited by Heidelore Böcker. Hamburg: Kovač, 2011.

Georgi, Christian Siegismund. *Wittenbergische Klage-Geschichte.* Wittenberg: Ahlfeld, 1760. Reprint, Stuttgart: Siener, 1993.

Ginzburg, Carlo. *The Night Battles: Witchcraft and Agrarian Cults in the Sixteenth and Seventeenth Centuries.* Translated by John and Anne Tedeschi. Baltimore: Johns Hopkins University Press, 1983.

———. "Saccheggi rituali: Premesse a una ricerca in corso." *Quaderni storici* 65 (1987): 615–636.

Gläntzer, Volker. "Nord-Süd-Unterschiede städtischen Wohnens um 1800 im Spiegel der zeitgenössischen Literatur." In *Nord-Süd-Unterschiede in der städtischen und ländlichen Kultur Mitteleuropas,* edited by Günter Wiegelmann, 73–88. Münster: Coppenrath, 1985.

Goethe, Johann Wolfgang von. *The Sufferings of Young Werther.* Translated by Stanley Corngold. New York: Norton, 2012.

Goitein, Shelomo Dov. *A Mediterranean Society: The Jewish Communities of the Arab World as Portrayed in the Documents of the Cairo Geniza.* Berkeley: University of California Press, 1967–1993.

Goldman, Bernard. *The Sacred Portal: A Primary Symbol in Ancient Judaic Art.* Detroit: Wayne State University Press, 1966.

Goldthwaite, Richard A. *The Building of Renaissance Florence: An Economic and Social History.* Baltimore: Johns Hopkins University Press, 1982.

Gönnenwein, Otto. "Die Anfänge des kommunalen Baurechts." In *Kunst und Recht: Festgabe für Hans Fehr,* edited by Franz Beyerle and Karl S. Bader, 71–134. Karlsruhe: Müller, 1948.

Götz, Ute. "Die Bildprogramme der Kirchentüren des 11. und 12. Jahrhunderts." Ph.D. diss., University of Tübingen, 1971.

Grimm, Jacob. *Deutsche Rechtsalterthümer.* 4th ed. Leipzig: Weicher, 1899.

Groebner, Valentin. *Der Schein der Person: Steckbrief, Ausweis und Kontrolle im Europa des Mittelalters.* Munich: C. H. Beck, 2004.

Gude, Hans. *Das deutsche Schlosserhandwerk als Glied des eisenver-arbeitenden Metallgewerbes.* Stuttgart: Metzlersche Buchdrucke-rei, 1938.

Guldan, Ernst. "Das Monster-Portal am Palazzo Zuccari in Rom: Wandlungen eines Motivs vom Mittelalter zum Manierismus." *Zeitschrift für Kunstgeschichte* 32 (1969): 229–261.

Hahnloser, Hans R. "Urkunden zur Bedeutung des Türrings." In *Festschrift für Erich Meyer zum sechzigsten Geburtstag,* edited by Werner Gramberg et al., 125–146. Hamburg: Hauswedell, 1959.

Hakluyt, Richard. *The Principal Navigations, Voyages, Traffiques, and Discoveries of the English Nation.* Edited by Edmund Goldsmid. 16 vols. Edinburgh: Goldsmid, 1885–1890.

Hale, John R. *Renaissance Europe (1480–1520).* London: Collins, 1977.

Hall, Joseph. *The art of divine meditation: exemplified with two large patterns of meditation: the one of eternall life, as the end, the other of death, as the way.* London: Flesher, 1647.

———. *Occasional Meditations.* In *Bishop Joseph Hall and Protestant Meditation in Seventeenth-Century England: A Study with Texts of* The Art of Divine Meditation *(1606) and* Occasional Meditations *(1633).* Edited by Frank Livingstone Huntley. Binghamton, NY: Center for Medieval and Early Renaissance Studies, 1981.

Hanawalt, Barbara A. "The Contested Streets of Medieval London." In *Die Strasse: Zur Funktion und Perzeption öffentlichen Raums im späten Mittelalter,* edited by Gerhard Jaritz, 148–157. Vienna: Österreichische Akademie der Wissenschaften, 2001.

Härter, Karl. "Vom Kirchenasyl zum politischen Asyl: Asylrecht und Asylpolitik im frühneuzeitlichen Alten Reich." In *Das antike Asyl: Kultische Grundlagen, rechtliche Ausgestaltung und politische Funktion,* edited by Martin Dreher, 301–336. Cologne: Böhlau, 2003.

Hartmann, Wilfried. *Kirche und Kirchenrecht um 900: Die Bedeutung der spätkarolingischen Zeit für Tradition und Innovation im kirchlichen Recht.* Hannover: Hahn, 2008.

Hebräische Berichte über die Judenverfolgungen während des Ersten Kreuzzugs. Edited by Eva Haverkamp. Monumenta Germaniae Historica: Hebräische Texte 1. Hannover: Hahn, 2005.

Hecht, Peter. "Dutch Seventeenth-Century Genre Painting: A Reassessment of Some Current Hypotheses." *Simiolus* 21 (1992): 85–95.

Heidemann, Frank. *Akka Bakka: Religion, Politik und duale Souveränität der Badaga in den Nilgiri Süd-Indiens.* Berlin: Lit, 2006.

Heidrich, Hermann. "Grenzübergänge: Das Haus und die Volkskultur in der frühen Neuzeit." In *Bayerisches Volksleben vom 16. bis zum 19. Jahrhundert,* edited by Richard van Dülmen, 17–41. Munich: C. H. Beck, 1983.

Heinig, Paul-Joachim. "Die Türhüter und Herolde Kaiser Friedrichs III: Studien zum Personal der deutschen Herrscher im 15. Jahrhundert." In *Kaiser Friedrich III. (1440–1493) in seiner Zeit,* edited by Paul-Joachim Heinig, 355–375. Cologne: Böhlau, 1993.

Helmont, Johan Baptista van. *A Ternary of Paradoxes: The Magnetick Cure of Wounds, Nativity of Tartar in Wine, Image of God in Man.* Translated by Walter Charleton. London: Flesher, 1650.

Hergenröther, Joseph. *Handbuch der allgemeinen Kirchengeschichte.* 4th ed. 3 vols. Freiburg im Breisgau: Herder, 1902–1909.

Herte, Adolf. *Die Lutherkommentare des Johannes Cochläus.* Münster: Aschendorff, 1935.

Heyne, Moriz [*sic*]. *Das deutsche Wohnungswesen von ältesten geschichtlichen Zeiten bis zum 16. Jahrhundert.* Leipzig: Hirzel 1899. Reprint, Meerbusch: Erb, 1985.

Hillebrand, Friedrich. "Das Öffnungsrecht bei Burgen: Seine Anfänge und seine Entwicklung in den Territorien des 13. bis 16. Jahrhunderts, unter besonderer Berücksichtigung Württembergs." Ph.D. diss., University of Tübingen, 1967.

Hilliges, Marion. *Das Stadt- und Festungstor: Fortezza und sicurezza—semantische Aufrüstung im 16. Jahrhundert.* Berlin: Gebr. Mann, 2011.

Hills, Helen. *Invisible City: The Architecture of Devotion in Seventeenth-Century Neapolitan Convents.* Oxford: Oxford University Press, 2004.

Hippler, Christiane. *Die Reise nach Jerusalem: Untersuchungen zu den Quellen, zum Inhalt und zur literarischen Struktur der Pilgerberichte des Spätmittelalters.* Frankfurt am Main: Peter Lang, 1987.

Hirschmann, Frank G. *Die Stadt im Mittelalter.* Munich: Oldenbourg, 2009.

Hödl, Ludwig. *Die Geschichte der scholastischen Literatur und der Theologie der Schlüsselgewalt.* Münster: Aschendorff, 1960.

Hollander, Martha. *An Entrance for the Eyes: Space and Meaning in Seventeenth-Century Dutch Art.* Berkeley: University of California Press, 2002.

Höllinger, Franz. "The Experience of Divine Presence: Religious Culture in Brazil, the United States and Western Europe." In *What the World Believes: Analyses and Commentary on the Religion Monitor 2008,* ed. Matthias Jäger, 437–462. Gütersloh: Verlag Bertelsmann Stiftung, 2009.

Holsing, Henrike. "Luthers Thesenanschlag im Bild." In Ott and Treu, *Luthers Thesenanschlag,* 141–172.

Humboldt, Alexander von. *Die Wiederentdeckung der neuen Welt: Erstmals zusammengestellt aus dem unvollendeten Reisebericht und den Reisetagebüchern.* Edited by Paul Kanut Schäfer. Munich: Hanser, 1992.

Hüsch, Frank. *Türöffnung.* 2nd ed. Stuttgart: Kohlhammer, 2010.

Imhof, Arthur E. *Die gewonnenen Jahre: Von der Zunahme unserer Lebensspanne seit dreihundert Jahren, oder von der Notwendigkeit einer neuen Einstellung zu Leben und Sterben.* Munich: C. H. Beck, 1981.

Immenkötter, Herbert, and Wolfgang Wüst. "Augsburg: Freie Reichsstadt und Hochstift." In *Die Territorien des Reichs im Zeitalter der Reformation und Konfessionalisierung*, edited by Anton Schindling and Walter Ziegler, 6:10–35. Münster: Aschendorff, 1996.

Index der Gebodboeken der Stad Antwerpen, 1489–1794. "Antwerpsch Archievenblad" 1 (1864): 120–464; 2 (1864): 1–69; 9 (1934): 115–157; 186–236; 241–315. References are to the year (in parentheses) and the corresponding page number.

Infessura, Stefano. *Diario della città di Roma di Stefano Infessura scribasenato.* Edited by Oreste Tommasini. Rome: Forzani, 1890.

Ingram, Martin. *Church Courts, Sex and Marriage in England, 1570–1640.* Cambridge: Cambridge University Press, 1994.

Inventaire sommaire des registres de la Jurade, 1520 à 1783. Edited by Dast Le Vacher de Bosiville et al. 8 vols. Bordeaux: Gounouilhou, 1896–1913.

Iserloh, Erwin. *Luther zwischen Reform und Reformation: Der Thesenanschlag fand nicht statt.* 3rd rev. ed. Münster: Aschendorff, 1968.

Isidore of Seville. *The Etymologies of Isidore of Seville.* Translated by Stephen A. Barney et al. Cambridge: Cambridge University Press, 2006.

Jacoby, David. "Un agent juif au service de Venise: David Mavrogonato de Candie." *Thesaurismata* 9 (1972): 68–96.

Jahn, Ulrich. *Die deutschen Opfergebräuche bei Ackerbau und Viehzucht: Ein Beitrag zur deutschen Mythologie und Altertumskunde.* Breslau: Koebner, 1884.

Janssen, Johannes. *Geschichte des deutschen Volkes seit dem Ausgang des Mittelalters.* 8 vols. Freiburg im Breisgau: Herder, 1882–1894.

Japan Opened: Compiled Chiefly from the Narrative of the American Expedition to Japan in the Years 1852–3–4. London: Religious Tract Society, 1858.

Jongh, Eddy de. "Inleiding." In *Tot lering en vermaak. Betekenissen van Hollandse genrevoorstellingen uit de zeventiende eeuw*, published by the Rijksmuseum Amsterdam, 14–28. Amsterdam: Rijksmuseum, 1976.

Jonson, Ben. *Every Man out of His Humour*. Edited by Helen Ostovich. Manchester: Manchester University Press, 2001.

Jung-Inglessis, Eva-Maria. "La Porta Santa." *Studi Romani* 23 (1975): 473–485.

Jütte, Daniel. *The Age of Secrecy: Jews, Christians, and the Economy of Secrets, 1400–1800*. Translated by Jeremiah Riemer. New Haven, CT: Yale University Press, 2015.

———. "Defenestration as Ritual Punishment: A New Window on Political Culture in Early Modern Europe," accepted for publication.

———. "Schwang Luther 1517 tatsächlich den Hammer? Die berühmtesten und folgenreichsten Thesen der neueren Weltgeschichte—handwerklich gesehen." *Frankfurter Allgemeine Zeitung*, 18 June 2014.

Kafka, Franz. *The Complete Stories*. Edited by Nahum N. Glatzer. New York: Schocken, 1983.

Kant, Immanuel. *Theoretical Philosophy, 1755–1770*. Edited by David Walford. Cambridge: Cambridge University Press, 1992.

Kaplan, Benjamin J. *Divided by Faith: Religious Conflict and the Practice of Toleration in Early Modern Europe*. Cambridge, MA: Harvard University Press, 2007.

Karant-Nunn, Susan C. *The Reformation of Ritual: An Interpretation of Early Modern Germany*. London: Routledge, 2007.

Karasek, Dieter. "Konrad von Weinsberg: Studien zur Reichspolitik im Zeitalter Sigismunds." Ph.D. diss., University of Erlangen-Nuremberg, 1967.

Kasarska, Iliana, ed. *Mise en œuvre des portails gothiques: architecture et sculpture*. Paris: Éditions Picard, 2011.

Kaufhold, Martin. "Öffentlichkeit im politischen Konflikt: Die Publikation der kurialen Prozesse gegen Ludwig den Bayern in Salzburg." *Zeitschrift für Historische Forschung* 22 (1995): 435‒454.

Kaufmann, Jean-Claude. "Portes, verrous et clés: les rituels de fermeture du chez-soi." *Ethnologie française* 26 (1996): 280‒288.

Keane, Gustave R. "Architectural Criteria for Public Entrance Doors." In *Public Entrance Doors: Proceedings of a Conference Presented as Part of the 1961 Spring Conferences of the Building Research Institute*, 1‒10. Washington, DC: National Academy of Sciences—National Research Council, 1961.

Keil, Martha. "Orte der jüdischen Öffentlichkeit: Judenviertel, Synagoge, Friedhof." In *Ein Thema—zwei Perspektiven: Juden und Christen in Mittelalter und Frühneuzeit*, edited by Eveline Brugger and Birgit Wiedl, 170‒186. Innsbruck: Studienverlag, 2007.

Kemp, Wolfgang. "Die Mauern und Tore von Nancy und Potsdam: Über Stadtgrenzen, vor allem im 17. und 18. Jahrhundert." In *Die Grenze: Begriff und Inszenierung*, edited by Markus Bauer and Thomas Rahn, 237‒254. Berlin: Akademie, 1997.

Kilian, Imma. "Wohnen im frühen Mittelalter (5.‒10. Jahrhundert)." In *Hausen, Wohnen, Residieren, 500‒1800*. Vol. 2 of *Geschichte des Wohnens*, edited by Ulf Dirlmeier, 11‒84. Stuttgart: Deutsche Verlags-Anstalt, 1998.

Kinzelbach, Annemarie. *Gesundbleiben, Krankwerden, Armsein in der frühneuzeitlichen Gesellschaft: Gesunde und Kranke in den Reichsstädten Überlingen und Ulm, 1500‒1700*. Stuttgart: Steiner, 1995.

Kipling, Gordon. "The King's Advent Transformed: The Consecration of the City in the Sixteenth-Century Civic Triumph." In *Ceremonial Culture in Pre-modern Europe*, edited by Nicolas Howe, 89‒127. Notre Dame, IN: University of Notre Dame Press, 2007.

Kirby, Torrance. "Emerging Publics of Religious Reform in the 1530s: The Affair of the Placards and the Publication of Antoine de Marcourt's *Livre des marchans.*" In *Making Publics in Early Modern Europe: People, Things, Forms of Knowledge,* edited by Bronwen Wilson and Paul Yachnin, 37–52. New York: Routledge, 2010.

Kirchhof, Hans Wilhelm. *Wendunmuth.* Edited by Hermann Österley. 5 vols. Tübingen: Laupp, 1869.

Kirchner, Paul Christian. *Jüdisches Ceremoniel, oder, Beschreibung dererjenigen Gebräuche, welche die Jüden so wol inn-als ausser dem Tempel . . . in acht zu nehmen pflegen.* Nuremberg: Monath, 1726.

Klapisch-Zuber, Christiane. *La maison et le nom: stratégies et rituels dans l'Italie de la Renaissance.* Paris: Éditions de l'École des hautes études en sciences sociales, 1990.

Klappheck, Anna. "Vom Sinn des Tores." Afterword to Ewalt Mataré, *Türen und Tore,* 105–114. Krefeld: Scherpe, 1960.

Koeth, H. "Rohstoffbewirtschaftung." Chapter 23 of *Der Weltkrieg.* Vol. 2 of *Handbuch der Politik,* ed. Gerhard Anschütz et al. 3rd ed. Berlin: Rothschild, 1920.

Köhler, W. "Die Schlüssel des Petrus: Versuch einer religionsgeschichtlichen Erklärung von Matth. 16,18.19." *Archiv für Religionswissenschaft* 8 (1905): 214–243.

Kōichi Isoda. "Das Dilemma des Wohnbewußtseins." In *Wohnen in Japan: Ästhetisches Vorbild oder soziales Dilemma?,* edited by Renate Herold, 97–114. Berlin: Erich Schmidt, 1987.

Köstlin, Julius. *Friedrich der Weise und die Schlosskirche zu Wittenberg: Festschrift zur Einweihung der Wittenberger Schlosskirche.* Wittenberg: Herrosé, 1892.

Krafft, Hans Ulrich. *Reisen und Gefangenschaft Hans Ulrich Kraffts.* Edited by K. D. Hassler. Stuttgart: Litterarischer Verein, 1861.

Kramer, Karl-Sigismund. "Das Herausfordern aus dem Haus: Lebensbild eines Rechtsbrauchs." *Bayerisches Jahrbuch für Volkskunde* 1956: 121–138.

Krieg, Martin. "Die Einführung der Reformation in Minden." *Jahrbuch des Vereins für westfälische Kirchengeschichte* 43 (1950): 31–108.

Krois, John Michael. *Cassirer: Symbolic Forms and History.* New Haven, CT: Yale University Press, 1987.

Kroll, Stefan. *Stade um 1700: Sozialtopographie einer deutschen Provinzhauptstadt unter schwedischer Herrschaft.* Stade: Stadt Stade, 1992.

Krug-Richter, Barbara. "Du Bacchant, Quid est Grammatica?— Konflikte zwischen Studenten und Bürgern in Freiburg/Br. in der Frühen Neuzeit." In *Praktiken des Konfliktaustrags in der Frühen Neuzeit,* edited by Barbara Krug-Richter and Ruth-E. Mohrmann, 79–104. Münster: Rhema, 2004.

Krünitz, Johann Georg, ed. *Oekonomische Encyklopädie.* 242 vols. Berlin: Pauli, 1773–1858.

Kühnel, Harry. "Das Alltagsleben im Hause der spätmittelalterlichen Stadt." In *Haus und Familie in der spätmittelalterlichen Stadt,* edited by Alfred Haverkamp, 36–65. Cologne: Böhlau, 1984.

———. "Die Sachkultur bürgerlicher und patrizischer Nürnberger Haushalte des Spätmittelalters und der frühen Neuzeit." In *Haushalt und Familie in Mittelalter und früher Neuzeit,* edited by Trude Ehlert, 15–31. Sigmaringen: Thorbecke, 1991.

Kümin, Beat. "Wirtshaus und Gemeinde: Politisches Profil einer kommunalen Grundinstitution im alten Europa." In *Zwischen Gotteshaus und Taverne: Öffentliche Räume in Spätmittelalter und Früher Neuzeit,* edited by Susanne Rau and Gerd Schwerhoff, 75–97. Cologne: Böhlau, 2004.

Kurtzer Bericht von dem Ser^{mo} Herrn Georg Wilhelm Hertzogen zu Braunschweig und Lüneburg competirenden Jure Optionis, Krafft dessen S. Fürstl. Durchl. die nach dero Herrn Bruders Herrn Hertzog Christian Ludwigs . . . tödlichen Hintrit eröffnete Fürstenthümber Graff- und Herrschafften zu optiren berechtiget. Hannover: Grimm, 1665.

Labovitz, Gail. *Marriage and Metaphor: Constructions of Gender in Rabbinic Literature.* Lanham, MD: Lexington Books, 2009.

Lahnstein, Peter. *Das Leben im Barock: Zeugnisse und Berichte, 1640–1740.* Stuttgart: Kohlhammer, 1974.

———. *Report einer "guten alten Zeit": Zeugnisse und Berichte, 1750–1805.* Stuttgart: Kohlhammer, 1970.

Lambrecht, Karen. "'Jagdhunde des Teufels': Die Verfolgung von Totengräbern im Gefolge frühneuzeitlicher Pestwellen." In *Mit den Waffen der Justiz: Beiträge zur Kriminalitätsgeschichte des späten Mittelalters und der frühen Neuzeit,* edited by Andreas Blauert and Gerd Schwerhoff, 137–157. Frankfurt am Main: Fischer, 1993.

Landucci, Luca. *Diario fiorentino dal 1450 al 1516.* Florence: Sansoni, 1883. Reprint, Florence: Studio Biblos, 1969. Translated by Alice de Rosen Jervis as *A Florentine Diary from 1450 to 1516* (London: Dent, 1927).

Lang, Stefan. *Ausgrenzung und Koexistenz: Judenpolitik und jüdisches Leben in Württemberg und im "Land zu Schwaben," 1492–1650.* Ostfildern: Thorbecke, 2008.

La Roncière, Charles de. "Tuscan Notables on the Eve of the Renaissance." In Ariès and Duby, *A History of Private Life,* 2:157–309.

Latour, Bruno. "Mixing Humans and Nonhumans Together: The Sociology of a Door-Closer." *Social Problems* 35 (1988): 298–310.

Laube, Stefan. *Von der Reliquie zum Ding: Heiliger Ort, Wunderkammer, Museum.* Berlin: Akademie, 2011.

Lefebvre, Henri. *The Production of Space.* Translated by Donald Nicholson-Smith. Oxford: Blackwell, 1991.

Le Goff, Jacques. *The Birth of Purgatory.* Translated by Arthur Goldhammer. London: Scolar, 1984.

———. "Costruzione e distruzione della città murata: Un programma di riflessione e ricerca." In Seta and Le Goff, *La città e le mura,* 1–10.

Le Goff, Jacques, and Jean-Claude Schmitt, eds. *Le Charivari*. Paris: EHESS, 1981.

Leppin, Volker. "Die Monumentalisierung Luthers: Warum vom Thesenanschlag erzählt wurde—und was davon zu erzählen ist." In Ott and Treu, *Luthers Thesenanschlag*, 69–92.

Leucht, Christian Leonhard. *Tractatus novus de jure fenestrarum: vulgo vom Licht- und Fenster-Recht*. Nuremberg: Felsecker, 1717.

Levine, Lee I. "The City-Gate as Synagogue Forerunner." In Levine, *The Ancient Synagogue: The First Thousand Years*, 28–34. New Haven, CT: Yale University Press, 2005.

Liessem, Udo. "Eingemauerte Kugeln: Ein apotropäisches Phänomen." *Burgen und Schlösser* 23 (1982): 73–76.

Linnemeier, Bernd-Wilhelm. *Jüdisches Leben im Alten Reich: Stadt und Fürstentum Minden in der Frühen Neuzeit*. Bielefeld: Verlag für Regionalgeschichte, 2002.

Lipis, Mimi Levy. *Symbolic Houses in Judaism: How Objects and Metaphors Construct Hybrid Places of Belonging*. Surrey: Ashgate, 2011.

Lohrmann, Ulrich, and Hermann Kiessling. *Türme, Tore, Bastionen: Die reichsstädtischen Befestigungsanlagen Augsburgs*. Augsburg: Settele, 1987.

Lombaerde, Piet. *Antwerpen versterkt: De Spaanse omwalling vanaf haar bouw in 1542 tot haar afbraak in 1870*. Brussels: UPA, 2009.

Lottes, Günther. "Popular Culture and the Early Modern State in 16th-Century Germany." In *Understanding Popular Culture: Europe from the Middle Ages to the Nineteenth Century*, edited by Steven L. Kaplan, 147–188. Berlin: Mouton, 1984.

Lundin, Matthew. *Paper Memory: A Sixteenth-Century Townsman Writes His World*. Cambridge, MA: Harvard University Press, 2012.

Luther, Martin. *Werke. Kritische Gesamtausgabe* [Weimar edition]. Weimar, 1883–. Where applicable, English translations are taken from *Luther's Works*, edited by Jaroslav Pelikan and Helmut T. Lehmann (Saint Louis: Concordia, 1955–1986).

Lütolf, Alois. *Sagen, Bräuche und Legenden aus den fünf Orten Lucern, Uri, Schwyz, Unterwalden und Zug.* Lucerne: Schiffmann, 1865.

Machiavelli, Niccolò. *The Discourses.* Translated by Leslie J. Walker and Brian Richardson. Harmondsworth: Penguin 1970.

―――. *Florentine Histories.* Translated by Laura F. Banfield and Harvey C. Mansfield, Jr. Princeton, NJ: Princeton University Press, 1988.

Mączak, Antoni. *Travel in Early Modern Europe.* Cambridge: Polity, 1995.

Malipiero, Domenico. *Annali veneti dall'anno 1457 al 1500.* In *Archivio storico italiano* 7, 2 (1844).

Mandrou, Robert. *Introduction à la France moderne, 1500–1640: essai de psychologie historique.* Paris: Michel, 1998.

Manzoni, Alessandro. *The Betrothed.* Translated by Bruce Penman. London: Penguin, 1972.

Mare, Heidi de. "The Domestic Boundary as Ritual Area in Seventeenth-Century Holland." In *Urban Rituals in Italy and the Netherlands: Historical Contrasts in the Use of Public Space, Architecture and the Urban Environment,* edited by Heidi de Mare and Anna Vos, 109–131. Assen: Van Gorcum, 1993.

Masters, Betty R. *The Chamberlain of the City of London, 1237–1987.* London: Corporation of London, 1988.

Mazur, Grace Dane. *Hinges: Meditations on the Portals of Imagination.* Natick, MA: Peters, 2010.

Melville, Gert, and Peter von Moos, eds. *Das Öffentliche und Private in der Vormoderne.* Cologne: Böhlau, 1998.

Menninghaus, Winfried. *Schwellenkunde: Walter Benjamins Passage des Mythos.* Frankfurt am Main: Suhrkamp, 1986.

Mercier, Félix. *Contributions directes: révision de l'impôt de la propriété bâtie de la côte personnelle et mobilière de l'Impôt des Portes et Fenêtres et des Exemptions.* Beauvais: Imprimerie Avonde et Bachelier, 1903.

Michiko Meid, "Einfluß westlicher Architektur und Ausstattung in Japan." In *Wohnen in Japan: Ästhetisches Vorbild oder soziales Dilemma?,* edited by Renate Herold, 59–79. Berlin: Erich Schmidt, 1987.

Miethke, Jürgen. *Politiktheorie im Mittelalter: Von Thomas von Aquin bis Wilhelm Ockham.* Tübingen: Mohr Siebeck, 2008.

Milton, John. *Paradise Lost.* Edited by Alastair Fowler. Rev. ed. Routledge: New York, 2007.

Mintzker, Yair. "The Defortification of the German City, 1689–1866." Ph.D. diss., Stanford University, 2009.

Moeller, Bernd. "Thesenanschläge." In Ott and Treu, *Luthers Thesenanschlag,* 9–31.

Mohrmann, Ruth-Elisabeth. *Volksleben in Wilster im 16. und 17. Jahrhundert.* Neumünster: Wachholtz, 1977.

Montaigne, Michel de. *Travel Journal.* In *The Complete Works,* translated by Donald M. Frame, 1049–1270. New York: Knopf, 2003.

More, Thomas. *Utopia.* Edited by George M. Logan, Robert M. Adams, and Clarence H. Miller. Cambridge: Cambridge University Press, 1995.

Morhard, Johann. *Haller Haus-Chronik.* Published by Historischer Verein für Württembergisch Franken. Schwäbisch Hall: Eppinger, 1962.

Moser, Hans. "Zur Geschichte der Klöpfelnachtbräuche, ihrer Formen und ihrer Deutungen." *Bayerisches Jahrbuch für Volkskunde* 1951: 121–140.

Muchnik, Natalia. "Du secret imposé à la clandestinité revendiquée: les communautés cryptojudaïsantes madrilènes face à l'Inquisition (XVIe–XVIIIe siècle)." In *Clandestinités urbaines. Les citadins et les territoires du secret (XVIe–XXe),* edited by Sylvie Aprile and Emmanuelle Retaillaud-Bajac, 23–34. Rennes: Presses universitaires de Rennes, 2008.

Muir, Edward. "Presence and Representation in Italian Civic Rituals."
In *La ville à la Renaissance: espaces — représentations — pouvoirs*,
edited by Marie-Luce Demonet and Robert Sauzet, 81–97. Paris:
Honoré Champion, 2008.

—. *Ritual in Early Modern Europe*. 2nd ed. Cambridge: Cambridge University Press, 2005.

Müller, Rainer A. *Der Fürstenhof in der Frühen Neuzeit.* Munich: Oldenbourg, 2004.

Mumford, Lewis. *The City in History: Its Origins, Its Transformations,
and Its Prospects*. New York: Harcourt, Brace & World, 1961.

Mylius, Christian Otto, ed. *Corpus constitutionum magdeburgica-
rum novissimarum, oder Königl. Preuß. und Churfl. Brandenb.
Landes-Ordnungen, Edicta und Mandata im Hertzogthum Magdeburg* [. . .]. Magdeburg, 1714.

Naphy, William G. *Plagues, Poisons, and Potions: Plague-Spreading
Conspiracies in the Western Alps, c. 1530–1640*. Manchester: Manchester University Press, 2002.

Naumov, Goce. "Housing the Dead: Burials inside Houses and Ves-
sels in the Neolithic Balkans." In *Cult in Context: Reconsider-
ing Ritual in Archaeology*, edited by David A. Barrowclough and
Caroline Malone, 257–268. Oxford: Oxbow Books, 2007.

Neuman (Noy), Dov. "Motif-Index of Talmudic-Midrashic Literature." Ph.D. diss., Indiana University, 1954.

Neuner, Stefan. "Signatur bei Albrecht Dürer." Diplomarbeit, University of Vienna, 1998.

New Catholic Encyclopedia. 2nd ed. Detroit: Thomson/Gale, 2003.

Nicolini, Fausto. *Peste e untori nei "Promessi sposi" e nella realtà sto-
rica*. Bari: Laterza, 1937.

Nirenberg, David. *Communities of Violence: Persecution of Minorities
in the Middle Ages*. Princeton, NJ: Princeton University Press,
1996.

Nordman, Daniel. "Sauf-conduits et passeports, en France, à la Renaissance." In *Voyager à la Renaissance*, edited by Jean Ceard

and Jean-Claude Margolin, 145–158. Paris: Maisonneuve et La-
rose, 1987.

Oberman, Heiko. *Masters of the Reformation: The Emergence of a New
Intellectual Climate in Europe.* Translated by Dennis Martin.
Cambridge: Cambridge University Press, 1981.

Oelze, Patrick. "Fraischpfänder — ein frühneuzeitlicher Rechtsbrauch
im Südwesten des Alten Reiches." *Zeitschrift für Württembergi-
sche Landesgeschichte* 69 (2010): 249–261.

Oestreich, Gerhard. "Die antike Literatur als Vorbild der praktischen
Wissenschaften im 16. und 17. Jahrhundert." In Oestreich, *Struk-
turprobleme der frühen Neuzeit,* 358–366. Berlin: Duncker &
Humblot, 1980.

Ogle, M. B. "The House-Door in Greek and Roman Religion and
Folk-Lore." *American Journal of Philology* 32 (1911): 251–271.

Osenbrüggen, Eduard. *Der Hausfrieden: Ein Beitrag zur deutschen
Rechtsgeschichte.* Erlangen: Enke, 1857.

Ott, Joachim, and Martin Treu, eds. *Luthers Thesenanschlag — Fak-
tum oder Fiktion.* Leipzig: Evangelische Verlagsanstalt, 2008.

Paas, John Roger. *The German Political Broadsheet, 1600–1700.* Wies-
baden: Harrassowitz, 1985–.

Panofsky, Erwin. *Gothic Architecture and Scholasticism.* New York:
Meridian Books, 1957.

Patrologia Latina, edited by Jacques-Paul Migne. 221 vols. Paris:
Migne, 1844–1865.

Paulus Diaconus. *Historia Langobardorum.* In *Monumenta Germaniae historica: Scriptores rerum Langobardicarum,* edited by
Georg Waitz, 12–187. Hannover: Hahn, 1878.

Paviot, Jacques. "La destruction des enceintes urbaines dans les an-
ciens Pays-Bas, XIVᵉ–XVᵉ siècle." In Blieck et al., *La forteresse à
l'épreuve du temps,* 19–28.

Peck, Linda Levy. "Building, Buying, and Collecting in London, 1600–
1625." In *Material London, ca. 1600,* edited by Lena Cowen Orlin,
268–289. Philadelphia: University of Pennsylvania Press, 2000.

Pepper, Simon. "Siege Law, Siege Ritual, and the Symbolism of City Walls in Renaissance Europe." In Tracy, *City Walls,* 573–604.

Pepys, Samuel. *The Diary of Samuel Pepys.* Edited by Robert Latham and William Matthews. 11 vols. London: Bell, 1970–1983.

Perrot, Michelle. "Roles and Characters." In Ariès and Duby, *A History of Private Life,* 4:167–240.

Petrucci, Armando. *Public Lettering: Script, Power, and Culture.* Translated by Linda Lappin. Chicago: University of Chicago Press, 1993.

Philippa, Marlies, Frans Debrabandere, and Arend Quak, eds. *Etymologisch woordenboek van het Nederlands.* Amsterdam: Amsterdam University Press, 2003–.

Picard, Charles. *Les portes sculptées à images divines.* Paris: De Boccard, 1962.

Pinto, Isaac de. *Traité de la circulation et du crédit: contenant une analyse raisonnée des fonds d'Angleterre, & de ce qu'on appelle Commerce ou jeu d'actions.* Amsterdam: Rey, 1771.

Plato. *The Republic.* Translated by Tom Griffith. Cambridge: Cambridge University Press, 2000.

Pole, Lotte van de. *The Burgher and the Whore: Prostitution in Early Modern Amsterdam.* Translated by Liz Waters. Oxford: Oxford University Press, 2011.

Poling, Kristin Elisabeth. "On the Inner Frontier: Opening German City Borders in the Long Nineteenth Century." Ph.D. diss., Harvard University, 2011.

Pontano, Giovanni. *I libri delle virtù sociali.* Edited by Francesco Tateo. Rome: Bulzoni, 1999.

Pope, Alexander. *Selected Poetry and Prose.* Edited by Robin Sowerby. London: Routledge, 1988.

Pouchelle, Marie-Christine. *The Body and Surgery in the Middle Ages.* Translated by Rosemary Morris. Cambridge: Polity, 1990.

Quellen zur Geschichte der Juden in den Archiven der neuen Bundes-länder. Edited by Stefi Jersch-Wenzel and Reinhard Rürup. 6 vols. Munich: Saur, 1996–2000.

Radvansky, Gabriel A., Sabine A. Krawietz, and Andrea K. Tamplin. "Walking through Doorways Causes Forgetting: Further Explorations." *Quarterly Journal of Experimental Psychology* 64 (2011): 1632–1645.

Ranum, Orest. "The Refuges of Intimacy." In Ariès and Duby, *A History of Private Life*, 3:207–263.

Ratté, Felicity. "Images of City Gates in Medieval Italian Painting." *Gesta* 38 (1999): 142–153.

Rauwolf, Leonhart. *Aigentliche beschreibung der Raiß/so er vor diser zeit gegen Auffgang inn die Morgenländer* [. . .] *volbracht.* Lauingen: Georg Willer, 1583. Facsimile, Graz: Akademische Druck- und Verlagsanstalt, 1971.

Regino of Prüm. *Das Sendhandbuch des Regino von Prüm.* Translated and edited by Wilfried Hartmann. Darmstadt: Wissenschaftliche Buchgesellschaft, 2004.

Régnier-Bohler, Danielle. "Imagining the Self." In Ariès and Duby, *A History of Private Life*, 2:313–394.

"Reiche Ausbeute am Dürrnberg: 600 Skelette aus 360 Grabanlagen aus dem keltischen Salzbergbau nahe Hallein konnten bislang untersucht werden." *Universum: Das Magazin des Naturhistorischen Museums Wien*, June 2002, 9.

Reinle, Adolf. *Zeichensprache der Architektur: Symbol, Darstellung und Brauch in der Baukunst des Mittelalters und der Neuzeit.* Zürich: Artemis, 1976.

Ripamonti, Giuseppe. *De peste quae fuit anno MDCXXX libri V.* Milan: Malatesta, 1640.

Rittgers, Ronald K. *The Reformation of the Keys: Confession, Conscience, and Authority in Sixteenth-Century Germany.* Cambridge, MA: Harvard University Press, 2004.

Robbins, Kevin C. *City on the Ocean Sea: La Rochelle, 1530–1650: Urban Society, Religion, and Politics on the French Atlantic Frontier.* Leiden: Brill, 1997.

Roche, Daniel. *A History of Everyday Things: The Birth of Consumption in France, 1600–1800.* Translated by Brian Pearce. Cambridge: Cambridge University Press, 2000.

Roeck, Bernd. *Eine Stadt in Krieg und Frieden: Studien zur Geschichte der Reichsstadt Augsburg zwischen Kalenderstreit und Parität.* 2 vols. Göttingen: Vandenhoeck & Ruprecht, 1989.

Rogers, Clifford J. *The Military Revolution Debate: Readings on the Military Transformation of Early Modern Europe.* Boulder, CO: Westview, 1995.

Rohr, Julius Bernhard von. *Einleitung zur Ceremoniel-Wissenschaft der Grossen Herren.* Berlin: Rüdiger, 1733. Reprint, with commentary by Monika Schlechte, Leipzig: Edition Leipzig, 1990.

Rosselin, Céline. "The Ins and Outs of the Hall: A Parisian Example." In Cieraad, *At Home,* 53–59.

Rossi, Domenico de'. *Studio d'architettura civile.* Rome, 1702–1721. Reprint, Brookfield, VT: Gregg International, 1972.

Roth, Cecil. "The Eastertide Stoning of the Jews and Its Liturgical Echoes." *Jewish Quarterly Review* 35 (1945): 361–370.

Rowe, David Nelson. "A Comparative Analysis of the Historical Background of the Monroe Doctrine and the Open-Door Policy in the Far East." Ph.D. diss., University of Chicago, 1938.

Rüthing, Heinrich. *Höxter um 1500: Analyse einer Stadtgesellschaft.* Paderborn: Bonifatius, 1986.

Sahlins, Peter. *Boundaries: The Making of France and Spain in the Pyrenees.* Berkeley: University of California Press, 1989.

Saltonstall, Wye. *Clavis ad portam, or a Key Fitted to Open the Gate of Tongues.* Oxford: William Turner, 1634.

Sammlung der wichtigsten und nöthigsten, bisher aber noch nicht herausgegebenen kayser- und königlichen, auch hertzoglichen Pri-

vilegien, Statuten, Rescripten und Pragmatischen Sanctionen des Landes Schlesien. 2 vols. Breslau, 1736–1739.

Sand, Gérard, and F. W. Rubbrecht. *Clés et défense d'une ville: Bruxelles et son histoire.* Brussels: Crédit Communal, 1984.

Sand, Jordan. *House and Home in Modern Japan: Architecture, Domestic Space, and Bourgeois Culture, 1880–1930.* Cambridge, MA: Harvard University Press, 2003.

Sander, Stephan Karl. "Urban Elites in the Venetian Commonwealth: Social and Economic Mobility in Early Modern Dalmatia." Ph.D. diss., Karl-Franzens-Universität Graz, 2011.

Sandrart, Joachim von. *Teutsche Academie der Bau-, Bild- und Mahlerey-Künste.* 2 vols. Nuremberg: Miltenberger, 1675–1679.

Sanson, Henri, ed. *Memoirs of the Sansons: From Private Notes and Documents (1688–1847).* 2 vols. London: Chatto and Windus, 1876.

Sauer, Joseph. *Symbolik des Kirchengebäudes und seiner Ausstattung in der Auffassung des Mittelalters, mit Berücksichtigung von Honorius Augustodunensis, Sicardus und Durandus.* 2nd ed. Freiburg im Breisgau: Herder, 1924.

Scamozzi, Vincenzo. *L'idea della architettura universale.* Venice 1615. Reprint, Ridgewood, NJ: Gregg Press, 1964.

Schama, Simon. *The Embarrassment of Riches: An Interpretation of Dutch Culture in the Golden Age.* Berkeley: University of California Press, 1988.

Schiffhauer, Nils. "Du kriegst die Tür nicht auf: Karte, Chip und Ziffernfolgen ersetzen den Hotelschlüssel." *Frankfurter Allgemeine Zeitung,* 13 November 2012, T1.

Schivelbusch, Wolfgang. *Disenchanted Night: The Industrialisation of Light in the Nineteenth Century.* Translated by Angela Davis. Oxford: Berg, 1988.

Schmidt, Fritz, and Ulf Dirlmeier. "Geschichte des Wohnens im Spätmittelalter." In *Hausen, Wohnen, Residieren, 500–1800,* 229–346. Vol. 2 of *Geschichte des Wohnens,* edited by Ulf Dirlmeier. Stuttgart: Deutsche Verlags-Anstalt, 1998.

Schmidt, Gary D. *The Iconography of the Mouth of Hell: Eighth-Century Britain to the Fifteenth Century.* Selinsgrove, PA: Susquehanna University Press, 1995.

Schmidt, Günter. "Libelli famosi: Zur Bedeutung der Schmähschriften, Scheltbriefe, Schandgemälde und Pasquille in der deutschen Rechtsgeschichte." J.D. diss., University of Cologne, 1985.

Schmidt-Voges, Inken. "Nachbarn im Haus: Grenzüberschreitungen und Friedewahrung in der 'guten Nachbarschaft.'" In *Grenzen und Grenz-Überschreitungen: Bilanz und Perspektiven der Frühneuzeitforschung,* edited by Christine Roll, Frank Pohle, and Matthias Myrczek, 413–427. Cologne: Böhlau, 2010.

———. "Securitas domestica oder ius certum domus? Juristische Diskurse zur Sicherheit des Hauses um 1700." Unpublished manuscript, 26 July 2012.

———. "'Si domus in pace sunt . . .': Zur Bedeutung des 'Hauses' in Luthers Vorstellungen vom weltlichen Frieden." *Lutherjahrbuch* 78 (2011): 153–185.

Schmitt, Jean-Claude. "Schwelle." In *Handbuch der politischen Ikonographie,* edited by Uwe Fleckner, Martin Warnke, and Hendrik Ziegler, 2:341–349. Munich: C. H. Beck, 2011.

Schrader, Stephanie. "Master M.Z.'s Embrace: The Construction of a Visual Dialogue." *Allen Memorial Art Museum Bulletin* 47 (1993): 15–27.

Schramm, Helmar, Ludger Schwarte, and Jan Lazardzig, eds. *Collection, Laboratory, Theater: Scenes of Knowledge in the 17th Century.* Berlin: De Gruyter, 2005.

Schroeder Joy A. "The Rape of Dinah: Luther's Interpretation of a Biblical Narrative." *Sixteenth Century Journal* 28 (1997): 775–791.

Schudt, Johann Jacob. *Jüdische Merckwürdigkeiten . . . Was sich Curieuses und denckwürdiges in den neuern Zeiten bey einigen Jahrhunderten mit denen in alle IV. Theile der Welt sonderlich durch Teutschland zerstreuten Juden zugetragen.* 4 vols. Frankfurt am Main, 1714. Reprint, Berlin: Lamm, 1922.

Schukowitz, Hans. "Bauopfer." *Zeitschrift für österreichische Volks-kunde* 3 (1897): 367.

Schulthaiß, Christoph. *Konstanzer Bistumschronik des Christoph Schulthaiß*. Edited by J. Marmor. *Freiburger Diöcesan-Archiv* 8 (1874): 1–101.

Schütte, Ulrich. "Stadttor und Hausschwelle: Zur rituellen Bedeutung architektonischer Grenzen in der frühen Neuzeit." In *Zeremoniell und Raum*, edited by Werner Paravicini, 305–324. Sigmaringen: Thorbecke, 1997.

Schwarz, Dietrich W. H. *Sachgüter und Lebensformen: Einführung in die materielle Kulturgeschichte des Mittelalters und der Neuzeit*. Berlin: Erich Schmidt, 1970.

Schwarz, Klaus. *Die Pest in Bremen: Epidemien und freier Handel in einer deutschen Hafenstadt, 1350–1713*. Bremen: Staatsarchiv Bremen, 1996.

Schweizer, Stefan. *Zwischen Repräsentation und Funktion: Die Stadttore der Renaissance in Italien*. Göttingen: Vandenhoeck & Ruprecht, 2002.

Schwemmer, Wilhelm. *Tore und Türen an Alt-Nürnberger Profanbauten*. Nuremberg: Spindler, 1930.

Scotti, J. J., ed. *Sammlung der Gesetze und Verordnungen, welche in den ehemaligen Herzogthümern Jülich, Cleve und Berg und in dem vormaligen Großherzogthum Berg [. . .] ergangen sind*. Düsseldorf: Wolf, 1821.

Scribner, Robert. "Symbolising Boundaries: Defining Social Space in the Daily Life of Early Modern Germany." In *Symbole des Alltags, Alltag der Symbole*, edited by Gertrud Blaschitz et al., 821–841. Graz: Akademische Druck- und Verlagsanstalt, 1992.

Scully, Stephen. *Homer and the Sacred City*. Ithaca, NY: Cornell University Press, 1994.

Seitter, Walter. "Entfestigung: Zur Obszonität der Städte." *Daidalos* 13 (1984): 46–53.

Selbmann, Rolf. *Eine Kulturgeschichte des Fensters von der Antike bis zur Moderne.* Berlin: Reimer, 2010.

Seligmann, Claus. "What Is a Door? Notes toward a Semiotic Guide to Design." *Semiotica* 38 (1982): 55–76.

Selle, Gert. *Die eigenen vier Wände: Zur verborgenen Geschichte des Wohnens.* Frankfurt am Main: Campus, 1993.

Sennett, Richard. *Flesh and Stone: The Body and the City in Western Civilization.* New York: Norton, 1994.

Serlio, Sebastiano. *On Architecture.* Translated and edited by Vaughan Hart and Peter Hicks. New Haven, CT: Yale University Press, 1996–2001.

Seta, Cesare de, and Jacques Le Goff, eds. *La città e le mura.* Bari: Laterza, 1989.

Shalom of Neustadt. *Hilkhot u-minhage Rabenu Shalom mi-Noishtat.* Edited by Shlomo Spitzer. 2nd ed. Jerusalem: Machon Yerushalayim, 1977.

Shaw, Diane. "The Construction of the Private in Medieval London." *Journal of Medieval and Early Modern Studies* 26 (1996): 447–466.

Sherman, William H. "On the Threshold: Architecture, Paratext, and Early Print Culture." In *Agent of Change: Print Culture Studies after Elizabeth L. Eisenstein,* edited by Sabrina Alcorn Baron, Eric N. Lindquist, and Eleanor F. Shevlin, 67–81. Amherst: University of Massachusetts Press, 2007.

Shestov, Lev. *Potestas clavium.* Translated by Bernard Martin. Athens: Ohio University Press, 1968.

Siebenhüner, Kim. *Zechen, Zücken, Lärmen: Studenten vor dem Freiburger Universitätsgericht, 1561–577.* Freiburg im Breisgau: Haug, 1999.

Siegert, Bernhard. "Türen: Zur Materialität des Symbolischen." *Zeitschrift für Medien- und Kulturforschung* 1 (2010): 151–170.

Simmel, Georg. "Brücke und Tür." In *Gesamtausgabe.* Edited by Otthein Rammstedt, 12:55–61. Suhrkamp, 1989–. Translated by

Mark Ritter as "Bridge and Door," in *Theory, Culture & Society* 11 (1994): 5–10.

Simson, Otto von. *The Gothic Cathedral: Origins of Gothic Architecture and the Medieval Concept of Order.* New York: Harper & Row, 1962.

Smail, Daniel Lord. "Enmity and the Distraint of Goods in Late Medieval Marseille." In *Emotions and Material Culture,* edited by Gerhard Jaritz, 17–30. Vienna: Verlag der Österreichischen Akademie der Wissenschaften, 2003.

———. "Hatred as a Social Institution in Late-Medieval Society." *Speculum* 76 (2001): 90–126.

Spohn, Thomas. "Herein!—klopfen, schellen, klingeln." *Jahrbuch für Hausforschung* 50 (2004): 137–151.

The Sources of Swiss Anabaptism: The Grebel Letters and Related Documents. Edited by Leland Harder. Scottsdale, PA: Herald, 1985.

Stern, Selma. *Der Hofjude im Zeitalter des Absolutismus: Ein Beitrag zur europäischen Geschichte im 17. und 18. Jahrhundert.* Translated and edited by Marina Sassenberg. Tübingen: Mohr, 2001.

Stern, Tiffany. *Documents of Performance in Early Modern England.* Cambridge: Cambridge University Press, 2009.

Steward, Jill, and Alexander Cowan. Introduction to *The City and the Senses: Urban Culture since 1500,* edited by Jill Steward and Alexander Cowan, 1–22. Aldershot: Ashgate, 2007.

Stow, Kenneth. "Delitto e castigo nello Stato della Chiesa: Gli ebrei nelle carceri romane dal 1572 al 1659." In *Jewish Life in Early Modern Rome: Challenge, Conversion, and Private Life,* 173–192. Aldershot: Ashgate, 2007.

Strozzi Macinghi, Alessandra. *Selected Letters of Alessandra Strozzi.* Translated by Heather Gregory. Berkeley: University of California Press, 1997.

Stupperich, Robert. *Westfälische Reformationsgeschichte: Historischer Überblick und theologische Einordnung.* Bielefeld: Luther-Verlag, 1993.

Sturm, Leonhard Christoph. *Erste Ausübung der vortrefflichen und vollständigen Anweisung zu der Civil-Bau-Kunst Nicolai Goldmanns, bestehend zu neun ausführlichen Anmerkungen.* Brunswick: Keßler, 1699.

Sturm, Patrick. *Leben mit dem Tod in den Reichsstädten Esslingen, Nördlingen und Schwäbisch Hall: Epidemien und deren Auswirkungen vom frühen 15. bis zum frühen 17. Jahrhundert.* Ostfildern: Thorbecke, 2014.

Suger, Abbot of Saint Denis. *Abbot Suger on the Abbey Church of St.-Denis and Its Art Treasures.* Edited and translated by Erwin Panofsky. 2nd ed. Princeton, NJ: Princeton University Press, 1978.

Süßmann, Arthur. *Die Judenschuldentilgungen unter König Wenzel.* Berlin: Lamm, 1907.

Syndikus, Candida. "Porta und Arcus: Stadttor und Triumphbogen bei Alberti." In *Leon Battista Alberti: Humanist, Architekt, Kunsttheoretiker,* edited by Joachim Poeschke and Candida Syndikus, 257–278. Münster: Rhema, 2008.

Tanavoli, Parviz, and John T. Wertime. *Locks from Iran: Pre-Islamic to Twentieth Century.* Washington, DC: Smithsonian, 1976.

Tantner, Anton. *Die Hausnummer. Eine Geschichte von Ordnung und Unordnung.* Marburg: Jonas, 2007.

———. *Ordnung der Häuser, Beschreibung der Seelen. Hausnummerierung und Seelenkonskription in der Habsburgermonarchie.* Innsbruck: Studienverlag, 2007.

Teut, Anna. "Türen, Tore, Torsituationen: Zur Ikonographie eines unheimlichen Bau- und Raumsegments." *Daidalos* 13 (1984): 87–95.

Thébert, Yvon. "Private Life and Domestic Architecture in Roman Africa." In Ariès and Duby, *A History of Private Life,* 1:319–405.

Theophilus. *On Divers Arts: The Treatise of Theophilus.* Translated by John G. Hawthorne and Cyril Stanley Smith. Chicago: University of Chicago Press, 1963.

Thøfner, Margit. *A Common Art: Urban Ceremonial in Antwerp and Brussels during and after the Dutch Revolt.* Zwolle: Waanders, 2007.

Thomas, Keith. "Cleanliness and Godliness in Early Modern England." In *Religion, Culture and Societey in Early Modern Britain: Essays in Honour of Patrick Collinson,* edited by Anthony Fletcher and Peter Roberts, 56–83. Cambridge: Cambridge University Press, 1994.

Thompson, E. P. "Rough Music Reconsidered." *Folklore* 103 (1992): 3–26.

Thornton, Peter. *The Italian Renaissance Interior, 1400–1600.* London: Weidenfeld & Nicolson, 1991.

Tintó Sala, Margarita. *La història del Gremi de Serrallers i Ferrers de Barcelona: any 1380.* Barcelona: Litografia Rosès, 1980.

Tlusty, B. Ann. "'Privat' oder 'öffentlich'? Das Wirtshaus in der deutschen Stadt des 16. und 17. Jahrhunderts." In *Zwischen Gotteshaus und Taverne. Öffentliche Räume in Spätmittelalter und Früher Neuzeit,* edited by Susanne Rau and Gerd Schwerhoff, 53–73. Cologne: Böhlau 2004.

Torpey, John. *The Invention of the Passport: Surveillance, Citizenship and the State.* Cambridge: Cambridge University Press, 2000.

Trabandt, Joachim. "Der kriminalrechtliche Schutz des Hausfriedens in seiner geschichtlichen Entwicklung." Ph.D. diss., Universität Hamburg, 1970.

Trachtenberg, Joshua. *The Devil and the Jews: The Medieval Conception of the Jews and Its Relation to Modern Antisemitism.* New Haven, CT: Yale University Press, 1943. Reprint, with foreword by Marc Saperstein. Philadelphia: Jewish Publication Society, 1983.

Tracy, James D. Introduction to Tracy, *City Walls,* 1–15.

——, ed. *City Walls: The Urban Enceinte in Global Perspective.* Cambridge: Cambridge University Press, 2000.

Trébuchet, A. "Recherches sur l'éclairage public de Paris." *Annales d'hygiène publique et de médecine légale* 30 (1843): 5–27.

Trexler, Richard C. *Public Life in Renaissance Florence.* New York: Academic Press, 1980.

Trumbull, H. Clay. *The Threshold Covenant.* New York: Charles Scribner's Sons, 1896.

Tucher, Endres. *Baumeisterbuch der Stadt Nürnberg, 1464–1475.* Edited by Matthias Lexer. Stuttgart: Litterarischer Verein, 1862.

Turner, Victor. "Passages, Margins, and Poverty: Religious Symbols of Communitas." In *Dramas, Fields, and Metaphors: Symbolic Action in Human Society,* 231–271. Ithaca, NY: Cornell University Press, 1974.

Untersuchungen über den Charakter der Gebäude: über die Verbindung der Baukunst mit den schönen Künsten und über die Wirkungen, welche durch dieselbe hervorgebracht werden sollen. Lepizig: Haug, 1788. Reprint, Nördlingen: Uhl, 1986.

Unwin, Simon. *Doorway.* London: Routledge, 2007.

Urkundenbuch der Stadt Basel. Edited by the Historische und Antiquarische Gesellschaft zu Basel. 11 vols. Basel: Detloff, 1890–1910.

Van Goethem, Herman. *Photography and Realism in the 19th Century: Antwerp: The Oldest Photographs, 1847–1880.* Antwerp: Van de Velde, 1999.

Verzar, Christine B. "Medieval Passageways and Performance Art: Art and Ritual at the Threshold." *Arte Medievale* 3 (2004): 63–74.

Veyne, Paul. "The Roman Home." In Ariès and Duby, *A History of Private Life,* 1:315–317.

Vickery, Amanda. *Behind Closed Doors: At Home in Georgian England.* New Haven, CT: Yale University Press, 2009.

Vikan, Gary, and John Nesbitt. *Security in Byzantium: Locking, Sealing, and Weighing.* Washington, DC: Dumbarton Oaks Center for Byzantine Studies, 1980.

Voet, Leon. "Antwerp: The Metropolis and Its History." In *Antwerp: Story of a Metropolis (16th–17th Century)*, edited by Jan Van der Stock, 13–17. Ghent: Martial & Snoeck, 1993.

Völkel, Michaela. *Schloßbesichtigungen in der Frühen Neuzeit: Ein Beitrag zur Frage nach der Öffentlichkeit höfischer Repräsentation.* Munich: Deutscher Kunstverlag 2007.

Wagner, Adolph. *Specielle Steuerlehre: Die Besteuerung des 19. Jahrhunderts: Britische und französische Besteuerung.* Vol. 3 of *Finanzwissenschaft.* Leipzig: Winter, 1889.

Waterson, Roxana. *The Living House: An Anthropology of Architecture in South-East Asia.* Singapore: Oxford University Press, 1990.

Webb, Diana. *Privacy and Solitude in the Middle Ages.* London: Continuum, 2007.

Weber, Max. *Wirtschaft und Gesellschaft: Grundriß der verstehenden Soziologie.* Edited by Johannes Winckelmann. Tübingen: Mohr, 1985.

Wegs, Robert J. *Die österreichische Kriegswirtschaft (1914–1918).* Wien: Schendl, 1979.

Weiland, Pieter. *Nederduitsch taalkundig woordenboek.* Amsterdam: Allart, 1807.

Weilenmann, Alexandra, Daniel Normark, and Eric Laurier. "Managing Walking Together: The Challenge of Revolving Doors." *Space and Culture* 17 (2014): 122–136.

Weinsberg, Hermann. *Das Buch Weinsberg: Kölner Denkwürdigkeiten aus dem 16. Jahrhundert.* Edited by Konstantin Höhlbaum et al. 5 vols. 1886–1926. Reprint, Düsseldorf: Droste, 2000.

Wellisch, Hans H. "'Index': The Word, Its History, Meanings and Usages." *Indexer* 13 (1983): 147–151.

———. "The Oldest Printed Indexes." *Indexer* 15 (1986): 73–82.

Wiedl, Birgit. "Jews and the City: Parameters of Urban Jewish Life in Late Medieval Austria." In *Urban Space in the Middle Ages and the Early Modern Age,* edited by Albrecht Classen, 273–308. Berlin: De Gruyter, 2009.

Wiesner, Jonas. *Der Bann in seiner geschichtlichen Entwickelung auf dem Boden des Judenthumes.* Leipzig: Leiner, 1864.

Wildvogel, Christian [Praeses], and Johann Georg von Calm [Respondent]. *Janus patulcius & clusinus sive De Jure Portarum.* Jena: Müller, 1697.

Wilson, James Q., and George L. Kelling. "Broken Windows: The Police and Neighborhood Safety." *Atlantic Monthly,* March 1982, 29–38.

Winkler, Friedrich. *Die Zeichnungen Albrecht Dürers.* 4 vols. Berlin: Deutscher Verein für Kunstwissenschaft, 1936–1939.

Wipfler, Esther P. "Luthers 95 Thesen im bewegten Bild: Ein Beispiel für die Schriftlichkeit im Bild." In Ott and Treu, *Luthers Thesenanschlag,* 173–197.

Wittneben, Eva Luise. *Bonagratia von Bergamo: Franziskanerjurist und Wortführer seines Ordens im Streit mit Papst Johannes XXII.* Leiden: Brill, 2003.

Wolf, Norbert. *Albrecht Dürer. 1471–528: Das Genie der deutschen Renaissance.* Cologne: Taschen, 2012.

Wolf, Eric M. *Making an Entrance: Design Philosophy and the Entry in Western Architecture.* New York: New York School of Interior Design, 2007.

Wolfe, Michael. *Walled Towns and the Shaping of France: From the Medieval to the Early Modern Era.* New York: Palgrave Macmillan, 2009.

Wolff, Helmut. *Geschichte der Ingolstädter Juristenfakultät, 1472–1625.* Berlin: Duncker & Humblot, 1973.

Woolgar, C. M. *The Senses in Late Medieval England.* New Haven, CT: Yale University Press, 2006.

Wotton, Henry. *The Elements of Architecture.* London: Bill, 1624.

Wunderlich, Steffen. *Das Protokollbuch von Mathias Alber: Zur Praxis des Reichskammergerichts im frühen 16. Jahrhundert.* 2 vols. Cologne: Böhlau, 2011.

Yaari, Avraham, ed. *Zichronot Eretz Yisra'el.* 2 vols. Ramat Gan: Masada, 1974.

Zedler, Johann Heinrich, ed. *Grosses vollständiges Universal-Lexicon aller Wissenschafften und Künste, welche bißhero durch menschlichen Verstand und Witz erfunden und verbessert worden* [. . .]. 68 vols. Halle: Zedler, 1731–1754.

Zeller, Olivier. *Relations de cohabitation et formes d'usage des espaces publics et privés à Lyon (XVIIIe et XIXe siècles).* Paris: Ministère de la Culture/Conseil du Patrimoine ethnologique, 2003.

Zimmer, Eric. *Jewish Synods in Germany during the Late Middle Ages, 1286–1603.* New York: Yeshiva University Press, 1978.

Zorn, Friedrich. *Wormser Chronik (mit den Zusätzen Franz Bertholds von Flersheim).* Edited by Wilhelm Arnold. Stuttgart: Litterarischer Verein, 1857.

Zschocke, Helmut. *Die Berliner Akzisemauer: Die vorletzte Mauer der Stadt.* Berlin: Berlin Story, 2007.

Zur Nieden, Andrea. *Der Alltag der Mönche: Studien zum Klosterplan von St. Gallen.* Hamburg: Diplomica, 2008.

ILLUSTRATION CREDITS

Figure 1. V&A Images, London / Art Resource, NY

Figure 2. Scala / Art Resource, NY

Figure 3. Winfried Wilhelmy, ed., *Seliges Lächeln und höllisches Gelächter: Das Lachen in Kunst und Kultur des Mittelalters* (Regensburg: Schnell + Steiner, 2012), p. 151

Figure 4. Alixe Bovey, *Monsters and Grotesques in Medieval Manuscripts* (Toronto: University of Toronto Press, 2002), p. 37

Figure 5. Erich Lessing / Art Resource, NY

Figure 6. Julien Chapius, *Stefan Lochner: Image Making in Fifteenth-Century Cologne* (Turnhout: Brepols, 2004), table 2

Figure 7. Roland Halfen, *Chartres: Schöpfungsbau und Ideenwelt im Herzen Europas: Das Königsportal* (Stuttgart: Mayer, 2001), p. 10

Figure 8. Author

Figure 9. Author

Figure 10. Bibliotheca Hertziana, Max Planck Institute for Art History, Rome

Figure 11. Author

Figure 12. Erich Lessing / Art Resource, NY

Figure 13. HEW 5.9.20, Harry Elkins Widener Collection, Harvard University

Figure 14. © Bayerisches Nationalmuseum München. Photo: Gerda Schmitzlein

Figure 15. bpk, Berlin / Gemäldegalerie, Staatliche Museen, Berlin, Germany / Jörg P. Anders / Art Resource, NY

Figure 16. bpk, Berlin / Kupferstichkabinett, Staatliche Museen, Berlin, Germany / Volker-H. Schneider / Art Resource, NY

Figure 17. Deutsches Schloss- und Beschlägemuseum, Velbert

Figure 18. Courtesy of the Library of Congress, Washington DC, LC-USZ62−71792

Figure 19. Scala / Art Resource, NY

Figure 20. Germanisches Nationalmuseum, Nuremberg. Photo: G. Janssen

Figure 21. Biblioteka Jagiellońska, Kraków, Rkp. Przyb. 42a/60, fol. 107r

Figure 22. Jeff Veitch

Figure 23. Museum Schloß Burgk

Figure 24. Marie Andree-Eysn, *Volkskundliches aus dem bayrisch-österreichischen Alpengebiet* (Braunschweig: Vieweg und Sohn, 1910), p. 100

Figure 25. Wartburg-Stiftung Eisenach

Figure 26. Lutherstadt Wittenberg Marketing GmbH

Figure 27. Herzog August Bibliothek Wolfenbüttel: Gm 4865 (1)

Figure 28. Joost de Damhouder, *Praxis rerum criminalium* (Antwerp: Beller, 1601; reprint Clark, NJ: Lawbook Exchange, 2005), Figure 140

Figure 29. bpk, Berlin / Kupferstichkabinett, Staatliche Museen, Berlin, Germany / Jörg P. Anders / Art Resource, NY

Figure 30. Courtesy of the Library of Congress, Washington DC, LC-USZ62−60194

Figure 31. Herman van Goethem, *Photography and Realism in the 19th Century: Antwerp: The Oldest Photographs, 1847−1880* (Antwerp: Van de Velde, 1999), p. 98

Figure 32. Herzog August Bibliothek Wolfenbüttel: 14.3 Geom. (5)

Figure 33. Author

Figure 34. Author

Figure 35. Herman van Goethem, *Photography and Realism in the 19th Century: Antwerp: The Oldest Photographs, 1847–1880* (Antwerp: Van de Velde, 1999), p. 101

Figure 36. Herman van Goethem, *Photography and Realism in the 19th Century: Antwerp: The Oldest Photographs, 1847–1880* (Antwerp: Van de Velde, 1999), p. 232

Figure 37. Author

INDEX

Page numbers in *italic* type indicate illustrations.

excrement, 204–5

executioners. *See* death penalty

Exodus, 158

Ezekiel, 38

Faber, Johann Ernst, 160

façade, 54, 62–63, 196

faith, 62, 119

"False Waldemar," 224

family. *See* marriage and family life

Febvre, Lucien, 6

feces, 204–5

Fehdebriefe, 202–3

feuds, 68–69, 201–3

Filarete, 213

fire prevention, 91, 262n12

First Crusade (1096), 70

Florence, 56, 75, 87–88, 209; Baptistery bronze doors, 24, *25*, 26, 27; chain and lock, 213, *214*; city gates, 225, 226–28; keys to city ceremony, 223; Medici-Pazzi conflict, 143–46, 225; plague account, 169; sixteenth-century guide to, 23–24

folklore, 11, 86–87, 90–91, 146. *See also* proverbs; superstitions

forcible entry, 65–66, 68–69, 93–94

foreigners, 18, 131, 231, 232, 233–34, 240, 249–50

fortification. *See* city gates and walls

Fra Angelico, *Christ's Harrowing of Hell*, *36*

Fraischpfänder, 74–75

France, 75, 92, 93, 110, 145, 201–2, 210, 230; church asylum, 49–50; defortification, 245–46; knocking practices, 140; locks and keys, 94–95

Franciscan order, 186

Frankenstein (Silesia), 169–70

Frankfurt am Main, 73, 187, 304n109, 305n123

Frederick the Wise, Elector of Saxony, 191

Freiburg im Breisgau, 236, 243; cathedral, 188

front porch, 104–5

Furttenbach, Joseph, 217–18, *219*

Gaidoz, Henri, 11

garden of Eden, 28

gated communities, 251

gatekeeper (person), 226, 232, 233–35, 238, 239

"gatekeepers" (quality standards), 80

gates, 3, 9, 53, 58, 75–80, 254–56; castle, 137–38; digital, 80, 133; of honor, 143, 222, 254; to sacraments, 39. *See also* city gates and walls

gates of heaven (*porta caeli*), 7, 13–14, *25*, 26–28, 30, *37*, 75, *115*, 212, 255; Christ's selective opening of, 136–37; eroded belief in, 122, 258; gates of paradise vs., 28; keys of the kingdom and,

Pope's Sacrilege and St. Peter's Rage over the Binding and Loosing Key of Our Lord Christ, The (anon. broadsheet), *120*

porch, 104–5

porta caeli. See gates of heaven

portal, 8, 24, 36–48, 50, 53, 61, 189, 191; bridal, 46, *46*, *47*; cathedral, 40–41, *41*; digital, 80, 133, 256; as knowledge metaphor, 78; as oversize mouth, 54, *55*

porte ascessorie, 53

porter, 43

Portugal, 162

power of keys (secular). *See* holder of the keys

Power of the Keys (*potestas clavium*), 27, 113–23, *120*, 227, 253, 258; modern view of, 121–23; Protestant view of, 118–19, 121

Prato cathedral, 204

printing press, 80, 180

privacy, 13, 14, 18, 26, 96, 258

private house door, 1–3, 10–11, 18, 52–77, 159, 173, 174, 210; antechamber and, 103–5; chippings from, 74; cleanliness and, 163–68; defamation of, 64–70, 181, 196–203, 205, 255; domestic sanctuary behind, 64–66, 68–69, 98; entrance procedure, 134–38, 149–51 (*see also* knocking); fears projected onto,

173–74; as honor/status reflection, 14, 26, 55, 61–62, 69, 70–71, 75, 126, 141, 143, 145, 195–97, 254; inscriptions on, 60, *61*, 62–63, 160; interior doors and, 17, 55–56, 89; Japanese culture and, 17, 123, 125–28; Jewish mezuzah and, 158–62, 174; magic spells and, 162–63; metal fixtures confiscation, 1–3, 5, 13, 22, 257–58; as mouth of house, 54–55, *55*, 166; nighttime locking of, 88–89, 92; ornamentation of, 56, 58–63, *61*, 195, 254; plague signs on, 155–56, 167–68; protective rites for, 152–63, *157*, 254; reading of, 174, 194–96, 203–8, 255; security of, 6, 13, 95–96, 173–74, 253, 258; women's status and, 98–105. *See also* closed door; open door; threshold

processions, 230

professions, "honorable" and "dishonorable," 205–6

property, 14, 71–75, 123, 129–30, 141

prostitutes, 103, 140, 204, 238

Protestantism, 36–37, 129–30, 187, 189, 201–2, 229–30; church doors and, 191; church interiors and, 187; core belief of, 62–63, 119; entrance to heaven and, 27; entrance to hell and, 32;